B
832
S296

Scheffler, Israel.

Four pragmatists

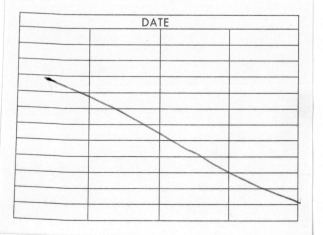

Four Pragmatists

International Library of Philosophy and Scientific Method

Editor: Ted Honderich

A catalogue of books already published in the
International Library of Philosophy and Scientific Method
will be found at the end of this volume.

Four Pragmatists

A Critical Introduction to Peirce, James, Mead, and Dewey

Israel Scheffler

Professor of Education and Philosophy
Harvard University

HUMANITIES PRESS

NEW YORK

First published in the United States of America 1974
by Humanities Press, Inc.
171 First Avenue,
Atlantic Highlands, N.J. 07716
Copyright © Israel Scheffler 1974
No part of this book may be reproduced in
any form without permission from the
publisher, except for the quotation of brief
passages in criticism

ISBN 0 391 00351 8

Library of Congress Catalog Card Number 74-12430

Printed in Great Britain

For
Fanny and Julius Zuckerbrod

CONTENTS

vii

Contents

PART THREE GEORGE HERBERT MEAD

PART FOUR JOHN DEWEY

PREFACE

Pragmatism is not only, as it has often been described, a distinctively American contribution to philosophy. In its effort to clarify and extend the methods of science, and to strengthen the prospects of freedom and intelligence in the contemporary world, it represents also a philosophical orientation of urgent general interest. Comprehensive in its thought, it bears the imprint of traditional modes of argumentation, but also of advanced logical and methodological ideas; it addresses itself not only to problems of philosophers but also to problems of men. In its search for an integrated interpretation of human life, it strives to relate mind and nature, language and thought, action and meaning, knowledge and value, emphasizing always the primary significance of critical thought, logical method, and the test of experience in all realms of endeavour.

I have tried, in this book, to portray the major themes of the four main thinkers of pragmatism, with special reference to their theories of thought and knowledge. I have attempted to offer not only a sympathetic interpretation but also a critical response, entering into discussion and argument with them on several points of doctrine. To this end, I have quoted liberally from their writings, hoping to provide the basis for a sympathetic view of their efforts as well as an anchor for critical evaluation.

Although I have sketched a general account of the pragmatic movement and provided some historical and biographical background, I have placed primary emphasis on the views of the individual thinkers themselves, considered both in an expository

A*

and a critical vein. I write not as an advocate of pragmatism, or as an interpreter merely, but primarily as a sympathetic critic. Although, as will become evident in the sequel, I am critical of a great many of the positions taken by the pragmatists discussed, I hold their positions always worthy of serious consideration. For they are addressed to significant problems which, if inadequately treated by pragmatism, remain as yet largely unsolved and continue to challenge our best efforts. Moreover, I applaud the conception of philosophy exemplified by the pragmatists' work. That philosophy ought to connect detail with principle, analysis with vision – that it should employ the resources of its tradition and its uncompromising logical criticism in illuminating the main realms of life and the problems of current thought and action – this attitude implicit in the pragmatic movement is one I fully share.

The treatment here presented grew, most immediately, out of lectures in courses on pragmatism that I have given for many years. For my earliest acquaintance with pragmatism, I am grateful to Sidney Hook and Ernest Nagel. I have since that time profited also from the writings of many scholars and interpreters in ways that cannot here be properly detailed and that are probably not adequately represented by footnote references. I must, however, mention especially the work of M. Fisch, W. B. Gallie, C. W. Morris, M. G. Murphey, R. B. Perry, and H. S. Thayer. For philosophical discussions, over the years, that have influenced my attitudes on various of the topics treated here, I am indebted to Henry D. Aiken, Nelson Goodman, Sidney Morgenbesser, Morton White, and the late Harold Weisberg.

Permission to quote from a variety of sources was granted by several publishers, to whom detailed acknowledgment is made. I am grateful for these permissions and wish also to thank Scott, Foresman for allowing me to draw upon my *Conditions of Knowledge* in developing certain portions of my treatment of James.

For support of my work on this book during 1972–3, I wish to thank the John Simon Guggenheim Memorial Foundation, as well as the Center for Advanced Study in the Behavioral Sciences, and I am grateful to Harvard University for granting me a sabbatical leave for this period. The administration and staff of the Center were unfailingly co-operative and helpful; I want especially to thank Betty Calloway, Margaret Amara and Pat Mastrandrea of the Center library, who made it possible for me to complete the checking of footnotes and sources with ease in the time at hand. I appreciate the help of Dorothy Spotts, of the Harvard staff, and Irene Bickenbach, of the Center, who typed various sections and versions of the manuscript. To Samuel Scheffler I am grateful for preparation of the index and for helpful critical comments. I thank Karen Hanson for her assistance with the proofs.

ACKNOWLEDGMENTS

The author and publishers would like to thank the following for kind permission to reproduce copyright material. All possible care has been taken to trace ownership of passages quoted and to make full acknowledgment for their use.

Macmillan Publishing Company, Inc. for extracts from *Democracy and Education* by John Dewey (1916, 1961), reprinted by permission of the publishers; Dover Publications, Inc. for extracts from *Peirce and Pragmatism* by W. B. Gallie, New York, 1966, reprinted by permission of the publisher; Appleton-Century-Crofts for extracts from *A History of Experimental Psychology* by Edwin G. Boring, copyright © 1929 by the Century Co., copyright © 1951 by Appleton-Century-Crofts, Inc.; Appleton-Century-Crofts, Inc. and Max H. Fisch for extracts from *Classic American Philosophers*, ed. Max H. Fisch, copyright © 1951 by Appleton-Century-Crofts, Inc.; George Braziller, Inc. for extracts from *The Pragmatic Movement in American Philosophy* by Charles Morris (1970); Penguin Books Ltd for extracts from *William James* by Margaret Knight (1950); extract from *Conditions of Knowledge* by Israel Scheffler, copyright © 1965 by Scott, Foresman & Co., reprinted by permission of the publisher; extract from *The Quest For Certainty* by John Dewey, reprinted by permission of G. P. Putnam's Sons, copyright 1929 by John Dewey, renewal © 1957 by Frederick A. Dewey; the Belknap Press of Harvard University Press for extracts from the *Collected Papers of Charles Sanders Peirce*, vols I–VI, ed. C. Hartshorne and P. Weiss, vols VII and VIII, ed. A. W. Burks (1931–58); Harvard University Press for extracts from *The*

Development of Peirce's Philosophy by Murray G. Murphey (1961); extracts from *John Dewey as Educator* by Arthur G. Wirth reprinted by permission of John Wiley & Sons, Inc.; copyright © 1966 John Wiley & Sons, Inc.; University of Chicago Press for extracts from *Mind, Self and Society* by George H. Mead, edited and with introduction by Charles W. Morris, copyright © 1934 University of Chicago Press; the Society for the Advancement of Education for extracts from John Dewey's article 'Democracy and educational administration' in *School and Society* 45 (13 April 1937); Cambridge University Press (New York) and the Macmillan Publishing Company, Inc. for extracts from *Science and the Modern World* by Alfred North Whitehead, copyright © 1925; Dodd, Mead & Co. for extracts from *Alice James, Her Brothers – Her Journal*, ed. Anna R. Burr (1934); Simon & Schuster, Inc. for extracts from *Human Knowledge* by Bertrand Russell © 1948; the Washington Square Press, a division of Simon & Schuster, Inc. for extracts from *John Dewey* by Richard J. Bernstein © 1966; Atlantic-Little, Brown for extracts from *Jeffersonian Principles and Hamiltonian Principles* by James Truslow Adams (1932), and from *The Thought and Character of William James* by Ralph Barton Perry (1935); extracts from *Human Nature and Conduct* by John Dewey © 1922 reproduced by arrangement with Holt, Rinehart & Winston, Inc., New York; letter dated 3 April 1883 quoted by George Dykhuizen in 'John Dewey: The Vermont Years' in *Journal of the History of Ideas*, vol. xx (1959) reproduced by permission of Professor Laura Buckham and Professor Philip P. Wiener; Oliver Wendell Holmes Jnr's letter (1919) to Morris R. Cohen quoted in *Journal of the History of Ideas*, vol. ix (1948) reproduced by permission of Harvard University; letter from John Dewey to W. T. Harris (1 May 1881) quoted by George Dykhuizen in 'John Dewey: the Vermont years' in *Journal of the History of Ideas*, vol. xx (1959) and letter from John Dewey to William Ernest Hocking quoted in *The Autobiography of Bertrand Russell: 1914–1944* (Little, Brown & Co., Boston, 1968), both reproduced by permission of the John Dewey Foundation.

ABBREVIATIONS

CP   Charles Hartshorne and Paul Weiss, eds, vols I–VI, and Arthur W. Burks, ed., vols VII and VIII, *Collected Papers of Charles Sanders Peirce* (Cambridge, Mass.: Harvard University Press, 1931–58). References are to volume and paragraph.

HNC   John Dewey, *Human Nature and Conduct: an Introduction to Social Psychology* (New York: Modern Library, 1922, 1930).

MSS   George H. Mead, *Mind, Self and Society: from the Standpoint of a Social Behaviorist* (edited, with Introduction, by Charles W. Morris) (University of Chicago Press, 1934).

PP   William James, *The Principles of Psychology* (New York: Dover, 1950).

QC   John Dewey, *The Quest for Certainty: a Study of the Relation of Knowledge and Action* (New York: Minton, Balch, 1929).

W   Philip P. Wiener, ed., *C. S. Peirce: Selected Writings* (New York: Dover, 1966).

INTRODUCTION

Pragmatism is widely described as America's distinctive philosophy and the most important influence on its educational theory. But it has, in general, not been understood *as* a philosophy; rather, it has been taken casually as an attitude: an emphasis on action, practice, society, a concern with what works.

I want, in this book, to deal with pragmatism as a group of related philosophical doctrines, comprising theories of meaning, knowledge and conduct, rooted in the philosophical tradition, growing out of a distinctive intellectual and historical context, and appealing to rational arguments. I shall deal with four philosophers in detail: Peirce, James, Mead, and Dewey, concentrating on certain of their writings and attending to the substance of their ideas and arguments, with only minimal glances at biographical backgrounds and historical influences and continuities.

It will be useful, however, to offer a preliminary word about the context and tendency of the movement as a philosophy of the nineteenth century. It faced a world in which many oppositions were apparent – science versus religion, positivism versus romanticism, intuition versus sense experience, the secular and democratic ideals of the Enlightenment versus the aristocratic and religious reaction of the turn of the century. It took the form of a *mediating* philosophy, striving to unify science and religion, theory and practice, speculative thought and analysis, tender-minded and tough-minded temperaments (James), and (with Dewey) school and life.

A major effort of pragmatism has been to assimilate modern science within philosophy, and to criticize traditional philosophical outlooks in the light of new scientific developments. But, un-like the tendency of positivism, pragmatism does not reduce or subordinate philosophical and other human interests to a simpli-fied model of positive science. In the first place, it is the theory of evolution and the new statistical modes of reasoning that have exercised the greatest impact upon pragmatism, and that have led it to criticize inherited conceptions of science itself. In the second place, pragmatism takes quite seriously the legitimate demands of other modes of human experience – morality and social practice; art, poetry, history; religion and philosophical speculation. It does not use *de facto* science as a device for excluding or downgrading these other modes. Rather, it takes science as suggestive of more general concepts of critical thought, in terms of which the con-tinuities among all modes may be revealed, and in light of which they may all be refined and advanced.

Thus, Charles Sanders Peirce develops the notion of *logical method* as an underlying conception capable of unifying the various oppositions we have mentioned. William James stresses the appeal to *experience* as a common test to which all constructions are to be brought. The various speculative philosophies, for example, are like so many separate hotel rooms, all differently furnished, to be sure, but connected by a common corridor of experience, through which they may be put into communication.[1] George H. Mead lays primary stress upon *symbolism* as the indispensable basis for human selfhood as well as for more differentiated and sophisti-cated forms of human consciousness. And John Dewey elaborates a theory of *intelligence* in offering a unified conception of thinking as an active interchange between organism and environment – an interchange which reveals the continuity between the humblest bit of learning by a child exploring its room and the most refined piece of theorizing by an experimental scientist investigating the natural world.

The *mediating or unifying* cast of pragmatism has not been much in evidence in post-Deweyan philosophy in America. As Morton White remarks, 'after John Dewey, American philosophy entered a new phase in which it altered its conception of its responsibilities'.[2] In this phase, philosophers gave their primary attention to

---

[1] William James, *Pragmatism* (New York: Longmans, Green, 1907, 1910), 54.
[2] Morton White, *Science and Sentiment in America* (New York: Oxford University Press, 1972), 3.

epistemological and semantic questions. Such concerns put them 'at the opposite end of the spectrum from pundits and sages who immerse themselves so deeply in the spiritual issues of their time that they make hardly any effort to reason systematically'.[1] In 'the middle band', however, belongs the emphasis of pragmatic philosophers as well as certain of their contemporaries:[2]

> In the middle of the spectrum . . . between highly specialized epistemologists and great-souled sages, there are philosophers who have their epistemologies all right, but who keep them warm by linking them to reflections on the great disciplines and institutions of civilization. They try to discourse intelligibly on the nature of mathematics, natural science, metaphysics, morals, history, art, law, politics, education, or religion; they advance views on man's condition and his fate; they offer analyses and assessments of their times; they are technicians but not mere technicians; they are seers but not madmen.

The broad scope of pragmatism reflected enormous social and intellectual changes in America during the period that Max H. Fisch calls our 'classical period':[3] from the end of the Civil War to the eve of the Second World War – changes in which science played a major role. Fisch catalogues these changes as follows:[4]

> the industrialization and urbanization of American society; the exploitation of our natural resources; the spreading and merging of railroads and other systems of transport and communication; the surge toward bigness in industry, business, capital, labor, and education; the management problems of large-scale organization; the drift toward specialization in all occupations; and the rise of an administrative and managerial class.

To personalize these changes, consider the comparison suggested by Gail Kennedy between Thomas Jefferson and John Dewey: 'During the generations that intervened between these two men the fringe of small rural communities on the Atlantic seaboard

[1] Ibid., 4.
[2] Ibid.
[3] Max H. Fisch, gen. ed., *Classic American Philosophers* (New York: Appleton-Century-Crofts, 1951, 1966), Preface and General Introduction.
[4] Ibid., 9.

which was the America that Jefferson knew developed into a great urban and industrial country, a world power.'[1] Jefferson wrote to Madison:[2]

> I think our governments will remain virtuous for many centuries; as long as they are chiefly agricultural; and this will be as long as there shall be vacant lands in any part of America. When they get piled upon one another in large cities, as in Europe, they will become corrupt as in Europe. Above all things I hope that the education of the common man will be attended to; convinced that on their good sense we may rely with the most security for the preservation of a due degree of liberty.

As Kennedy comments, 'What Jefferson would have prevented inexorably occurred. And its occurrence generated the fundamental concern of Dewey's philosophy, to discover the means of realizing the ideals of Jefferson in an urban and industrial civilization.'[3]

Dewey's own life saw the latter part of the great transformation in America:[4]

> He was born on the eve of the great war that was to ensure the triumph in America of industrialism and economic enterprise, in the year that Darwin published his *Origin of Species*, the book which marked the coming of age of modern science. He grew up in the environment of the older America, in the Vermont town of Burlington. Here life was still largely unaffected by the newer science and by modern industrialism. From this small community with its simple and intimate round of handicraft and agricultural occupations, the form of society that Jefferson knew, he was to go out into the complex world created by modern science and mass-production industries, to the first American university, the newly founded Johns Hopkins, to the fermenting democracy of the Middle West, in his years of teaching at the Universities of Michigan and Minnesota, then to the great industrial and commercial

---

[1] Gail Kennedy, 'Introduction to John Dewey', in Fisch, op. cit., 328.
[2] Quoted in ibid., from James Truslow Adams, *Jeffersonian Principles and Hamiltonian Principles* (Boston: Little, Brown, 1932), 18.
[3] Kennedy, op. cit., 328.
[4] Ibid., 328–9.

cities of Chicago and New York. Dewey has said in an autobiographical essay that the forces which influenced him came 'from persons and from situations' rather than from books. It was the transition from the America of his boyhood to the new America of his maturity that created the basic problems and formed the central theme of his philosophy.

The changes wrought by science were not merely social, they were intellectual. They posed a challenge not only to traditional religion and to traditional conceptions of the personal and moral life – they also seemed to undermine classical philosophical conceptions of knowledge. As Oliver Wendell Holmes, Jnr, a friend of William James and member of the Metaphysical Club in the early 1870s, wrote to Morris R. Cohen in 1919:[1]

My father was brought up scientifically – i.e. he studied medicine in France – and I was not. Yet there was with him as with the rest of his generation a certain softness of attitude toward the interstitial miracle – the phenomenon without phenomenal antecedents, that I did not feel. The difference was in the air, although perhaps only the few of my time felt it. . . . I think science was at the bottom.

The most influential idea was that of evolution, 'expelling from nature the last fixity, that of species',[2] including man in nature, and forcing the consideration of a biological view of man's intelligence itself. The rise of experimental physiology and experimental psychology as well as the historically-oriented sciences of man (anthropology, social psychology, comparative religion and folklore, institutional and historical economics) reinforced the evolutionary ideas of *process*, as well as *continuity* between mankind and the lower animals, between higher mental faculties and animal instinct. Moreover, the concepts of *probability* and statistical *inference*, underlying the kinetic theory of gases and thermodynamics as well as evolutionary doctrine, seemed to call for a revision in traditional conceptions of logic and of science. Finally, while pervasive social changes were complicating conditions of life and making individuality, liberty, and authenticity more prob-

[1] 'The Holmes–Cohen Correspondence' (edited with a foreword by Felix S. Cohen), *Journal of the History of Ideas*, IX (1948), 14; quoted in Fisch, op. cit., 9.
[2] Fisch, 'The Classic Period in American Philosophy', in *Classic American Philosophers*, 10. I have also drawn upon 11–12 for other points in the present paragraph.

lematic, the new sciences of man generated the prospect of deliberate alteration of social arrangements to cope with social problems. Responsibility for social arrangements replaced reliance on unalterable tradition as a consequence of the new conceptions of a *social* science. Knowledge and *action* now needed to be seen as intimately related. Knowledge, it seemed evident, arises in a biological and social context as a result of *experimentation*, that is, an active transformation of the environment directed toward the resolution of the problems of life. Knowledge, moreover, in so far as it increases the possibilities of deliberate social change and control, increases our *moral* responsibility for the *actions* we take in determining the conditions of social life.

The far-reaching social and intellectual changes we have touched upon were interpreted by the pragmatists as raising the following urgent problems: First, how are we to assimilate the new scientific emphases on change, on process, on action, on biological and social factors, and on probable reasoning? Clearly, a revision of classical conceptions of knowing would seem to be required. For these conceptions have interpreted knowing as the work of the individual mind either eliciting eternal truths from within, or passively registering ideas sent to it from without and reflecting an alien form of substance.

Second, and more generally, how are we to connect the life of man with the natural world in which he arises, the knowledge he acquires with the values he espouses, the concepts and abstractions in which his cognition is couched with the realms of willing, feeling, and doing which, no less than cognition, are parts of his life as an organism? The need, as pragmatists construed it, was to overcome inherited dualisms – between knower and known, fact and value, mind and matter, acting and feeling, abstract and concrete. To take the latter pair as an example, the pragmatists were at one with Whitehead in condemning 'the fallacy of misplaced concreteness',[1] by which abstractions important for special purposes were taken for the reality from which they were abstracted. Whitehead, criticizing the traditional scientific outlook, thus sums up the seventeenth-century view that survived until the end of the nineteenth century:[2]

---

[1] Alfred North Whitehead, *Science and the Modern World* (New York: Macmillan, 1925), 72.
[2] Ibid., 77.

The primary qualities are the essential qualities of substances
whose spatio-temporal relationships constitute nature. . . .
The occurrences of nature are in some way apprehended by
minds, which are associated with living bodies. . . . But the
mind in apprehending also experiences sensations which,
properly speaking, are qualities of the mind alone. These
sensations are projected by the mind so as to clothe appropriate bodies in external nature. Thus the bodies are perceived
as with qualities which in reality do not belong to them,
qualities which in fact are purely the offspring of the mind.
Thus nature gets credit which should in truth be reserved
for ourselves: the rose for its scent: the nightingale for his
song: and the sun for his radiance. . . . Nature is a dull affair,
soundless, scentless, colourless; merely the hurrying of
material, endlessly, meaninglessly.

The problem of overcoming this 'bifurcation of nature'[1] is to be
met by achieving a new conception of the relativity of abstractions
and the functional nature of thought.

Third, how are we to find new sources of stability of belief in
the face of change? This problem was set not merely by scientific
emphases on change in nature, or by accelerating changes of scientific beliefs, but by rejection of the 'quest for certainty' characteristic
of classical philosophy and the adoption of an experimental frame
of mind. Giving up the security of certainties and eternal truths in
favour of what Peirce called 'fallibilism',[2] how could sufficiently
stable beliefs and ideals yet be formed to sustain the life of the
intellect, of action, of education, and of morality?

Fourth, how are we to conceive individual selfhood and community in a form consonant with the new science and with the
new social conditions? How are we to construe social policy
under conditions of increased powers of social control, so that
control may be vested in those whom policy affects? How is the
advancement of knowledge to be connected with humane purposes in its application? What, in general, are the prospects of

[1] Alfred North Whitehead, *The Concept of Nature* (Cambridge University Press,
1926), 26ff.
[2] Charles Hartshorne and Paul Weiss, eds, vols I–VI, and Arthur W. Burks, ed.,
vols VII and VIII, *Collected Papers of Charles Sanders Peirce* (Cambridge, Mass.:
Harvard University Press, 1931–58) (*CP*), I.171; see also I.8–14.

individuality and critical intelligence in the new circumstances of industrial society?

Various facets of the pragmatic response to the foregoing problems will be explored in detail in the discussions to follow. Several major themes characterizing this response are, however, worth mentioning here, in a summary way. A dominant theme is the *rejection of Cartesian thought*, with its construal of knowledge as a mathematical structure resting upon a foundation of certainty in the intuition of the individual mind, the mind itself understood as constituted of a substance utterly discrete from the physical world. Flowing from this rejection are several pragmatic emphases comprising pervasive special themes: the *functional view of thought*, relating cognition to the biological, social, and purposive life of the organism; the *fallibilistic view of knowledge* as a provisional scheme of hypotheses resting, at best, upon probable reasoning; the *social and experimental conception of science* as the effort, not of an individual, but of an 'ideal' community of investigators dedicated to learning from the consequences of artful transformations of nature; and the *representative character of thinking*, always dependent, as it is, upon networks of sign-processes, and hence incapable of absolute fixity or absolute certainty.

The interpretation of *thought as intimately interwoven with action* in a purposive context is stressed by pragmatism as indicating the *continuity of mind and nature*: the mind acquires knowledge through physical interactions within its environment, but the conceptions of nature ingredient in such knowledge always mirror the active and purposive life of the knowing organism. 'What now is a *conception*?' asks William James. 'It is a *teleological instrument*. It is a partial aspect of a thing which *for our purpose* we regard as its essential aspect, as the representative of the entire thing.'[1]

With certainty precluded as a goal of individual thought, and science reinterpreted as the activity of an ideal community dedicated to continuous learning from experience, the *primacy of intellectual method* comes to receive fundamental emphasis. For particular conclusions of inquiry are all to be regarded as provisional, hence incapable of yielding stability and continuity over time. Such stability and continuity are rather to be sought in those critical methods that define the community of investigation itself.

---

[1] William James, *Collected Essays and Reviews* (New York: Longmans, Green, 1920), 86–7; quoted in Fisch, op. cit., 26.

It is allegiance to critical methods of learning from experience that unifies the generations of scientists despite the revisions of their substantive views. Such methods, moreover, reach beyond the special sciences in their significance and relate these sciences to critical thought in the spheres of art, practice, and education. The function of the latter, indeed, is to foster those habits of mind capable of sustaining *critical thinking* in all areas of life.

As the notion of scientific method is broadened to embrace critical thought generally, the concept of the *scientific community is taken as a suggestive analogue of democratic society*. In both cases, there is a basic unity, not of doctrine, but of method and procedure. Science institutionalizes procedures for the critical scrutiny and testing of ideas of nature, and democratic society institutionalizes procedures for the critical examination of social ideas, plans, and policies. In science, provisional substantive agreements are sufficient to promote intellectual advance, but the underlying unity of method requires all such substantive agreements to remain subject to the continuing test of experience. In democratic society, provisional agreements on particular ideas and policies are sufficient to organize relevant efforts, but all such ideas and policies are to be considered *hypotheses*: that is, they remain subject to the continuing test of experience, to be revised critically, in the light of experience and in accordance with the underlying unity of democratic methods.

The foregoing sketch of pragmatic themes is, of course, not intended as a systematic argument. Nor does it define a strictly uniform doctrine held in common by the pragmatic thinkers we shall be concerned with. Rather, it provides an initial glimpse of ideas associated with these thinkers, but elaborated by them severally in partial and variant ways which we shall explore in the chapters to follow. To the first of these thinkers we now turn – to the founder of pragmatism, Charles Sanders Peirce.

PART ONE
CHARLES SANDERS PEIRCE

I

BIOGRAPHICAL COMMENTS

Peirce was born in Cambridge, Massachusetts, in 1839, the second
son of Benjamin Peirce, professor of mathematics and astronomy
at Harvard and one of America's leading mathematicians. He was
educated at Harvard College, graduating in 1859 – one of the
youngest graduates, 'with one of the poorest records in his class'.[1]
He got much of his education from his father, with whom he
enjoyed an affectionate as well as an intensely intellectual relationship, which could not, however, have been wholly beneficial to
the son.

After graduation, Peirce spent a year surveying in Louisiana.
In 1861, he began work with the U.S. Coast and Geodetic Survey,
where he continued, while doing other things, until 1891. Peirce
took his M.A. at Harvard in 1862; and in 1863, he received the
Sc.B. degree in chemistry, *summa cum laude*.[2]

During the 1860s, he gave occasional lecture courses on logic
and philosophy. In 1864–5, he lectured on philosophy of science at
Harvard, although, as he later wrote in a letter to F. E. Abbot,
'My lectures fell through for want of an audience.'[3] In 1866–7, he
gave the Lowell Institute Lectures in Boston on 'The Logic of
Science and Induction' and, in 1869–70, he delivered fifteen University Lectures in philosophy. In 1871, Peirce founded the

---

[1] H. S. Thayer, *Meaning and Action: a Critical History of Pragmatism* (Indianapolis:
Bobbs-Merrill, 1968), 68. See also Paul Weiss's biographical sketch of Peirce in
Dumas Malone, ed., *Dictionary of American Biography*, vol. XIV (New York: Scribner,
1934), 398–403. I have drawn upon these sources for other points in this section.

[2] Weiss, op. cit., 399.

[3] Thayer, op. cit., 69.

Metaphysical Club, where pragmatism originated in a paper he read to the Club in 1872.[1]

'It was in the earliest seventies', writes Peirce, 'that a knot of us young men in Old Cambridge, calling ourselves, half-ironically, half-defiantly, "The Metaphysical Club" – for agnosticism was then riding its high horse, and was frowning superbly upon all metaphysics – used to meet, sometimes in my study, sometimes in that of William James.'[2] The Club included, aside from Peirce and James, Chauncey Wright, Oliver Wendell Holmes, Jnr, and Nicholas St John Green, a lawyer and disciple of Bentham, who, as Peirce says,[3]

> often urged the importance of applying Bain's definition of belief as 'that upon which a man is prepared to act'. From this definition, pragmatism is scarce more than a corollary; so that I am disposed to think of him as the grandfather of pragmatism. . . . Wright, James, and I were men of science, rather scrutinizing the doctrines of the metaphysicians on their scientific side than regarding them as very momentous spiritually. The type of our thought was decidedly British. I, alone of our number, had come upon the threshing-floor of philosophy through the doorway of Kant, and even my ideas were acquiring the English accent. Our metaphysical proceedings had all been in winged words . . . until at length, lest the club should be dissolved, without leaving any material *souvenir* behind, I drew up a little paper expressing some of the opinions that I had been urging all along under the name of pragmatism. This paper was received with such unlooked-for kindness, that I was encouraged, some half-dozen years later . . . to insert it, somewhat expanded, in the *Popular Science Monthly* for November, 1877 and January, 1878.

The original paper written for the Club has not survived. The published version referred to, somewhat expanded, appeared as two essays, under the titles, 'The Fixation of Belief' and 'How to

---

[1] See Max H. Fisch, General Introduction, *Classic American Philosophers* (New York: Appleton-Century-Crofts, 1951, 1966), 12. See also Murray G. Murphey, *The Development of Peirce's Philosophy* (Cambridge, Mass.: Harvard University Press, 1961), 98, n.6.

[2] *CP*, V.12.

[3] Ibid., 12-13.

Make Our Ideas Clear'. The second of these essays contains the pragmatic maxim (though not the word 'pragmatism').

The 1860s were years of promise, for Peirce, still a young man, was acclaimed and recognized as a man of great gifts. He was appointed an Assistant at the Harvard Observatory in 1869, and his work there led to his *Photometric Researches* (1878);[1] this book of his was the only one he saw published during his lifetime.

In 1875, Peirce sailed to Liverpool. One of his fellow passengers, W. H. Appleton, invited him to contribute to the *Popular Science Monthly*. His series of six articles, 'Illustrations of the Logic of Science', of which 'The Fixation of Belief' and 'How to Make Our Ideas Clear' were the first two, was the result. During his stay in England, Peirce visited Cambridge University and attended meetings of the Royal Society, engaging in discussions with James Clerk Maxwell and W. K. Clifford, among others.

Peirce's early promise never culminated in years of satisfaction or happiness. Although he continued to write and to work, he never succeeded in completing his system of philosophy. He could not get along well with other people, and gained the reputation of being a difficult person. He never got a university position of a permanent sort, the only extended teaching he did having been during the period from 1879 to 1884 on a logic lectureship at Johns Hopkins. There he was apparently considered an able and popular teacher, among whose students, incidentally, were Josiah Royce, John Dewey, Thorstein Veblen, and Joseph Jastrow. Peirce was, however, dismissed from Johns Hopkins in 1884 in circumstances that have never been fully disclosed, and he was never able to regain another academic post.

He continued his lecturing and scientific work. In 1892 and 1903 he again lectured at the Lowell Institute. He served as American delegate to the International Geodetic Conference in 1875, and was in charge of weights and measures for the U.S. Coast and Measure Survey in 1884-5. In 1891, his active scientific work and government career ended when he left the Coast Survey, having 'quarreled with his superiors' there.[2] His wife, whom he had married in 1862, left him in 1876, and he divorced her in 1883, remarrying soon thereafter.

---

[1] *Photometric Researches*, vol. 9 of *Annals of the Astronomical Observatory of Harvard College* (Leipzig, 1878).
[2] Thayer, op. cit., 70.

In 1887, having inherited a small bequest, Peirce retired to Milford, Pennsylvania, where he spent the rest of his time in almost complete isolation, working on his philosophical system. But he never produced any systematic books, and he was plagued by ever-worsening financial difficulties, though he tried to make some money by writing reviews for the *Nation*, and he also contributed to the *Century Dictionary* and Baldwin's *Dictionary of Philosophy and Psychology*. William James continued to help him and arranged occasional lectures for him. He died in 1914, 'a frustrated, isolated man, still working on his logic, without a publisher, with scarcely a disciple, unknown to the public at large'.[1]

Peirce was a difficult man, and the puzzle of his personality is not yet solved. One scholar describes the character that emerges from reports of him (including Peirce's own) as: 'highly emotional, vain, snobbish, morose, quarrelsome, intellectually arrogant, and quick to take offense, and, at the same time, . . . easily duped, hopelessly unpractical about money matters, and with a remarkable capacity for forgetting appointments'.[2] On the other hand, he was capable of insightful irony and self-criticism: 'I insensibly put on a sort of swagger here . . . which is designed to say: "You are a very good fellow in your way; who you are I don't know and I don't care, but I, you know, am Mr. Peirce, distinguished for my varied scientific acquirements, but above all for my extreme modesty in which respect I challenge the world." '[3] Peirce was also capable of being charming and witty and of inspiring affection as well as respect in his friends. And his philosophical temperament, as revealed in his writings, is broad, generous, self-critical, and totally problem-centred, without a trace of pettiness.

Despite his abrasive personality and lack of university backing, he influenced the eminent philosophers James and Royce, and achieved a certain fame through his papers. He published nearly eighty philosophical papers (if we include his contributions to Baldwin's *Dictionary*) and about twenty papers and a small book (*Photometric Researches*) on topics in the physical sciences and the theory of measurement. Between 1891 and 1906, he contributed about 180 reviews to the *Nation*.[4]

[1] Weiss, op. cit., 403. See also Thayer, op. cit., for materials in this paragraph.
[2] W. B. Gallie, *Peirce and Pragmatism* (New York: Dover, 1966), 37.
[3] Ralph Barton Perry, *The Thought and Character of William James*, vol. I (Boston: Little, Brown, 1935), 538.
[4] Gallie, op. cit., 36.

His inability to complete the systematic books he promised was in part due to his temperamental difficulties, no doubt, and in part also to his failure to secure a university position, through alienation of such persons as President Eliot of Harvard, for example. But a deeper reason, it has been suggested, lies in his abstract interests and his researcher's temperament. As Peirce himself put it in comparing himself to William James, 'Who, for example, could be of a nature so different from his as I? He is so concrete, so living; I a mere table of contents, so abstract, a very snarl of twine.'[1] A philosopher's philosopher, Peirce was too self-critical and too involved in the deepening of various special researches to which his work led him to be able to systematize and expound his achievements adequately.

Despite all these difficulties, Peirce's fame and influence continue to grow with the years. At his death, he left a huge collection of original manuscripts, now in the care of the Harvard Philosophy Department. As H. S. Thayer remarks,[2]

In attempting to get at Peirce's philosophic thought in these volumes of ambitious but incomplete writings, one is often in a position not unlike Peirce's creditors who came to the Milford house to collect on their bills. Peirce had an attic study accessible only by ladder, and there he retreated to uninterrupted philosophizing by drawing up the ladder behind him.

In 1916, C. I. Lewis's *Survey of Symbolic Logic* set forth Peirce's contributions as foremost among founders of that subject. In 1923, Morris R. Cohen's *Chance, Love, and Logic* appeared and made Peirce widely available to students for the first time. In 1931, the first six volumes of the *Collected Papers* started to appear, edited by Charles Hartshorne and Paul Weiss. Later, two additional volumes appeared, edited by Arthur Burks. And Professor Max Fisch has been at work on the several boxes of manuscripts still at Harvard, to produce final volumes and a biography.

Philosophically, it is difficult to get a uniform reading of Peirce, for he was clearly a very complex man with an acute intellect, great erudition and originality, and possessed of a speculative

---

[1] *CP*, VI.184.
[2] Thayer, op. cit., 71.

flair. Moreover, there are genuine difficulties, ambiguities, and tensions in Peirce's thought. To take but one example, his pragmatic maxim imposes a hardheaded criterion for the clarification of terms, akin to what has later become known as 'operational definition', and he stressed the need for statements to be evaluated by reference to their experimentally verifiable consequences. Yet his speculations on the origin of the universe hardly meet such criteria.

Was he primarily a logician and methodologist of science or a speculative metaphysician? Commentators diverge. Buchler[1] sees him primarily as the former, while Feibleman[2] sees him as the latter. Goudge[3] argues that there are two Peirces, one a naturalist and the other a transcendentalist, who cannot be reconciled. Murphey[4] emphasizes the development of his thought, taking him to be attempting, at each stage, to construct a system, but failing, and bequeathing difficulties to be overcome at the next stage. Gallie[5] recognizes the internal difficulties in Peirce's thought, but strives for a sympathetic interpretation of both his logical and his speculative sides.

It seems to me clear, in any case, that Peirce was critical both of nineteenth-century positivism and romanticism, and hoped to develop *logic* as something that would unify science and life. The essence of general education, for Peirce, was logical method, attention to clarity of concepts, and cogency of argument. But logic, for him, was scientific logic and not merely dialectic. This was, for him, a broad notion, connecting ideas with experience, with the public community of investigators, and with the impersonal reality towards which science directs its study.

In an age of rugged individualism, Peirce deplored the uses of science in support of individualism, phenomenalism, sensationalism, and materialism – all labelled by him 'nominalism', in favour of a conception of science that would in contrast be 'realistic', that is, would emphasize the abstract, the general, and the social.[6]

[1] Justus Buchler, *Charles Peirce's Empiricism* (New York: Harcourt, Brace, 1939).
[2] James K. Feibleman, *An Introduction to the Philosophy of Charles S. Peirce: Interpreted as a System* (first published 1946), (Cambridge, Mass.: M.I.T. Press, 1969).
[3] Thomas A. Goudge, *The Thought of C. S. Peirce* (University of Toronto Press, 1950).
[4] Murphey, op. cit.
[5] Gallie, op. cit.
[6] See Murphey, op. cit., 99ff.

As a scientist among scientists [writes Murphey[1]] he was impressed by the lack of individualism, the selfless devotion to the discovery of truth, which he observed among his colleagues. The sense of cooperation, the respect for the opinions of colleagues, and the ceaseless striving to reach agreement seemed to him the exact antithesis of the individualism which the results of science were being used to support. The true spirit of science it seemed to him was the spirit of religious devotion to the discovery of universal truth. And the same spirit he found exemplified in the work of the medieval Scholastic philosophers.

Think of the spirit in which Duns Scotus must have worked, who wrote his thirteen volumes in folio, in a style as condensed as the most condensed parts of Aristotle, before the age of thirty-four.[2]

'Indeed', says Peirce,[3]

if anyone wishes to know what a scholastic commentary is like, and what the tone of thought in it is, he has only to contemplate a Gothic cathedral. . . . Nothing is more striking in either of the great intellectual products of that age, than the complete absence of self-conceit on the part of the artist or philosopher. That anything of value can be added to his sacred and catholic work by its having the smack of individuality about it, is what he has never conceived. His work is not designed to embody *his* ideas, but the universal truth; . . . Finally, there is nothing in which the scholastic philosophy and the Gothic architecture resemble one another more than in the gradually increasing sense of immensity which impresses the mind of the student as he learns to appreciate the real dimensions and cost of each.

'Peirce was convinced', says Murphey, 'that modern science was

---

[1] Ibid., 101.

[2] *CP*, VIII.11. See also Philip P. Wiener, ed., *C. S. Peirce: Selected Writings* (New York: Dover, 1966) (*W*), 78. Wherever possible, I will also give references to the Wiener collection, which is more easily accessible to students than the *Collected Papers*.

[3] *CP*, VIII.11; *W*, 78. These cited passages are from Peirce's review of A. C. Fraser's edition of *The Works of George Berkeley*, in the *North American Review*, 113 (October 1871), 449–72.

just as realistic and just as fundamentally opposed to nominalism as had been the philosophy of the Scholastics, and it became the labor of his life to prove that the one afforded the only true basis for the other.'[1]

In sum, the antitheses within Peirce arise from two motives: first, to develop scientific logic and apply it to the revision of philosophy; second, to construct a broad enough and realistic enough interpretation of scientific logic to avoid the reductiveness of positivism and what he called 'nominalism'. Whether Peirce succeeded in satisfying these two motives is exceedingly doubtful. But that both motives were at work within him and guided his various reflections seems to me very hard to doubt, and serves to present a unified picture of his thought, at least in its intention. Thus, I take him to be both a logician and a metaphysician, attempting to construct a metaphysics inspired by the new science and at the same time to present a logical interpretation of science that would broaden out to a metaphysical orientation to the whole of reality. It is, of course, compatible with such a view of his intentions that he did not fully succeed in satisfying them, that he succeeded better in respect of certain of his projects than others, and that he focused attention on one or another particular project at different stages of his work. It is also true, I believe, that his *efforts* along the various lines he took are instructive to us, irrespective of his successes or failures.

Peirce offers a theory of thought, in which the pragmatic maxim is the most widely noted ingredient, the main emphasis of his theory falling on the connection between ideas and practice, between beliefs and habits. His theory, however, springs from reflection on scientific practice, and relates also to his rejection of philosophical views of the individual thinker as drawing up truths from within or receiving atomic sensations from without. Renouncing, in particular, Cartesian doubt and certainty, intuitionism and individualism, Peirce emphasizes *real doubt* as arising in a context of prior habit and belief, *fallibilism and probable reasoning*, and the *ideal community of investigators* as the context of individual research efforts. Rejecting rationalistic conceptions of thought and reasoning, he rejects also the rationalistic world-picture of a perfectly clear and sharply defined mechanical universe, fixed in its operations, which needs only to be observed and conceived

[1] Murphey, op. cit., 102.

clearly to yield scientific truth. The rationalistic conception of thought and the mechanistic world-picture feed on each other, in his view. Introducing fallibilism and probability into the former is paralleled by a loosening up and blurring of the conception of nature as well – an introduction of real chance, a rejection of necessity and determinism, and an application of genetic and anthropomorphic categories to the world at large. I do not claim that the connections here are logically air-tight, but only that there is a plausible connection between these themes that were psychologically active in the development of Peirce's thought.

The direction of development in Peirce's thought is, roughly speaking, from the epistemological to the cosmological. His important pair of papers, 'Questions Concerning Certain Faculties Claimed for Man',[1] and 'Some Consequences of Four Incapacities',[2] appeared in 1868, and provide a fundamental critique of the Cartesian theory of knowledge. Peirce's theory of inquiry and his pragmatic doctrine, properly so-called, appeared in 'The Fixation of Belief'[3] and 'How to Make Our Ideas Clear',[4] published in 1877 and 1878, respectively. The cosmological reflections occur in his five *Monist* papers of the 1890s: 'The Architecture of Theories' (1891),[5] 'The Doctrine of Necessity Examined' (1892),[6] 'The Law of Mind' (1892),[7] 'Man's Glassy Essence' (1892),[8] and 'Evolutionary Love' (1893).[9]

In treating Peirce's philosophical thought, I shall, however, not follow the chronological order. Rather, I discuss first his cosmological views, next his criticisms of Cartesianism, and then his own positive views relating to inquiry and to the pragmatic clarification of ideas. The order here is not historical but schematic: it is a working inward, as it were, starting with the universe at large, passing through consideration of a major philosophical tradition,

[1] *Journal of Speculative Philosophy*, II (1868), 103–14. See also *CP*, V.213–63; *W*. 15–38.
[2] *Journal of Speculative Philosophy*, II (1868), 140–57. See also *CP*, V.264–317; *W*, 39–72.
[3] *Popular Science Monthly*, XII (November 1877), 1–15. See also *CP*, V.358–87; *W*, 91–112.
[4] *Popular Science Monthly*, XII (January 1878), 286–302. See also *CP*, V.388–410; *W*, 113–36.
[5] *Monist*, I (January 1891), 161–76. See *CP*, VI.7–34; *W*, 142–59.
[6] *Monist*, II (April 1892), 321–37. See *CP*, VI.35–65; *W*, 160–79.
[7] *Monist*, II (July 1892), 533–59. See *CP*, VI.102–63.
[8] *Monist*, III (October 1892), 1–22. See *CP*, VI.238–71.
[9] *Monist*, III (January 1893), 176–200. See *CP*, VI.287–317.

and ending with Peirce's own views about thought. The reasons for such a development are these: I think many of Peirce's substantive themes as well as his speculative boldness and scientific cast of mind are seen most directly and strikingly in his cosmology. Moreover, the latter aspect of his work is so often presented apologetically as the quirk of a great mind that the balance needs to be redressed. The critique of Descartes is also not widely emphasized in most general presentations, although it seems to me of quite fundamental importance.

Thus, I treat the cosmology first in the hope that it will provide an introduction to Peirce's themes, style, and concerns. Next, I discuss the papers criticizing Descartes, and thereafter I turn to that part of Peirce's work which has received the most attention by far – his notion of inquiry and his pragmatism. Finally, I shall discuss briefly some of Peirce's writings on social topics, in particular, his comments on religion and on education.

As a consequence of this ordering of topics, we must be on guard against anachronism, that is, the suggestion of false conceptions of historical sequence. Provided this caution is kept in mind, the topical treatment will, I hope, not mislead. Its aim is not to give a *historical* account of Peirce's thought process, but to provide a *critical appreciation* of his thinking on selected problems.[1] In the treatment of Peirce's contributions relating to these several problems, I shall therefore not only expound and interpret his ideas, but I shall offer critical remarks of my own.

[1] The development of Peirce's thought is treated in the important work of Murray G. Murphey, op. cit., to which I am indebted.

II

PEIRCE'S COSMOLOGY

Peirce is concerned to attack the inherited picture of a perfectly clear, sharply defined, mechanical universe, governed by deterministic and unchanging laws accessible to careful observation and clear conception to within limits of subjective error. The picture is that of nature as an ideal mechanism, a perfect clock: ideal and perfect since real mechanisms wear out and real clocks break down. The *change* in our knowledge of the clockwork is a change in us; the clockwork itself is perfectly constant – *it* has no history. The limitations in our knowledge at any given time are equally to be assigned to us rather than to nature: *incompleteness* of our explanatory schemes does not imply the lack of relevant regulating principles in nature; *blur* of measurement is a matter of the observer's limitations rather than the inconstancy of measured magnitudes; *deviations from deterministic formulations* are results of our ignorance and do not indicate that nature itself is anywhere free of the sway of perfect necessity.

As against this conception, Peirce proposes a radically divergent view. According to this view, nature itself is infected with an objective indeterminacy; there is an element of absolute chance in the world. The regularities we find in nature are not to be automatically extrapolated backwards and forwards in time; rather, like habits, they are themselves to be explained as having evolved out of states of greater spontaneity and are to be expected to precede further states of increasing regularity. Deviations from determinism and incompleteness of explanation are not products simply of our ignorance: they betoken an objective and ineradicable 'element of pure chance'[1] in the career of natural phenomena. The imprecision of measurement cannot, for example, be reduced without increasing irregularity in the association of measured values. Indeed, says Peirce,[2]

> Try to verify any law of nature, and you will find that the more precise your observations, the more certain they will be to show irregular departures from the law. We are accustomed to ascribe these, and I do not say wrongly, to errors of observation; yet we cannot usually account for such errors in any antecedently probable way. Trace their causes back far enough and you will be forced to admit they are always due to arbitrary determination, or chance.

The blur in a snapshot may be due to movement of the camera, or it may be produced by the scene itself – consider a photograph of a London street in a fog.[3] We may not be able to tell in given cases what the cause in fact was, but we could say in principle how to find out. However, the blur of knowledge dependent upon measurement is different; it cannot even in principle be eliminated. That is, we may reduce departures from law by increasing the imprecision of our observations, or reduce observational imprecision by increasing irregular deviations from law. Nor is there any way of *showing* the blur to belong in certain cases to the object and in certain others to the observer. Observation certainly cannot approach near enough to decide the matter. 'The essence of the necessitarian position is that certain continuous quantities have certain exact values,' says Peirce. 'Now, how can observation determine the value of such a quantity with a probable error absolutely *nil*?'[4] There is, further, no theoretical reason to attribute the blur to the observer alone. The fluctuation is a product of the interaction of observation itself, as attributable to perturbations in the phenomena measured as to the limitations of the observer.

Among the arguments that Peirce offers for his view, aside from the considerations relating to measurement just noted, is the

---

[1] *CP*, VI.33; *W*, 159.

[2] *CP*, VI.46; *W*, 170.

[3] This example was suggested by a comment with rather different intent in Max Black, *Language and Philosophy* (Ithaca, New York: Cornell University Press, 1949), 28.

[4] *CP*, VI.44; *W*, 169.

claim that science requires a new principle of method for its further development, and that this principle needs to be a developmental or evolutionary one. Until now, he suggests, science has
been able to progress by intuition, because the scientists' intuition
has itself been formed by the very phenomena upon which it has
been directed.[1]

> A modern physicist on examining Galileo's works is surprised
> to find how little experiment had to do with the establishment
> of the foundations of mechanics. His principal appeal is to
> common sense and *il lume naturale*. He always assumes that
> the true theory will be found to be a simple and natural one.

But the intuition of simplicity is itself due to the fact that our
minds have been formed in, and adapted to, an environment in
which objects acted under the rule of intuited laws.[2]

> Thus it is that, our minds having been formed under the
> influence of phenomena governed by the laws of mechanics,
> certain conceptions entering into those laws become im-
> planted in our minds, so that we readily guess at what the
> laws are. Without such a natural prompting, having to search
> blindfold for a law which would suit the phenomena, our
> chance of finding it would be as one to infinity. The further
> physical studies depart from phenomena which have directly
> influenced the growth of the mind, the less we can expect to
> find the laws which govern them 'simple', that is, composed
> of a few conceptions natural to our minds.

The natural light with its intuition of simplicity will thus cease
to be a reliable principle of investigation, and some substitute will
need to be supplied if theorizing is not to be wholly haphazard or
fruitless. Such a substitute is to be sought, Peirce suggests, in a
theory of evolutionary cosmology. 'When we come to atoms', for
example, says Peirce, 'the presumption in favor of a simple law
seems very slender.'[3]

> To find out much more about molecules and atoms we must
> search out a natural history of laws of nature which may
> fulfill that function which the presumption in favor of simple

[1] *CP*, VI.10; *W*, 145–6.
[2] *CP*, VI.10; *W*, 146.
[3] *CP*, VI.11; *W*, 147.

laws fulfilled in the early days of dynamics, by showing us what kind of laws we have to expect and by answering such questions as this: Can we, with reasonable prospect of not wasting time, try the supposition that atoms attract one another inversely as the seventh power of their distances, or can we not?[1]

Peirce sees clearly that science is not a matter of routinely constructing theories out of accumulated facts. Theories are always underdetermined by available facts and there is an indefinitely large number of theories capable of accounting for these facts at any time. Reliance on intuition is not the same thing as applying a routine method or decision procedure, but it has in the past been helpful in dealing with gross principles of the environment, because intuition has been adapted by evolution to that environment. When we theorize about remote or unfamiliar phenomena, what guide do we have? These reflections led Peirce to anticipate the actual departure from familiar intuitive principles in further physical theorizing. Murphey comments on this point as follows:[2]

To appreciate the significance of Peirce's argument, one must bear in mind what the situation was in the physical sciences in the early 1890's. The reign of Newtonian mechanics was rapidly drawing to a close, and many of the fundamental difficulties were already known which within fifteen years would lead to the complete revision of physical theory. The Michelson–Morley experiment was already four years old, and with it the demonstration that there was something fundamentally wrong with our theories of the ether. The crisis thus introduced into physics was among the most serious in the history of science, involving a conflict between the two sets of equations which scientists regarded as expressing the most fundamental laws of nature – Newton's laws and Maxwell's equations. At the same time, problems had also arisen in the area of atomic physics which indicated that the classical laws of mechanics might not be applicable in this domain, and indeed some scientists had even been led to assert that no explanation of these phenomena was possible at all.

[1] *CP*, VI.12; *W*, 147–8.
[2] Murray G. Murphey, *The Development of Peirce's Philosophy* (Cambridge, Mass.: Harvard University Press, 1961), 327–8.

The solution of these problems came almost simultaneously in both macro- and microphysics with the work of Einstein and Planck in and about 1905, and in both cases it is true that the new theories did involve fundamental departure from what can be called the realm of common sense ideas. In fact, Peirce saw the actual situation with remarkable clearness, although his explanation of it leaves a great deal to be desired.

One shortcoming of Peirce's explanation, pointed out by Murphey, is the attribution of the naturalness of Newtonian explanations to an 'innate proclivity of the human mind'.[1] Here he betrays an insensitivity to cultural and historical relativity. Newton's laws were not, for example, intuitive to Aristotle, and '*il lume naturale* notwithstanding, Galileo's insight that the natural state of a terrestial body could be uniform rectilinear motion was perhaps the most important intellectual feat in the history of Europe'.[2] A second shortcoming is indicated by the fact that the resolution of the physical crisis was not, after all, accomplished by theorizing under the guidance of some grand evolutionary cosmology. And a final shortcoming – in itself decisive – is the fact that Peirce's own attempt at such a cosmology is hopelessly vague, beset with logical difficulties, and incapable of being put to the test.

Beyond Peirce's argument, just reviewed, to the effect that some new guiding principle is needed to replace the natural light, what reason does he offer for expecting such a principle to be of *evolutionary* form? He argues that, far from universal laws of nature providing ultimate explanatory accounts,[3]

Uniformities are precisely the sort of facts that need to be accounted for. That a pitched coin should sometimes turn up heads and sometimes tails calls for no particular explanation; but if it shows heads every time, we wish to know how this result has been brought about. Law is *par excellence* the thing that wants a reason.

Now the only possible way of accounting for the laws of

[1] Ibid., 328.
[2] Ibid., citing Herbert Butterfield, *The Origins of Modern Science* (New York: Macmillan, 1956, 1960), 2ff.
[3] *CP*, VI.12–13; *W*, 148.

nature and for uniformity in general is to suppose them results of evolution.

Against Herbert Spencer's attempt to explain evolution itself by appeal to mechanical principles, Peirce argues that, while law requires explanation by some genetic account, evolution 'requires no extraneous cause, since the tendency to growth can be supposed itself to have grown from an infinitesimal germ accidentally started'.[1] Finally, he argues that law alone cannot account for the manifest heterogeneity in nature, nor can mechanical principles explain irreversible processes such as phenomena of growth.

In 'The Doctrine of Necessity Examined', Peirce continues the negative arguments just noted by a full-scale attack on the thesis of complete determinism, i.e., 'the common belief that every single fact in the universe is precisely determined by law'.[2] His criticisms of this belief are three: (1) It is not self-evident or an *a priori* truth. It has in fact not been held by all rational men, as Aristotle's rejection of it shows. (2) It is not required as a postulate of science, or presupposition of induction. (3) It cannot be established by observation.

Let us take a closer look at (2): the defence of determinism or the uniformity of nature as a presupposition of science has been very widespread, down to our own times. If such a defence is the best that can be offered for it, Peirce argues (rightly in my opinion):[3]

the belief is doomed. Suppose it be 'postulated': that does not make it true, nor so much as afford the slightest rational motive for yielding it any credence. It is as if a man should come to borrow money, and when asked for his security, should reply he 'postulated' the loan. To 'postulate' a proposition is no more than to hope it is true.

Bertrand Russell, in 1919, commented in a similar vein, 'The method of "postulating" what we want has many advantages; they are the same as the advantages of theft over honest toil.'[4] Twenty-nine years later, however, in his *Human Knowledge*, Russell

[1] *CP*, VI.14; *W*, 148.
[2] *CP*, VI.36; *W*, 162.
[3] *CP*, VI.39; *W*, 164.
[4] Bertrand Russell, *Introduction to Mathematical Philosophy* (London: Allen & Unwin, 1919), 71.

departed from his own criticism and devoted the critical section of his analysis of knowledge to an outline of what he called 'Postulates of Scientific Inference'.[1] Peirce is more thorough-going in his rejection. All scientific reasoning, according to him, rests upon non-deductive or 'ampliative' inference of three kinds: induction, hypothesis, and analogy.[2] All in turn rest upon the logic of sampling, ideally requiring randomness and 'predesignation of the character sampled for',[3] but in no case involving any deterministic postulate whatever.

In his critical argument (3) mentioned above, Peirce denies that determinism can either be proved or rendered probable by observation:[4]

> To one who is behind the scenes, and knows that the most refined comparisons of masses, lengths, and angles, far surpassing in precision all other measurements, yet fall behind the accuracy of bank accounts, and that the ordinary determinations of physical constants, such as appear from month to month in the journals, are about on a par with an upholsterer's measurements of carpets and curtains, the idea of mathematical exactitude being demonstrated in the laboratory will appear simply ridiculous.

What observations show is simply that 'there is an element of regularity in nature, and have no bearing whatever upon the question of whether such regularity is exact and universal, or not. Nay, in regard to this *exactitude*, all observation is directly opposed to it.'[5] An element of absolute chance must rather be acknowledged in nature, along with the element of regularity: this is Peirce's notion of *tychism*.

Having disposed of the three arguments for determinism, Peirce advances five positive reasons in favour of his alternative view: (1) Mechanical forces cannot explain diversity, which must be independently assumed, but, more important, cannot explain *increasing* diversity over time, facts of growth or evolution, which are, unlike mechanical processes, irreversible. (2) The ordinary

[1] Bertrand Russell, *Human Knowledge: Its Scope and Limits* (New York: Simon & Schuster, 1948), 419ff.
[2] *CP*, VI.40; *W*, 165.
[3] *CP*, VI.42; *W*, 168.
[4] *CP*, VI.44; *W*, 169.
[5] *CP*, VI.46; *W*, 170.

view must admit diversity, without explanation, or suppose it introduced at once at the beginning of time, whereas to admit a continuous action of spontaneity 'though restrained within narrow bounds by law' accounts for increasing diversity 'in the only sense in which the really *sui generis* and new can be said to be accounted for'.[1] (3) Determinists do not explain diversity, but they equally do not explain law, which is to be taken, according to them, as an ultimate and immutable fact. Now to explain law, argues Peirce, it must be shown to develop out of non-law, and the hypothesis of spontaneity provides for just such an explanation. Here Peirce repeats his earlier argument that it is *primarily* law that wants explanation:[2]

> That single events should be hard and unintelligible, logic will permit without difficulty: we do not expect to make the shock of a personally experienced earthquake appear natural and reasonable by any amount of cogitation. But logic does expect things *general* to be understandable. To say that there is a universal law, and that it is a hard, ultimate, unintelligible fact, the why and wherefore of which can never be inquired into, at this a sound logic will revolt, and will pass over at once to a method of philosophizing which does not thus barricade the road of discovery.

(4) Necessitarianism cannot account for mind, feeling and consciousness, which do not follow strict causation, but rather 'the law of mind' – 'that ideas tend to spread continuously and to affect certain others which stand to them in a peculiar relation of affectibility'.[3] Finally, (5) Peirce says that his hypothesis yields consequences which can be empirically verified. But he does not specify in detail what these are.[4]

The total picture of Peirce's world-view, in admittedly tentative form, is given in the striking conclusion to 'The Architecture of Theories'. The metaphysics he there outlines[5]

> would be a Cosmogonic Philosophy. It would suppose that in the beginning – infinitely remote – there was a chaos of

---

[1] *CP*, VI.59; *W*, 175.
[2] *CP*, VI.60; *W*, 176.
[3] *CP*, VI.104.
[4] See *CP*, VI.62, and editors' footnote.
[5] *CP*, VI.33; *W*, 158–9.

unpersonalized feeling, which being without connection or regularity would properly be without existence. This feeling, sporting here and there in pure arbitrariness, would have started the germ of a generalizing tendency. Its other sportings would be evanescent, but this would have a growing virtue. Thus, the tendency to habit would be started; and from this, with the other principles of evolution, all the regularities of the universe would be evolved. At any time, however, an element of pure chance survives and will remain until the world becomes an absolutely perfect, rational, and symmetrical system, in which mind is at last crystallized in the infinitely distant future.

III

PEIRCE'S COSMOLOGY: CRITICAL REMARKS

In presenting Peirce's cosmology, I have emphasized his cosmogonic doctrine and have so far omitted mention of his three categories of *First, Second,* and *Third.* These categories are intended as aspects of (or forms of analysis applicable to) all situations. I shall here comment only on their relation to Peirce's cosmogonic views and not attempt a general account. For the categories are in themselves rather obscure and they are put to a variety of uses by Peirce, not always consistently. Suffice it then to say that, as he explains the matter in 'The Architecture of Theories',[1]

> First is the conception of being or existing independent of anything else. Second is the conception of being relative to, the conception of reaction with, something else. Third is the conception of mediation, whereby a first and second are brought into relation.

In his cosmogonic philosophy, there would then 'be an evolution from Firstness (feeling) through Secondness (actual occurrences which are repeated) to Thirds (laws)'.[2] Peirce, however, confuses matters by also saying: 'Chance is First, Law is Second, the tendency to take habits is Third.'[3] And, as Gallie points out, despite Peirce's claim that his three categories are *universal,* the beginning

---

[1] *CP,* VI.32; *W,* 158.
[2] Murray G. Murphey, *The Development of Peirce's Philosophy* (Cambridge, Mass.: Harvard University Press, 1961), 349.
[3] *CP,* VI.32; *W,* 158.

state he envisions is one of pure spontaneity, i.e., all First, and no Second or Third, so that 'in applying his doctrine of categories in his cosmology Peirce has virtually gone back on its primary thesis, viz. that each of his three categories is universal'.[1]

Rather than press this sort of criticism, however, which pertains more to the categories than to the cosmogonic doctrine, I want now to take a critical look at the cosmogonic philosophy itself. A fundamental claim of Peirce's, as we have seen, is that it is uniformities that especially require explanation, rather than particulars, so that primacy must be given to a *genetic account* of the emergence of uniformity out of pure spontaneity.

Now there is a logical gap between premiss and conclusion in the argument just mentioned. Suppose it is true that 'uniformities are precisely the sort of facts that need to be accounted for'.[2] How does it follow that an evolutionary or genetic explanation is 'the only possible way'[3] of providing such an account? It is not also possible to explain a given uniformity by showing how to derive it from another, more comprehensive, uniformity? Indeed, is it not a typical process of scientific explanation to subsume reliable, low-level generalizations under the scope of broader laws or more abstract theoretical formulations? We may certainly agree with Peirce that 'law . . . wants a reason'[4] – that is to say, scientists strive to account for particular laws and do not ever suppose that available laws must be taken as absolutely inexplicable. But the explanation of particular laws characteristically calls upon other lawlike statements – generalizations, laws, or theories.

Peirce in fact glides from the question of explaining particular laws to that of explaining regularity in general. Thus, he says, 'Law is *par excellence* the thing that wants a reason. Now the only possible way of accounting for the laws of nature *and for uniformity in general* is to suppose them results of evolution' (my italics).[5] His idea seems to be that explaining uniformity in general cannot itself rest upon uniformity, for such a procedure would be circular; the explanation must therefore be evolutionary or genetic. But even if this be granted, it does not at all follow that it is equally circular

[1] W. B. Gallie, *Peirce and Pragmatism* (New York: Dover, 1966), 225.
[2] *CP*, VI.12; *W*, 148.
[3] *CP*, VI.13; *W*, 148.
[4] *CP*, VI.12; *W*, 148.
[5] *CP*, VI.12–13; *W*, 148.

to explain a *given law of nature* by invoking another. There is no fallacy in the process whereby any *particular* law is accounted for by subsuming it under further general statements, and therefore no good reason to hold that all such laws require evolutionary explanation. Moreover, from the premiss that scientists hold uniformities, in the plural, to be 'precisely the sort of facts that need to be accounted for',[1] it does not at all follow that scientists hold *uniformity in general* to be the sort of fact that needs to be accounted for. Nor is it clear how even to conceive the explanation of uniformity in general as a scientific problem if we understand science as offering theoretical, i.e., general, explanations.

Peirce argues further that, unless one adopts his proposed genetic derivation of regularity from chance, one is driven inevitably into dogmatic arrest of the process of scientific discovery:[2]

> To say that there is a universal law, and that it is a hard, ultimate, unintelligible fact, the why and wherefore of which can never be inquired into, at this a sound logic will revolt, and will pass over at once to a method of philosophizing which does not thus barricade the road of discovery.

But the process of scientific explanation by subsumption is not in fact committed to dogmatism. Explanation of any given fact or law must, of necessity, rest upon explanatory assumptions: if nothing is taken for granted as explanatory, nothing can be explained. It does not follow, however, that what is taken for granted for the purposes of a given problem of explanation must be held immune to future criticism or investigation. On the contrary, the assumptions of a particular scientific problem are often thrown into question in further investigations. Thus, if scientific explanations rest upon lawlike premises in every case, it does not follow that some such premises are held to be hard, ultimate, unintelligible facts, the why and wherefore of which can never be inquired into. At any given time, certain lawlike statements and theories are used to explain and are thought to provide insight into the phenomena they subsume. At no time, however, is it supposed that such statements and theories may not be reexamined or taken, in turn, as elements to be explained. Science, to be sure, does not attempt to explain all regularities at once, but,

---

[1] *CP*, VI.12; *W*, 148.
[2] *CP*, VI.60; *W*, 176.

at any given time, assumes some to explain others. This process is neither circular nor committed to dogmatism.

Peirce, however, has another argument in favour of genetic explanation and against subsumptive explanation, even if the latter is rescued from his earlier criticisms. His further argument is that particular events need no explanation, whereas uniformities do. Thus, if a given explanation rests upon appeal to uniformities, these will in turn require explanation, whereas if a given explanation appeals only to particular happenings in a genetic story, these particular happenings will be accepted as not requiring further explanation.

Now, in the first place, even if assumed uniformities require explanation, it does not follow that they themselves do not explain. Nor does it follow that appeal to such uniformities affords no insight unless they are first subsumed under larger uniformities in an infinite regress without beginning. Nor does an event, because it is an effect, cease to be itself a cause capable of illuminating its own effects. In the second place, Peirce's suggestion that particular events are happily accepted without explanation seems to be simply false. Particular assumptions, like lawlike ones, may serve in given explanations as premises, but they may always be challenged and they may, in fact, be overthrown should sufficient doubt be cast upon them in later inquiry. Alternatively, they may be retained and explained further, should the occasion arise and the explanatory resources become available.

Peirce's two examples to the contrary are those of the pitched coin and the earthquake. Consider first the pitched coin example: 'That a pitched coin should sometimes turn up heads and sometimes tails calls for no particular explanation; but if it shows heads every time, we wish to know how this result has been brought about.'[1] Now *each toss* resulting in heads is a particular happening and, although we do not normally have sufficient information about its background circumstances to explain the result, and are, moreover, not normally interested in providing such an explanation, the question may be raised, and it theoretically has an answer. But Peirce, I suggest, is not concerned with the *single toss* at all: he contrasts the case of the coin showing heads every time with the case of its showing heads sometimes and tails other

[1] *CP*, VI.12; *W*, 148.

times. This contrast is not, I submit, a contrast of the general with the particular. Both cases are general if either one is.

Presumably, the explanation as to why the coin shows heads every time is that it is loaded; but then the explanation as to why it shows now heads, now tails, is that it is not loaded but fair. Or, if the proportions of heads and tails are unequal, the explanation consists in assigning to the coin suitable theoretical probabilities for each alternative, the assignment in turn open to explanation by likely physical factors of one or another kind. It is true that we normally take it for granted that coins are fair, and so are not surprised when they yield now heads, now tails. Nor do we normally raise the question why they do. But the normal assumption of fairness is available to us as a potential explanation should the question arise.

Consider now Peirce's earthquake example: 'That single events should be hard and unintelligible, logic will permit without difficulty: we do not expect to make the shock of a personally experienced earthquake appear natural and reasonable by any amount of cogitation.'[1] This argument seems, however, utterly beside the point. Certainly explanation cannot eliminate the objects it is designed to explain. The shock is what needs explaining, and explanation of the shock will need to take it as a fact and account for it. Such an account will of course not soothe it away and assimilate the experience to the familiar and expected course of events. Nor will it show the shock to be *reasonable* in the sense of a deliberate action undertaken to achieve some objective. It can, however, strive to understand the reaction by relating it to the antecedent quake, viewed as belonging to a suitable class of severe environmental changes generally producing startle reactions. I conclude that there is no difference with respect to explanatory ultimacy as between uniformities and particular events. We may explain particulars and we may explain uniformities, and the explanatory premises we assume for a particular case may be thrown into question at a later time.

In upholding subsumption as a legitimate form of scientific explanation, we must, however, avoid the supposition that what *we take to be a law* at any given time will in fact be sustained *as a law* by future inquiry – so that further subsumption is the *only* course of development to be expected. This supposition would be another

[1] *CP*, VI.60; *W*, 176.

form of dogmatism, milder than the first, but still to be deplored. It would hold that every statement we now take to express a genuine law really does express a genuine law – we can, to be sure, embed it in more comprehensive uniformities but we cannot ever give it up. Subsumptive explanation does not, in fact, imply this supposition. In employing lawlike premisses it *takes these* to express relationships holding universally. It is, however, prepared to surrender such claims if the relationships in question are later judged to fail of universality. Such provisionality means we must be prepared to revise our judgments as to what is, in fact, a law. It does not imply that the very notion of a law as expressing a universal relationship must be given up in favour of an evolving regularity. Peirce seems to miss this point. He argues against the idea 'that there is a universal law, and that it is a hard, ultimate, unintelligible fact, the why and wherefore of which can never be inquired into'.[1] We need, however, to distinguish between there being a universal law and our taking some particular statement to express such a law. The striving to find genuine, universal, laws is perfectly compatible with our rejection of those statements we have hitherto taken to express such laws. This striving therefore does not, in itself, commit us even to a mild form of dogmatism. Indeed it forces us to test current universal hypotheses to see how well they hold up.

Sometimes they do hold up, and can themselves be explained by incorporation into suitable sets of general assumptions. Sometimes, however, they do not sustain their status as genuinely universal under test: experiment shows, for example, that an asserted function holds only over a certain range of values or that an ascribed property or relation fails outside the original domain of investigation. Such a breakdown of universality shows the hypothesis to be local, temporally bounded, or otherwise restricted. It gives it a history or a locality, so to speak: in this way the universal hypothesis may indeed be said to be superseded by a 'genetic' account. We need *not* therefore say, as Peirce suggests, that here a law has itself changed; we say rather that what we have taken to be a law has been shown to be restricted, hence not a law at all.

The latter formulation has the advantage of according better with scientific practice in this respect: when a restriction in universality has been shown in the manner above described, scientists do

[1] *CP*, VI.60; *W*, 176.

not, as Peirce suggests, simply accept the brute fact of restriction; they do not rest content with circumscription of initially asserted relations. Rather, they now strive to explain why the scope is restricted in specified ways, why the relation breaks down where it does. They seek to determine relevant variations that make the breakdown intelligible. In so doing, they propose new and more fundamental generalizations, which become new candidates for the status of genuine laws.

It is true that the usage of the term 'law' is loose, and that the term is often employed to cover both genuinely universal statements and restricted ones. Any definite proposal will therefore be likely to depart from ordinary linguistic practice. But the issue is substantive, not verbal, if the proposal is taken to reflect the character of scientific explanation. In particular, the doctrine of evolving laws provides support for Peirce's emphasis on the primacy of genetic explanations. And the latter emphasis conflicts with the fact that genetic (or other) circumscriptions of the range of hypotheses do not, in general, arrest the striving for explanation. On the contrary, such striving for explanation persists and seeks unrestricted theoretical foundations. The point was well expressed by Philipp Frank, who, in countering the view that relativism in science is subjectivistic, argued that it seeks rather the introduction of a richer language capable of unambiguously stating the plain truth about the universe. Accordingly, Frank chose as the title of one of his books: *Relativity – a Richer Truth*.[1]

Internal difficulties also beset Peirce's cosmogonic philosophy. Paul Carus, for example, urged the point that evolution itself requires a law:[2]

> How little after all we can escape the determinism of law as being a feature of the world will be seen from the fact, that the explanation for the evolution of law is presented by Mr. Peirce as being itself a law, i.e. a formula describing a regularity supposed to obtain in facts.

An evolutionary account or genetic story is not simply a listing of temporally sequential events; it yields insight only if some general form of change is supposed or, at least, intimated. And Peirce

---

[1] Philipp Frank, *Relativity – a Richer Truth* (London: Cape, 1951), see esp. p. 30.
[2] Paul Carus, 'Mr. Charles S. Peirce's Onslaught on the Doctrine of Necessity', *Monist*, II (1891–2), 574.

indeed suggests such generality in saying of the arbitrary sporting of feelings that it '*would have* started the germ of a generalizing tendency' (my italics).[1] Thus, he has not, after all, explained all regularity on the basis of pure spontaneity alone.

Moreover, Peirce's notion that the initial state was one of absolute chance seems inconsistent with Peirce's denial, elsewhere, of the logical possibility of absolute disorder. Any such state, he there argues, would be one in which 'everything conceivable' would be found 'with equal frequency'. This, however, 'would not be disorder, but the simplest order'.[2] This point was also urged by Carus, who reminded Peirce of his own statement that 'a contradiction is involved in the very idea of a chance-world'.[3] Peirce replied that this statement posed no difficulty since his view supposed the initial chaos to be 'without existence'.[4] But this reply is utterly unconvincing. For either the initial chaos is logically self-contradictory and non-existent, in which case it cannot explain at all, or else it is ordered in some way, hence allows at the very outset *some* unexplained uniformity.[5]

Gallie argues, more generally, that notions of chance are always contextually bound by implicit or explicit references to specific orders:[6]

As ordinarily employed, the idea of pure chance, or of a purely random distribution of characteristics, presupposes the ideas of (a) a law determining how the purely random character of the distribution shall be ensured, and (b) certain actual physical conditions whose persistence (predictably regular persistence) will ensure the applicability of the law that determines the randomness of the distribution. At least, without these conditions the idea of pure chance has no experimental basis whatever. The truth seems to be that pure chance or randomness is not an isolable conception; on the contrary, it seems inevitably to involve its complementary

---

[1] *CP*, VI.33; *W*, 159.

[2] *CP*, V.345.

[3] Ibid., V.404.

[4] Ibid., VI.609, citing the passage at the end of 'The Architecture of Theories', that the 'chaos ... being without connection or regularity would properly be without existence' (ibid., 33).

[5] See also Manley Thompson, *The Pragmatic Philosophy of C. S. Peirce* (University of Chicago Press, 1953, 1963), 115ff.

[6] Gallie, op. cit., 226.

opposite, the idea of regularity. But how in that case can the idea of pure chance be applied, with any definite meaning, to Peirce's supposed primordial state of sheer indeterminacy?

Gallie also refers to the difficulty mentioned above that a purely chaotic state could hardly be conceived as *'giving rise* to a "tendency to habit" ' (my italics).[1] Gallie's comment suggests the following dilemma: either the tendency to habit just occurred, in which case the habits themselves might just as well have been assumed without explanation, or else there was some regularity by which the tendency arose, in which case the initial state was infected with regularity.

Peirce argues that Spencer's attempt to explain evolution mechanistically is illogical, fundamentally because mechanism cannot explain irreversible processes such as growth.[2] But this in itself does not show that the only alternative to Spencer's attempt is a genetic account of all laws. It is also possible to suppose that nature requires explanation by a *variety* of sorts of law, 'some reversible, some irreversible, some absolute [deterministic], some statistical tendencies'.[3] However, Peirce's cosmology surely calls attention, in a striking way, to certain elements of this variety that had not, in his day, received sufficient consideration. And this thought opens the possibility of a sympathetic view of his cosmology despite all the difficulties outlined above.

For it is not (despite what Peirce himself thought) properly viewed as a grand scientific theory of the universe. Rather it is a metaphysical or cosmological story that serves to highlight certain categories and strategies as important in the future direction of scientific research. Einstein, to take a modern example, said that God does not play dice with the world; he thus expressed his determination to seek explanations beyond the quantum-mechanical and not to rest satisfied with the ultimacy of statistical accounts of nature.[4] His statement was not part of scientific theory, but rather an expression of Einstein's scientific faith. It expressed his conviction as to how science ought to proceed. Rival schools of science operate with rival directive convictions whose signifi-

---

[1] Ibid.
[2] *CP*, VI.14; *W*, 148.
[3] Murphey, op. cit., 348.
[4] See, e.g., Stephen Toulmin, *The Philosophy of Science* (London: Hutchinson, 1953), 123.

cance reaches into the future of the science in question. These differences may be encapsulated in picturesque stories and metaphors, but their function is to express a strategic faith – they do not explain. Yet science cannot do without such faith, for it must always proceed boldly into terrain as yet unexplored. Peirce's cosmology, viewed in this light, constituted a forceful challenge to the older mechanistic and deterministic faith, and provided striking expression of new and fruitful convictions as to the further growth of scientific thought.

IV

PEIRCE'S CRITIQUE OF DESCARTES

Peirce's cosmological ideas are anthropomorphic; they interpret the universe as if it were a growing organism. Applied *directly* to the growing organism, these ideas show a high degree of plausibility. The child, for example, begins at birth with a state of spontaneity or randomness of response. Each such response is specific: it has no sign-function, it does not represent anything else to which it is linked. Analogously, stimuli are also specific: they are not classified by common meaning or function, and they do not signify for the child. Eventually, increasing order and generality replace randomness and specificity. Habits arise which link stimuli to responses under given circumstances. Stimuli and responses are grouped, respectively, and take on representative functions. Meaning begins to develop. Regular habits parallel the growth of a regular and stable environment. However, some element of spontaneity in conduct always remains. Character never becomes wholly rigid, nor does the environment ever become totally predictable and intelligible.

What is the source of this growth of habit, the 'germ of a generalizing tendency'?[1] Peirce supposes a law of mind according to which feelings and ideas tend to generalize. The feelings of discomfort produced by an irritating stimulus tend to spread until activity succeeds in overcoming it. The successful response is most often repeated and correspondingly facilitated; thus habit is built up in relation to the circumstances productive of irritation. These

[1] *CP*, VI.33; *W*, 159.

42

circumstances themselves, accordingly, take on a general meaning or significance. They are classified into various groups and call forth responses of relevant sorts. They take on functions of *representation*, signifying probable consequences in behaviour.

To illustrate these ideas concretely, let us consider a cat placed for the first time in a closed puzzle box. The box is constructed with a latch which opens the door when struck. Not having been fed for a while, the cat is hungry, and it sees the cream which has been placed outside the door. Now this initial situation has a *perceptual* and a *motivational* side: the cat perceives its physical surroundings; moreover, it sees the cream. It also wants the cream. Not being able to get it, however, the cat is hungry. Its hunger is an irritating stimulus. Initially specific in location, its pangs spread their effects, producing a set of movements – a kind of thrashing about – that is virtually unordered or random. This activity continues until some movement happens to strike the latch, releasing the cat from the box and enabling it to appease the hunger which initiated the active phase of the episode. In subsequent trials, the activity phase becomes shorter, the movements less random. Finally, the cat learns to manipulate the latch in a direct and economical manner when put into the same situation again.

When the cat has indeed learned to manipulate the latch, it has acquired a habit linked to the puzzle-box situation: given this situation S, with perceptual and motivational features p and m, it responds appropriately with response R, to achieve the desired and perceptible consequence K. The link of habit is the general if-then connection between S and R, but R is a condition facilitating K. Moreover, it is the prospective link of R with K that enables the learning of R in the situation S. R mediates between the initial condition of irritation and the sought-for condition in which irritation is overcome. The general linkage of R to S provides a form of transition from 'problem' to 'solution'. A rough diagram is as follows:

$$S(p,m) \to R \to K$$

The cat, having acquired the habit in question, abstracts from the utter specificity of the initial situation. The situation loses its 'fullness' and becomes a *cue* or *signal*, the cat now responding to S *in light of* potential desired consequences that are contingent on what it does. In acquiring the habit, the cat has, in a rudimentary but appropriate sense, grasped the meaning or significance of the situation. Its regularity of action now parallels a regular and conceptualized stability of the initial environment.

This general picture of learning is applied by Peirce to *thought*, with the consequence that a theory of knowledge emerges at radical variance with both rationalist and empiricist philosophy. In place of Descartes's emphasis on *radical doubt*, and Locke's emphasis on *sensations*, Peirce emphasizes *belief*. Moreover, renouncing the intellectualistic conception of belief as a mental state segregated from the physical world, Peirce connects belief with action. Finally, in opposition to the classical stress on intuition and certainty, he rejects both in a fundamental way. Like the cat, we begin in the middle of things. Thought or *inquiry* arises in a perceptual and motivational context, and it is precipitated by doubt. But doubt is a real, active state of irritation, not the mere absence of belief. Inquiry is the active process of passing from doubt to belief. Unlike doubt, belief is a calm, settled state of readiness, in the nature of a habit. It is not an occurrence but more like a set. It is that upon which we are prepared to act; thus, it orients us to future experience and is always open to upset by experience. It is constituted of signs, with implicit reference to other signs; thus it is always mediated, never direct, hence not intuitive and incapable of certainty. In place of certainty, Peirce stresses his doctrine of *fallibilism*.[1]

Peirce develops the bases of these ideas in his two important papers of 1868, critical of Descartes, and he carries them forward in 'The Fixation of Belief' and 'How to Make Our Ideas Clear'. We shall here consider the papers of 1868. In the first of these, 'Questions Concerning Certain Faculties Claimed for Man', Peirce sets himself to criticize the doctrine of intuition or immediate knowledge. By implication, he criticizes all doctrines of direct knowledge, from the Greek idea of science as resting upon first principles to contemporary epistemological ideas of knowledge as resting on some basis of certainty. He expands this criticism also to embrace the deductive or mathematical model of reasoning evident in Descartes and influential generally in philosophy.

Do we, asks Peirce in Question 1 of his paper, have the faculty of intuitively distinguishing intuitions from other cognitions?

[1] *CP*, I.8–14 and I.171.

44

What evidence is there that we do? Apparently that we feel we do. But is this feeling itself 'the result of education, old associations, etc.'?[1] If so, it would hardly be decisive. But can we rule these possibilities out by holding that we have the faculty of *telling intuitively* that the *feeling is intuitive*? This would utterly beg the question.

If 'the power of intuitively distinguishing intuitions from other cognitions'[2] indeed exists, one might have supposed a historically evidenced agreement as to *which* cognitions *are* intuitive. But history shows no such agreement. Moreover, common experience with testimony in the law courts or with cases of perceptual illusion reveals how great is the gap between the actual facts and the description of an intelligent witness.[3]

> This certainly seems to show that it is not always very easy to distinguish between a premiss and a conclusion, that we have no infallible power of doing so, and that in fact our only security in difficult cases is in some signs from which we can infer that a given fact must have been seen or must have been inferred.

Far from having an infallible power of telling the difference between the seen and the inferred, we need in fact to rely upon signs, that is, circumstantial and inferential evidence, to make such a distinction in any given case.

Other examples Peirce considers are: (1) *Dreams:* the distinguishing of dreams from reality is not intuitive or direct and infallible, but is rather circumstantial. (2) *Children's explanations:* the child's understanding of how he knows what he knows is often fanciful.[4]

> In many cases, he will tell you that he never learned his mother tongue; he always knew it, or he knew it as soon as he came to have sense. It appears, then, that *he* does not possess the faculty of distinguishing, by simple contemplation, between an intuition and a cognition determined by others.

[1] *CP*, V.214; *W*, 19.
[2] *CP*, V.215; *W*, 19.
[3] *CP*, V.216; *W*, 20.
[4] *CP*, V.218; *W*, 21.

(3) *The third dimension of space:* Berkeley's *New Theory of Vision* showed this third dimension to be inferred rather than intuited, contrary to the prevalent conviction prior to publication of his theory: 'We had been *contemplating* the object since the very creation of man, but this discovery was not made until we began to *reason* about it.'[1] (4) *Blind spot on the retina:* Peirce instructs his reader how to locate the blind spot, concluding that the space we see is not, after all, continuous. Rather it is, as Peirce says,[2]

> a ring, the filling up of which must be the work of the intellect. What more striking example could be desired of the impossibility of distinguishing intellectual results from intuitional data by mere contemplation?

(5) *Texture:* different textures may be distinguished by touch but this cannot be done immediately, for the subject must move his fingers across the surface, 'which shows that he is obliged to compare the sensations of one instant with those of another'.[3] (6) *Pitch:* the pitch of a tone depends, says Peirce, 'upon the rapidity of the succession of the vibrations which reach the ear'. Each vibration 'produces an impulse upon the ear', and each such impulse is known, experimentally, to be perceived.[4]

> There is, therefore, good reason to believe that each of the impulses forming a tone is perceived. . . . Therefore, the pitch of a tone depends upon the rapidity with which certain impressions are successively conveyed to the mind. These impressions must exist previously to any tone; hence, the sensation of pitch is determined by previous cognitions. Nevertheless, this would never have been discovered by the mere contemplation of that feeling.

(7) *Two dimensions of space:* the perception of two dimensions of space is thought to be an immediate intuition but the retina is not spread out; it consists rather 'of innumerable needles pointing towards the light'.[5] Even if each of these nerve points gave the sensation of a small surface, we would immediately see 'not a continuous surface, but a collection of spots'. Moreover, it is

[1] *CP*, V.219; *W*, 21.
[2] *CP*, V.220; *W*, 22.
[3] *CP*, V.221; *W*, 22.
[4] *CP*, V.222; *W*, 22.
[5] *CP*, V.223; *W*, 22.

quite unlikely that the excitation of a single nerve 'can produce an idea as complicated as that of a space, however small'. And if this is so for each nerve point, that is, if no one of these immediately conveys the impression of space, 'the excitation of all cannot do so'. Imagine, says Peirce, that a momentary image is made on the retina. Since no single sensation tells us how many nerves or nerve points are excited, the impression produced is 'indistinguishable from what might be produced by the excitation of some conceivable single nerve'.

> It is not conceivable that the momentary excitation of a
> single nerve should give the sensation of space. Therefore,
> the momentary excitation of all the nerve-points of the retina
> cannot, immediately or mediately, produce the sensation of
> space.[1]

Conceptions of space and of time arise not through intuition but rather because of their utility in reducing the extreme complexity of phenomena to a manageable order.

The various facts reviewed, concludes Peirce in reply to his Question 1, are all 'most readily explained on the supposition that we have no intuitive faculty of distinguishing intuitive from mediate cognitions'.[2]

In Questions 2, 3, 4, he considers next the strongest sources of the claim for intuitive knowledge. First, in Question 2, he asks whether we have an intuitive self-consciousness: a knowledge of ourselves. The question concerns 'the recognition of my *private* self. I know that *I* (not merely *the* I) exist. The question is, how do I know it; by a special intuitive faculty, or is it determined by previous cognitions?'[3] In view of the negative answer to Question 1, we cannot, says Peirce, claim it is *self-evident* that we have an intuitive self-consciousness. Thus, whether we have or not[4]

> is to be determined upon evidence, and the question is
> whether self-consciousness can be explained by the action of
> known faculties under conditions known to exist, or whether
> it is necessary to suppose an unknown cause for this

[1] *CP*, V.223; *W*, 22–3.
[2] *CP*, V.224; *W*, 25.
[3] *CP*, V.225; *W*, 26.
[4] *CP*, V.226; *W*, 26–7.

cognition, and, in the latter case, whether an intuitive faculty of self-consciousness is the most probable cause which can be supposed.

Peirce then proposes a remarkable miniature theory of the development of self-consciousness without presupposition of an intuitive *faculty* to this purpose. The sense of self is not inborn but develops, as evidenced by the late use of the word 'I'. 'From the child's point of view, [its] body is the most important thing in the universe.' This is so since it is so important to feelings, colours, tastes. 'Only what it touches has any actual and present feeling; only what it faces has any actual color; only what is on its tongue has any actual taste.'[1] Furthermore, the body is soon discovered to be peculiarly related to things the child perceives as fit to be changed. With the advent of language, his world is enlarged through testimony, which is 'even a stronger mark of fact than *the facts themselves*'.[2] With testimony and the enlargement of the child's world comes a corresponding realization of ignorance and 'it is necessary to suppose a *self* in which this ignorance can inhere. So testimony gives the first dawning of self-consciousness.'[3]

It also gives rise to the conception of privacy and error, which requires the supposition of a self that is fallible. This sketch of a theory, calling only upon known faculties (children's knowledge of ignorance and error) would thus explain the rise of self-consciousness. Still we do not know that the process works in exactly the manner suggested. Nevertheless, argues Peirce, the supposition that it does 'is infinitely more supported by facts than the supposition of a wholly peculiar faculty of the mind'.[4]

Finally, in a very striking, and important, passage, Peirce considers a general argument for an intuitive self-consciousness: 'We are more certain of our own existence than of any other fact; a premiss cannot determine a conclusion to be more certain than it is itself; hence, our own existence cannot have been inferred from any other fact.'[5] He admits the first premiss, but rejects the second: a conclusion, he argues, may indeed become stronger than any

---

[1] *CP*, V.229; *W*, 27.
[2] *CP*, V.233; *W*, 28.
[3] Ibid.
[4] *CP*, V.236; *W*, 29.
[5] *CP*, V.237; *W*, 29.

one of the facts upon which it rests. If a dozen witnesses testify to some occurrence,[1]

> my belief in that occurrence rests on the belief that each of those men is generally to be believed upon oath. Yet the fact testified to is made more certain than that any one of those men is generally to be believed. In the same way, to the developed mind of man, his own existence is supported by *every other fact,* and is, therefore, incomparably more certain than any one of these facts. But it cannot be said to be more certain than that there is another fact, since there is no doubt perceptible in either case.

Thus, Peirce concludes that self-consciousness may well be inferential, hence there is no need to postulate an intuitive self-consciousness.

In Question 3, he considers whether we have an intuitive capacity to distinguish between the subjective character, i.e., what may be termed the mode, of our various cognitions. 'Every cognition', he says, 'involves something represented, or that of which we are conscious, and some action or passion of the self whereby it becomes represented. The former shall be termed the objective, the latter the subjective, element of the cognition.'[2] The question is, then, whether we can directly intuit the mode of a given cognition to be that 'of dreaming, imagining, conceiving, believing, etc.'.[3] Relying again on the negative reply to Question 1, he argues that we cannot simply uphold a positive reply on the basis of self-evidence. Do we then have good reason to postulate such a faculty or can we explain the facts without such postulation? To this he replies that we can adequately explain the manifest facts without special postulation. The difference in the *objects* of sense and imagination, of dream and experience of reality, is sufficient to explain our recognition of these different modes. As for distinguishing belief from conception, either we judge the mode again by reference to an accompanying characteristic *object*, e.g., a sensation of conviction, or we take belief to be instanced in action, so that the existence of belief may be inferred from actions.

In Question 4, Peirce considers 'whether we have any power of

[1] *CP*, V.237; *W*, 29–30.
[2] *CP*, V.238; *W*, 30.
[3] Ibid.

introspection, or whether our whole knowledge of the internal world is derived from the observation of external facts'.[1] Sensations are, to be sure, partly determined by internal conditions; thus redness as a sensation depends on the constitution of the mind. But to infer anything about the mind from the sensation would involve an 'inference from redness as a predicate of something external'.[2] Peirce apparently means that we attribute redness to external objects in the first instance. Well then, what of the emotions, which seem to 'arise in the first place, not as predicates at all, and to be referable to the mind alone'? Do they then not yield a direct access to the mind, yielding a knowledge of it not based on 'outward things'?[3]

We cannot, argues Peirce, suppose a positive answer to be self-evident. For the negative answer to Question 3 already has shown that we cannot intuitively distinguish modes of consciousness; we cannot therefore suppose it obvious that we have a power of introspection. The answer, if positive, must be shown to be required in order to give a reasonable explanation of the facts. Here Peirce argues that even emotions are external in reference. Their reference is relative to particular circumstances, but no less external for that. To feel angry is, in effect, to suppose the objective circumstances to be of appropriate sort, and the object of anger to have appropriate features. Thus anger, and other emotions, are not simply internal mental states available for introspection. Volition Peirce takes as a kind of concentration of attention or abstraction, which presumably focuses on the end desired. Now desire, as an emotion, has already been dealt with. And volition as the power of abstraction is inferred from abstract objects, 'just as the knowledge of the power of seeing is inferred from colored objects'.[4] Peirce denies, then, any reason to postulate introspection and concludes that the only way to study a psychological question is by inference from external facts.

In discussing Question 5: 'Whether we can think without signs',[5] he argues that all thought is embodied in signs since, following the conclusion of Question 4 and seeking 'the light of

---

[1] *CP*, V.243; *W*, 32.
[2] *CP*, V.245; *W*, 32.
[3] Ibid.
[4] *CP*, V.248; *W*, 33.
[5] *CP*, V.249; *W*, 34.

external facts, the only cases of thought which we can find are of thought in signs'.[1] He further argues, in discussing his Question 6, that no sign can have meaning if it is defined as the sign of something absolutely incognizable. For all conceptions are traceable to cognitions arising in judgments of experience and nothing absolutely incognizable occurs in experience, so there can be no conception of it. 'But the meaning of a term is the conception which it conveys. Hence, a term can have no such meaning.'[2]

In Question 7, finally, Peirce raises the question whether there is any cognition not determined by a previous one: surely there must have been a first in this series? His reply is rather obscure but it seems to amount to the suggestion that thoughts are continuous so that the series requires no first term. Gallie remarks that the reply is weak since it offers no positive ground for holding that thought-sequences *are* continuous.[3] And Murphey comments that Peirce's argument presupposes that thought may be represented by a line not containing its own limit. That is, 'granted that there is no least finite interval required for a cognition, the series may converge to a limit outside itself'.[4] But, as Murphey notes, this argument assumes just what is at issue – 'that there is no minimum finite interval'.[5] I do not myself believe Peirce's argument can be rescued, unless (as Peirce himself refused to do) we give up the *temporal* question altogether and emphasize solely the *logical* one. If thought, that is to say, is embodied in signs, there is a mutual and general determination of meanings and logical relations, and it makes no sense to say that some special thoughts are privileged. As Peirce says in discussing Question 5, 'From the proposition that every thought is a sign, it follows that every thought must address itself to some other, must determine some other, since that is the essence of a sign.'[6] All thoughts are in the same boat, all fallible, all interdependent. It is here that we come to Peirce's most important divergence from Cartesianism elaborated in the second essay of 1868.

What Peirce hopes to have shown in the first of these essays, in

[1] *CP*, V.251; *W*, 34.
[2] *CP*, V.255; *W*, 35.
[3] W. B. Gallie, *Peirce and Pragmatism* (New York: Dover, 1966), 70.
[4] Murray G. Murphey, *The Development of Peirce's Philosophy* (Cambridge, Mass.: Harvard University Press, 1961), 110.
[5] Ibid., 111.
[6] *CP*, V.253; *W*, 34.

sum, is that there are no absolute cognitive starting points, i.e., points not determined by prior or other cognitions, certifiable through direct and infallible inspection of them. We cannot tell by intuitive inspection if we have such a starting point. Further, all cognitions are expressed in signs and so implicitly refer to others and are fallible. Finally, self-consciousness is not intuitively known but built up by inference from external facts, so even the Cartesian *cogito* is thrown into doubt.

In 'Some Consequences of Four Incapacities', Peirce sets himself to elaborate further his alternative to Cartesianism, here concentrating on issues of logic and methodology, rather than on the question of intuition. In what one imagines to be a partly ironic statement, Peirce declares that Cartesianism differs from the scholasticism it displaced in advocating four points which form the platform of modern philosophy, whereas modern science and logic require a reversal of all four points. Peirce is not, of course, here urging a return to scholasticism, but rather a recognition of certain logical and methodological virtues of the latter, which, as he argues, it shares with the logic of modern science.

The 'spirit of Cartesianism' is summed up by Peirce in the following four points:[1]

1. It teaches that philosophy must begin with universal doubt; whereas scholasticism had never questioned fundamentals.
2. It teaches that the ultimate test of certainty is to be found in the individual consciousness; whereas scholasticism had rested on the testimony of sages and of the Catholic Church.
3. The multiform argumentation of the middle ages is replaced by a single thread of inference depending often upon inconspicuous premisses.
4. Scholasticism had its mysteries of faith, but undertook to explain all created things. But there are many facts which Cartesianism not only does not explain but renders absolutely inexplicable, unless to say that 'God makes them so' is to be regarded as an explanation.

In commenting on these four teachings, Peirce rejects each. First, he argues that 'we cannot begin with complete doubt'.[2] Doubt requires a positive reason. In philosophy, we must begin

[1] *CP*, V.264; *W*, 39.
[2] *CP*, V.265; *W*, 40.

where we are, for there is no other place to begin. 'Let us not pretend to doubt in philosophy what we do not doubt in our hearts.' Radical Cartesian doubt, since it is in fact impossible, must be formal only, hence self-deceptive, since not real doubt. In fact the Cartesian method ends by recovering all the beliefs with which the doubter began. Real doubt, by contrast, has the capacity to alter the beliefs of the doubter; it is motivated by positive reason, and it is also directed or specific.

As to the second point, Peirce argues fundamentally against the individualism of the Cartesian criterion: 'Whatever I am clearly convinced of, is true.' This individualism, he suggests, renders the criterion also formal and hence not decisive, therefore also in a critical sense self-deceptive. Can I really hold that whatever I am clearly convinced of is true? Were I really convinced, I should require no further justification or criterion; 'I should have done with reasoning'.[1] In the sciences, such a criterion would be totally ineffective, for 'when a theory has been broached it is considered to be on probation until . . . agreement is reached. After it is reached, the question of certainty becomes an idle one, because there is no one left who doubts it.'[2] To make the individual consciousness the test of truth is, Peirce seems to say, to define a pursuit in which this social dimension is ignored, and in which the ideal of agreement is surrendered, with the consequence that real and specific doubts arising from disagreements with one's peers are overridden. 'The result is that metaphysicians will all agree that metaphysics has reached a pitch of certainty far beyond that of the physical sciences – only they can agree upon nothing else.'[3] Peirce remarks that this state of affairs is pernicious, but I interpret this remark not as a simple value judgment, but as a conclusion from the judgment that this state of affairs is formal and self-deceptive in fact.

What, however, is the alternative? To honour the ideal of agreement is to allow that the individual consciousness, no matter how firmly convinced, can never be decisive; the author of a theory ought, in principle, to allow always for the possibility of a reconsideration and revision of his views in light of the investigations of others. Here again is the notion of fallibilism; it means giving

[1] Ibid.
[2] Ibid.
[3] Ibid.

up the virtuoso ideal of philosophy, according to which philosophers hope individually 'to attain the ultimate philosophy'. On the contrary, says Peirce, 'We can only seek it . . . for the *community* of philosophers.'[1] The collaborative and community aspects of science are here thus contrasted with Cartesianism. Certainty is removed from the actuality of the individual's experience; ultimacy becomes an ideal of the investigative community. The result is that actual agreements operate, in a provisional and short-term way, to settle debates over scientific theories until such time as genuine doubts arise, occasioning particular reconsiderations.

As to the third point, Peirce argues against the mathematical method of 'linear' deduction, at least as applied in philosophy. Philosophy, he insists, ought rather to take the successful sciences as a whole, inclusive of the empirical sciences, as a model for its reasonings. It ought 'to trust rather to the multitude and variety of its arguments than to the conclusiveness of any one'.[2] The notion of a deductive chain of inference anchored to fixed and certain premises, and capable only of transmitting what is already contained in those premises, must be surrendered as a model of philosophical reasoning. Such reasoning should not be construed to 'form a chain which is no stronger than its weakest link, but a cable whose fibers may be ever so slender, provided they are sufficiently numerous and intimately connected'.[3] The cable *is* stronger than its weakest fibre; it gathers and goes beyond the individual strengths of its single fibres. As Peirce argued earlier that, in general, a premiss *can* determine a conclusion to be more certain than it is itself, so he here opposes the cable metaphor to that of the chain, to bring home the point: scientific reasoning is circumstantial, multiform, hypothetical, explanatory. Though it builds only on modestly firm data, the web it forms is extremely powerful.

Peirce's emphasis here accords well with contemporary understandings. Physical science may be presented in axiomatic or deductive form, but this by no means implies that the axioms are fixed and certain, and that the theorems gain their credibility through deductive channels from these axioms. The various factual statements accepted in a science at a given time have, gener-

---

[1] Ibid.
[2] *CP*, V.265; *W*, 40–1.
[3] *CP*, V.265; *W*, 41.

ally, independent and diverse warrants of their own. Generally these statements may be ordered or systematized in various ways. Generally, too, the fundamental theoretical axioms are not thought to be indubitable. Typically, they are proposed provisionally as hypotheses for the ordering of firmer experimental, or more confidently held, theorems. The theorems are typically thought to support the hypotheses that successfully and elegantly axiomatize them, rather than gaining their own credibility from those hypotheses. In short, the function of deduction is not to transmit certainty from a direct, intuitive starting point, but rather to systematize and connect various factual beliefs so that they may serve to test one another, the tested network thus formed acquiring a strength beyond that of any constituent element.

These comments relate, finally, to Peirce's fourth point: the rejection of unanalysable and inexplicable ultimates. The explanation he gives seems to me somewhat obscure, but I take it as an elaboration of the point that axioms or first principles never constitute absolutely firm starting points. Indeed, as remarked earlier, they are typically hypothetical, and warranted by their capacity to explain a variety of facts. At the same time, each of these facts is partly warranted by its place in the order and partly by independent, e.g. experimental, means. Thus, no part of the whole web stands outside the possibility of control by the rest; no part is immune to revision for cause. Yet the web as a whole may gather enormous strength since the strands provide one another with mutual support.

'It would be difficult to find', says Gallie, 'in the whole history of philosophy, a battery of criticisms more devastating and complete than those [of] the second of Peirce's papers of 1868.'[1] There are certainly frequent obscurities and flaws here – to take but two examples, the confusion noted earlier between the *temporal* and *logical* interdependence of cognitions, and the notion of thought as mathematically continuous. Many passages are puzzling, several are too condensed to evaluate, and still others are unconvincing in substance. Despite these defects, the 1868 papers are very important. They express, in pioneering manner, a clearly modern philosophy, one that proposes fundamentally new ways of thinking about knowledge, based upon deep reflection on the import of modern empirical science.

[1] Gallie, op. cit., 78.

Symbolic of Peirce's new ways of thinking is his substitution of the cable metaphor for that of the chain. It is interesting to note how this shift of metaphors strikingly foreshadows analogous figures in the thought of later philosophers. The most obvious comparison, perhaps, is with Wittgenstein. In forming a more complex notion of classifying similarities, the latter thinker thus discusses the extension of the concept of number:[1]

> And we extend our concept of number as in spinning a thread we twist fibre on fibre. And the strength of the thread does not reside in the fact that some one fibre runs through its whole length, but in the overlapping of many fibres.

More pertinent to modern science, however, are the images proposed by Russell, Popper, and Neurath; these point to the same features addressed by Peirce: the interdependence of scientific statements, the lack of certainty at any point in science and the development of strong systematic structures out of relatively weak components.

Russell says:[2]

> Given a number of propositions, each having a fairly high degree of intrinsic credibility, and given a system of inferences by virtue of which these various propositions increase each other's credibility, it may be possible in the end to arrive at a body of interconnected propositions having, as a whole, a very high degree of credibility. Within this body, some are only inferred, but none are only premises, for those which are premises are also conclusions. The edifice of knowledge may be compared to a bridge resting on many piers, each of which not only supports the roadway but helps the other piers to stand firm owing to interconnecting girders. The piers are the analogues of the propositions having some intrinsic credibility, while the upper portions of the bridge are the analogues of what is only inferred. But although each pier may be strengthened by the other piers, it is the solid

---

[1] Ludwig Wittgenstein, *Philosophical Investigations* (translated by G. E. M. Anscombe) (Oxford: Blackwell, 1953), para. 67.

[2] Bertrand Russell, *Human Knowledge: Its Scope and Limits* (New York: Simon & Schuster, 1948), 395-6.

ground that supports the whole, and in like manner it is intrinsic credibility that supports the whole edifice of knowledge.

Popper writes:[1]

The empirical basis of objective science has thus nothing 'absolute' about it. Science does not rest upon rock-bottom. The bold structure of its theories rises, as it were, above a swamp. It is like a building erected on piles. The piles are driven down from above into the swamp, but not down to any natural or 'given' base; and when we cease our attempts to drive our piles into a deeper layer, it is not because we have reached firm ground. We simply stop when we are satisfied that they are firm enough to carry the structure, at least for the time being.

Neurath, finally, compares us to 'sailors who must rebuild their ship on the open sea, never able to dismantle it in dry-dock and to reconstruct it there out of the best materials'.[2] We must stay afloat, repairing any part of the ship that springs a leak by using material from the rest of the boat, relying on the rest to keep us afloat during the process of repair. The process may be continued without end, yet nowhere is there the possibility of rebuilding afresh.

All these images purport to capture that elusive, yet profoundly important capacity of science to construct, without certain foundations or indubitable beginnings, a firm habitation for man's knowledge, capable, moreover, of continuous use and continuous repair. It is Peirce's merit to have offered the earliest of such figures, but more significantly, to have appreciated the need for philosophy to rethink its conceptions of knowledge in the light of a new understanding of scientific thought.

[1] Karl R. Popper, *The Logic of Scientific Discovery* (New York: Basic Books, 1959), 111.
[2] Otto Neurath, 'Protocol Sentences' (published originally in *Erkenntnis*, III (1932–3)), translated by Frederick Schick; in A. J. Ayer, ed., *Logical Positivism* (Chicago: Free Press, 1959), 201.

V

PEIRCE'S THEORY OF INQUIRY

We have earlier remarked the importance of Bain's theory of belief in the development of pragmatism. Peirce indeed considered the latter doctrine to be 'scarce more than a corollary'[1] of Bain's conception. What was the nature of this conception? Bain laid special emphasis on the relation of belief to action, characterizing belief as ' "an attitude or disposition of preparedness to act" when occasion offers'. He also denied that doubt could be identified with mere disbelief. Doubt and belief are felt to be different in quality, 'belief' being the 'name for a serene, satisfying, and happy tone of mind', whereas the state of doubt 'is one of discomfort in most cases, and sometimes of the most aggravated human wretchedness'.[2] The impulse[3]

> to escape doubt and reach belief is . . . inherent in man; indeed, belief is our natural state, for we have an initial trust or belief in the continuation of the present state and the continued efficacy of our mode of behavior. But experience disappoints us and so generates doubt, which must continue until a new pattern is established which does yield the desired result.

Among the reasons why Bain's theory appealed to Peirce, as suggested by Murphey, was the fact that it combined so well with

---

[1] *CP*, V.12.

[2] Alexander Bain, *The Emotions and the Will* (1859); quoted in Max H. Fisch, 'Alexander Bain and the Genealogy of Pragmatism', *Journal of the History of Ideas*, XV (June 1954), 419–20; also quoted in Murray G. Murphey, *The Development of Peirce's Philosophy* (Cambridge, Mass.: Harvard University Press, 1961), 160–1.

[3] Ibid., 161, citing Fisch, op. cit., 420f.

the 1868 papers we have been discussing. Bain, in effect 'supplies a psychological foundation for Peirce's denial of Cartesian doubt, for Bain holds that men are naturally believers and that doubt is produced only by events which disrupt our beliefs – not by pretense'.[1] Rather than supposing that the 'natural' state is utter lack of belief, i.e., *radical* doubt, so that every belief we have requires justification from scratch, Bain offers Peirce a theory that reverses the order of naturalness, as the modern concept of inertia reversed the natural state from rest to motion. The natural state is now held to be that belief, with no possibility of wholesale and radical justification. Rather, doubt arising in the body of belief now wants a positive reason, and finds its resolution in the recapture of belief.

Moreover, using Bain's ideas, Peirce can[2]

fit his whole theory of inquiry into an evolutionary frame of reference. Beliefs may be regarded as adjustive habits while failure of adjustment leads to doubt. And the superior adjustive power of an organism endowed with the capacity to correct its patterns of action by experience makes it possible to utilize an argument from natural selection to explain how we come to be so admirably constituted. . . . Moreover, the addition of this biological perspective permits Peirce to strengthen some of his earlier doctrines. For in the first place, it provides him with a new definition of the nature of a problem – a definition subsequently developed by Dewey. A problem situation exists whenever we find our established habits of conduct inadequate to attain a desired end, regardless of how the inadequacy comes about, and the effect of a problem situation upon us is the production of doubt. This being the case, Cartesian doubt is nonsense, for there is no problem situation. But secondly, the theory provides a clarification of the nature of an answer. An answer is any rule of action which enables us to attain our desired ends. Accordingly, our objective is to find a rule which will always lead us to that which we desire. So in the investigation of a real object, our objective is a knowledge of how to act respecting that object so as to attain our desired ends. Thus,

[1] Murphey, op. cit., 161.
[2] Ibid., 163.

as pragmatism asserts, the concept of the object can mean nothing to us but all the habits it involves. The attainment of a stable belief – belief that will stand in the long run – is thus the goal of inquiry. Such belief we define as true, and its object as reality.

'The Fixation of Belief' presents a statement of Peirce's theory of inquiry. Doubt differs from belief in three respects: (a) 'there is a dissimilarity between the sensation of doubting and that of believing.'[1] (b) 'The feeling of believing is a more or less sure indication of there being established in our nature some habit which will determine our actions. Doubt never has such an effect.'[2] (c) 'Doubt is an uneasy and dissatisfied state from which we struggle to free ourselves and pass into the state of belief, while the latter is a calm and satisfactory state which we do not wish to avoid, or to change to a belief in anything else. On the contrary, we cling tenaciously, not merely to believing, but to believing just what we do believe.'[3]

Inquiry is the struggle to overcome doubt and attain belief, and it has in doubt its 'only immediate motive'.[4] It begins with doubt, and ends only with the cessation of doubt. Hence, says Peirce, 'the sole object of inquiry is the settlement of opinion'.[5] When opinion is settled, and 'real and living doubt'[6] overcome, genuine inquiry cannot arise. When no *actual* doubt affects any given proposition, this proposition may be employed as a premiss, no matter how it might be imagined to be doubtful by hypothetical considerations.

If the function of inquiry is the settlement of opinion or the fixation of belief, the question arises as to the relative effectiveness of alternative methods by which this function may be carried out. Peirce considers this question and proceeds to a comparison of four such methods: (1) the method of tenacity, (2) the method of authority, (3) the *a priori* method, and (4) the method of science.

The method of *tenacity* consists in a reiteration of the belief, 'dwelling on all which may conduce to that belief, and learning to

---

[1] *CP*, V.370; *W*, 98.
[2] *CP*, V.371; *W*, 98–9.
[3] *CP*, V.372; *W*, 99.
[4] *CP*, V.374–5; *W*, 100.
[5] *CP*, V.375; *W*, 100.
[6] *CP*, V.376; *W*, 100.

turn with contempt and hatred from anything which might disturb it'. This method, which, as Peirce says, 'is really pursued by many men' offers 'great peace of mind' despite some inconveniences. Moreover, one could hardly argue against it that it is irrational, for its proponent 'does not propose to himself to be rational, and indeed, will often talk with scorn of man's weak and illusive reason'.[1]

Now the latter point seems somewhat peculiar in the context of Peirce's discussion. For the proponent of tenacity may not be interested in effective settlement of opinion either, and this does not deter Peirce from arguing against the effectiveness of tenacity. Presumably, what Peirce is really after is not a *debate* with proponents of his various methods, aimed at persuasion, but rather an *investigation* into relative effectiveness which we ourselves, undecided at the outset, may find instructive once we have realized that the sole function of inquiry is the settlement of opinion. And Peirce indeed claims that tenacity is ineffective for 'the social impulse is against it'.[2] Finding oneself confronted with the differing opinions of other men, one's confidence in one's own tenaciously held beliefs is shaken. Nor can we shield ourselves from contacts with others unless we become hermits. The method of tenacity thus leaves us vulnerable to continual unsettlement of our beliefs.

Imagine, then, a transfer of tenacity from the individual to the group, in particular the state, with institutions for inculcating the preferred doctrines and stamping out contrary views as well as possibly unsettling counter-evidence. Imagine systematic censorship, indoctrination, and terror as systematically instituted, with occasional massacres as needed, for these have proved 'very effective means of settling opinion in a country'.[3] This method, which Peirce denotes 'the method of authority',[4] is capable of the most horrible atrocities, 'for the officer of a society does not feel justified in surrendering the interests of that society for the sake of mercy, as he might his own private interests'.[5] It is, from the point of view of effectiveness, certainly superior to the method of

---

[1] *CP*, V.377; *W*, 101–3.
[2] *CP*, V.378; *W*, 103.
[3] *CP*, V.379; *W*, 103.
[4] *CP*, V.380; *W*, 104.
[5] *CP*, V.379; *W*, 104.

tenacity, for it shields the individual, by and large, from encounters with differing opinions. Though the official beliefs of such a system undergo change, moreover, these changes are generally so slow that the beliefs of any given person remain 'sensibly fixed'.[1]

Nevertheless, there are flaws. Social regulation cannot extend to all opinions whatever, and unregulated opinion of whatever sort poses a potential threat to stability. Individual men may reflect that other societies and other ages have held quite different beliefs, and must further consider that it is the mere accident of their own condition that has led them to the official doctrines they have. Doubts thus arise because of internal awareness of historical and social differences, and such doubts must affect 'every belief which seems to be determined by the caprice either of themselves or of those who originated the popular opinions'.[2]

We consider then a third method, which rejects both 'the willful adherence to a belief, and the arbitrary forcing of it upon others', a method which follows the natural preferences of 'men conversing together and regarding matters in different lights'. Examples of this method are to be found in 'the history of metaphysical philosophy', where beliefs have been formed not in the effort to account for observed facts but in the effort to formulate what seemed 'agreeable to reason'.[3] This *a priori* method, admittedly 'far more intellectual and respectable from the point of view of reason than either of the others'[4] already considered, nevertheless fails equally. For it assimilates inquiry to the development of taste, always a matter of fashion, and thus never culminating in agreement but always subject to pendulum swings over time. When we, moreover, reflect upon the diversity of fashions, and come to recognize that our own beliefs have been formed by the operation of such 'accidental causes',[5] we cannot prevent real doubts from arising within us.

We consider then, finally, the method of science, which purports to form beliefs by reference to external permanencies, rather than human causes. It supposes real things with properties 'entirely independent of our opinions about them'.[6] Moreover, al-

[1] *CP*, V.380; *W*, 104.
[2] *CP*, V.382; *W*, 105.
[3] *CP*, V.382; *W*, 105–6.
[4] *CP*, V.383; *W*, 106.
[5] *CP*, V.383; *W*, 107.
[6] *CP*, V.384; *W*, 107.

though our individual encounters with these things are indefinitely varied, we can ascertain their character through reasoning, since they affect our senses according to constant laws of perception and are thus accessible to any man who has enough experience and sufficient competence to reason about these matters.

What about this supposition of *realities*? If it underlies science, it cannot in turn be proved by science. Peirce offers four replies: (1) If science does not prove that there are real things, it at least does not disprove their existence. Thus, practice of the method of science does not lead us to doubt it, whereas practice of the other methods does lead us to doubt them, since (presumably) the realization that they are wilful, arbitrary, or capricious upsets our confidence in their general effectiveness. (2) The feeling that gives rise to any method of inquiry is a 'dissatisfaction at two repugnant propositions'. But this is already a 'vague concession that there is some *one* thing to which a proposition should conform'. *Nobody* can 'really doubt that there are realities'. There can therefore be no positive reason for doubt brought forth by the social impulse. (3) Everybody in fact uses the scientific method about many things, and 'only ceases to use it when he does not know how to apply it'. (4) 'Experience of the method has not led us to doubt it', but has served rather to increase our confidence in it, because of its triumphs in settling opinion. Thus to question the existence of real things *in general* is idle. 'If there be anybody with a living doubt upon the subject, let him consider it.'[1]

What is the fundamental contrast between the method of science and all the others? The main contrast Peirce offers is that the method of science is the only one that presents 'any distinction of a right and a wrong way'.[2] That is to say, the method is self-corrective, in that it acknowledges the possibility of errors in execution which may be located and corrected by the very use of the method itself. By contrast, the pursuit of any of the other methods is necessarily correct according to the method in question, so that no errors can be acknowledged, much less corrected, by that method itself.

The other methods have their virtues, and these should not be ignored, says Peirce, but a man should reflect that 'after all, he

---

[1] *CP*, V.384; *W*, 108.
[2] *CP*, V.385; *W*, 109.

wishes his opinions to coincide with the fact, and that there is no reason why the results of those first three methods should do so. To bring about this effect is the prerogative of the method of science.'[1]

[1] *CP*, V.387; *W*, iii.

VI

PEIRCE'S THEORY OF INQUIRY: CRITICAL REMARKS

The doubt-belief theory of inquiry itself raises several important issues, and the comparative examination of methods in 'The Fixation of Belief' raises others. I shall consider first those issues pertaining to Peirce's interpretation of doubt and belief, and shall then turn to a discussion of the essay itself.

Consider, first, Peirce's contrast between doubt and belief: doubt is an uneasy state of irritation, whereas belief is a calm state, a latency or disposition. Does it follow, then, that doubt is always conscious? Not necessarily, it might be supposed. For one might realize one's being in a state of doubt by inference from the disruption of conduct consequent upon the failure or contradiction of one's beliefs. Or one might infer one's doubt from the active thrashing about constituting the struggle to overcome it. Yet, Peirce does affirm a 'sensation of doubting'.[1] Does he allow, then, that one *might* not have the sensation but *only* the active disruption, and does he incline to call such a state 'doubt' or not? The answer is unclear.

As to belief, Peirce speaks also of a 'sensation of believing'.[2] Yet, since belief is a latent state of readiness for action, it is even more implausible to suppose that every such state is accompanied at all times by a sensation peculiar to it. It will be recalled that, in answer to Question 3 of 'Questions Concerning Certain Faculties',

---

[1] *CP*, V.370; *W*, 98.
[2] Ibid.

Peirce discussed the distinction of belief and conception, denying that such distinction required an intuitive awareness of subjective elements of cognition. Belief could, he argued, in most cases be judged by the feeling of conviction attending it (such feeling constituting an objective rather than a subjective element); in other cases, belief could be judged by inference from the action to which it tended, that is, from 'external facts'.[1] Peirce there explicitly distinguished *sensational* from *active* belief and asserted 'that neither of these necessarily involves the other'.[2] Yet here, in 'The Fixation of Belief', he affirms the sensation of believing apparently without qualification. Moreover, in 'How to Make Our Ideas Clear', the companion essay, he states flatly that belief has just three properties: 'First, it is something that we are aware of; second, it appeases the irritation of doubt; and third, it involves the establishment in our nature of a rule of action, or, say for short, a *habit*.'[3] From this we may infer he supposes belief to be always available to awareness. But this, aside from its conflict with other passages, is a difficult doctrine. Does Peirce then mean perhaps that belief can always be *called into* awareness at will? Even this will not be generally true for *active* belief, accessible through inference from 'external' conduct; such inference cannot be short-circuited by an act of will.

Peirce's second point above, that belief appeases the irritation of doubt, is in conflict, furthermore, with the idea (earlier propounded) that belief is prior to doubt, and constitutes the natural state before inquiry. Do all beliefs arise from inquiry? Peirce's theory clearly rests on a negative answer to this question, in view of the fact that he holds inquiry itself to presuppose belief, and rejects completely the radical doubt of Cartesianism. Yet we find him now saying that belief appeases the irritation of doubt. Perhaps he means only that it is *capable* of appeasing the irritation of doubt. If so, his statement is merely trivial, since the habit reflected in a belief is understood *ab initio* to preclude the active disruption of conduct comprising doubt. While belief reigns within a given region, doubt, by the same token, is excluded therefrom.

Finally, Peirce says belief involves the establishment of a rule of action or a habit. But not all habits are, or are associated with,

[1] *CP*, V.242; *W*, 32.
[2] *CP*, V.242; *W*, 31.
[3] *CP*, V.397; *W*, 121.

beliefs, so presumably beliefs are related to a subclass of habits. But what subclass? Not those habits we are aware of, or those which arise from inquiry, as we have just argued. Is there then some distinctive way of marking out the relevant subclass by the *capability* of appeasing the irritation of doubt? This does not seem likely either. For, in the first place, an analogous question arises with respect to doubt – that is, what sorts of disruptions of conduct are to be taken as constituting doubt? And, in the second place, even if we take the notion of doubt for granted, the proposal is confronted by counter-examples. A neurotic doubt may, for example, be appeased by a habit below the threshold of awareness, moreover one which has, at best, only 'symbolic meaning', for example, a tic or a characteristic blink. Does such a habit therefore constitute a belief? The matter remains obscure.

The problem of interpreting belief is, of course, still with us; it has not been solved by philosophies after Peirce. Indeed this problem is one of the most perplexing issues confronting contemporary philosophical analysis. We need to recognize Peirce's important contribution in bringing the concept of belief into relation with action, habit, and evolutionary notions, and, at the same time, to recognize fundamental difficulties in his specific formulations.

Peirce, as has been suggested, developed his doubt-belief theory of inquiry as a psychological foundation of his earlier epistemological critique of Descartes. But the latter is not necessarily affected by difficulties in the former. One may, in fact, try to read even the theory of inquiry as *epistemology* rather than *psychology*. Its import then is not to *describe* the course of thinking, but rather to say, for example, that *proper* scientific thought always is directed to specific questions, that it proceeds always by taking certain assumptions for granted, and that it is to be evaluated by how well it satisfies the questions from which it arose. Read thus, it rejects the idea that there can be scientific investigation without any assumptions whatever, as well as the idea that required assumptions must be absolutely indubitable.

Still there are special difficulties to be faced in interpreting Peirce's insistence on 'real and living doubt'[1] as the origin of inquiry. For there is, in fact, much *thinking* that does not originate in doubt. Imagination, recollection, perception, composition – all

[1] *CP*, V.376; *W*, 100.

67

seem to provide counter-instances. But, it will be said, Peirce speaks of *inquiry* specifically, not of thinking in general, and he is surely concentrating on scientific research as his model. Is it then true, at least, that all such research in fact originates or should, ideally, originate in real and living doubt? Does there need to be an active and real irritation, a breakdown in prior habits, before scientific research can begin? Does not theoretical curiosity or playfulness have a role in sparking scientific thought? The 'problem theory of thinking' which sprang from Peirce, and was later applied in progressive theories of education seemed, surely, to be insisting, to the contrary, that genuine thought arises from real and live difficulties in the environment rather than from abstract theoretical motives.

Yet Peirce himself speaks, in 'How to Make Our Ideas Clear', of *feigned hesitancy*, and says that 'whether feigned for mere amusement or with a lofty purpose', it 'plays a great part in the production of scientific inquiry'.[1] Moreover, in a note to 'The Fixation of Belief' added in 1893, he says that doubt is typically[2]

> anticipated hesitancy about what I shall do hereafter, or a feigned hesitancy about a fictitious state of things. It is the power of making believe we hesitate, together with the pregnant fact that the decision upon the merely make-believe dilemma goes toward forming a bona fide habit that will be operative in a real emergency.

And, in another note, he says further that 'for the sake of the pleasures of inquiry, men may like to seek out doubts'.[3] The effect of these qualifications is surely to deny that research must always spring from *actual* difficulties or failures of adjustment; it is also to insist that the researcher is motivated, not only to solve problems, but to seek them. His research activity does not subside when his problems are solved, unless we artificially *define* such activity as consisting in problem-solution only, to the exclusion of problem-finding.

Peirce's theory of inquiry, even taken epistemologically, thus

[1] *CP*, V.394; *W*, 119.
[2] *CP*, V.373, n.1; *W*, 99, n.9.
[3] *CP*, V.372, n.2; *W*, 99, n.7.

presents serious problems of interpretation; in particular, his treatment of doubt appears inconsistent. Moreover, his qualifications seem to undercut his earlier criticism of Descartes: having admitted that feigned or hypothetical doubt is typical and functional in science, how can Peirce dismiss Descartes's procedure as not properly based on real and living doubt?

I believe that Peirce's formulation: *that all inquiry must begin in real and living doubt,* is indeed faulty. For it implies that without real and living doubt, there can be no inquiry; yet Peirce admits the importance of inquiries springing from doubts that are merely feigned. The fundamental epistemological point that Peirce is concerned to make is rather that without real and living doubt, a proposition *may still be taken as an assumption* for the purposes of inquiry. It does not matter that a proposition is subject to feigned doubt; the mere fact that one might *hypothetically* doubt it does not *require us* to reject it as an assumption and seek to replace it or reinstate it through additional and special argumentation. We are *required* to reject propositions as usable assumptions, that is to say, only if they are subject to real and living doubts – doubts that are specific to the propositions in question and that rest on positive reasons. It is clearly compatible with this thesis to allow that a proposition we are not *required* to reject as an assumption may still be hypothetically rejected for the purposes of a given inquiry in which other assumptions not positively doubted are meanwhile taken for granted. In other words, inquiries may indeed originate in feigned doubt of particular propositions. Such feigning is not inconsistent with the use of the proposition as an assumption in other inquiries; the mere possibility of such feigning does not, in particular, render assumptions useless.

Peirce thus rejects the unconditional or wholesale doubt of radical scepticism and this rejection is the root of his criticism of Descartes's procedure. For Descartes's method is to reject all assumptions open to hypothetical doubt, allowing no assumption, therefore, unless it is not merely undoubted but also theoretically indubitable or self-evident. Peirce, on the contrary, insists that inquiry may rely upon assumptions not actually doubted even if not also indubitable. Standing on these assumptions, inquiry may proceed to investigate other assumptions taken as the focus of the problem for the present. The sceptic who doubts all assumptions short of self-evidence leaves himself, in effect, no room to stand

and allows himself no resources for dealing with the questions he raises. His doubt is therefore artificial and culminates, not in particular revisions of his initial beliefs, but in a wholesale reinstatement of them. The sceptic is wrong, not in his feigning, but in his demand that all hypothetically dubitable propositions be feigned useless as assumptions simultaneously. Scientific doubt, by contrast, is always specific, resting on provisional assumptions that serve usefully as premises even though they fall short of the impossible dream of absolute certainty. Nor is the scientific researcher's work done when his particular problem is solved, for he will, in general, be concerned to find, imagine, and construct problems of the widest critical significance: problems not like that of the sceptic, but specific problems formulable as hypothetically testable questions.

Let us turn now to a consideration of 'The Fixation of Belief', as a whole. Murphey regards this essay as 'one of the most curious and least satisfactory [papers] that Peirce ever wrote'.[1] He considers the first three methods discussed by Peirce simply straw men designed to show the superiority of the scientific method, and he moreover judges Peirce's specific arguments to be wholly, or almost wholly, without merit. I do not myself concur in this negative appraisal. Nevertheless, the essay does seem to me very puzzling.

In the first place, Peirce promises to compare his four methods solely by reference to their relative effectiveness in stabilizing belief, since 'the settlement of opinion is the sole object of inquiry'.[2] Yet, in defending the method of science, he does not even mention its superior *effectiveness*, but calls in a variety of new considerations, some metaphysical (relating to supposition of real things), some methodological (relating to self-correctiveness), some epistemological (relating to the need for opinions to aspire to coincidence with fact), and some even moral ('what is more wholesome than any particular belief is integrity of belief, ... to avoid looking into the support of any belief from a fear that it may turn out rotten is quite as immoral as it is disadvantageous').[3]

[1] Murray G. Murphey, *The Development of Peirce's Philosophy* (Cambridge, Mass.: Harvard University Press, 1961), 164.
[2] *CP*, V.377; *W*, 101.
[3] *CP*, V.387; *W*, 111.

In the second place, the defence of science as providing greater success in settling belief seems utterly wrongheaded. Science does not, like the method of tenacity, yield 'great peace of mind'.[1] In holding all its claims to be provisional and subject to the test of continuing experience, it places them all in jeopardy and makes them all vulnerable to unsettlement. Indeed, the rate of change of scientific opinions, in so far as one can judge these matters at all, would seem to be higher than that associated with any of the other methods. Peirce himself remarks, in discussing the method of authority, that 'the change [in an authoritative creed] is so slow as to be imperceptible during one person's life, so that individual belief remains sensibly fixed'.[2] Certain religious, ethical, and philosophical beliefs of hundreds, even thousands, of years ago retain for many men a significant measure of credibility, providing a relatively stable reference point amid contemporary change. By contrast, important scientific views of even twenty-five years ago are already obsolete, and the scientific doctrines of the ancients are, from a contemporary point of view, worthless. Physical theories undergo increasingly accelerating change, and contemporary biology is currently experiencing a revolutionary transformation. Moreover, the technological and social changes dependent upon scientific developments feed back into further alteration of our concepts of physical and human nature. One might imagine a plausible defence of science resting upon an appeal to the restless and adventurous impulses of man, his quest for novelty and exploration, his need to rebel against secure and familiar opinion. Science might thus be persuasively presented as a systematic method for unfixing belief and unsettling opinion, for dissolving encrusted deposits of doctrine. How could Peirce have hoped to succeed in the exactly opposite course?

It might be suggested that the mere fact of scientific change is not sufficient to upset the notion of science as stabilizing belief. For suppose that the change in question is 'progressive', that is, it adds more information to what is already known, leaving previous belief untouched, or it makes more precise the vaguer hypotheses of the past, or it increasingly reduces the variety of opinion in a process of approximation to an ideal limit. Such a conception is

[1] *CP*, V.377; *W*, 102.
[2] *CP*, V.380; *W*, 104.

reflected in the important passage in 'How to Make Our Ideas Clear', in which Peirce says that truth is 'the opinion which is fated to be ultimately agreed to by all who investigate . . . and the object represented in this opinion is the real'.[1] Scientists, he says, 'may at first obtain different results, but, as each perfects his method and his processes, the results will move steadily together toward a destined center'.[2]

This suggestion is, however, vulnerable to two criticisms: first of all, the concept of *approximation*, although it may plausibly apply to the increasing precision of measurements, cannot generally be applied to scientific opinion as a whole, inclusive of theories. For, as Quine has said, 'the notion of limit depends on that of "nearer than", which is defined for numbers and not for theories'.[3] Second, science does not simply accumulate information; it often rejects previous beliefs. New theories do not, in every case, build on old ones but often replace them completely rather than simply absorbing them into ever more comprehensive frameworks. Thus science is not, in the relevant sense, progressive. At each period there is, to be sure, a considerable consensus, but the consensus is always subject to processes of change which are not merely cumulative of information, or generally conceivable as approaching an ideal limit.

Such reflections have in recent years been pressed by a number of writers critical of naïve conceptions of scientific progress. Of these writers, T. S. Kuhn[4] is perhaps the best known; he insists that periods of scientific revolution see the *replacement* of one dominant paradigm by another, and not the progressive incorporation of a given paradigm by the next. Nevertheless, it might be argued, the fact that science *as a whole* does not generally develop by accumulation does not imply that there is nothing *in* science that accumulates. Technological, experimental, and observational knowledge, it may be suggested, does tend to accumulate and its numerical bases do tend to become progressively more precise even though theoretical interpretations of such knowledge

---

[1] *CP*, V.407; *W*, 133.

[2] Ibid.

[3] W. V. Quine, *Word and Object* (New York: Technology Press of M.I.T. and John Wiley, 1960), 23.

[4] Thomas S. Kuhn, *The Structure of Scientific Revolutions* (Chicago and London: University of Chicago Press, 1962).

are not, in general, conserved. Thus, if we separate theory from what we might generically denote as 'experimental' knowledge, we may perhaps interpret Peirce as holding that science is, in fact, stabilizing and conserving with respect to such knowledge. Moreover, in so far as contemporary theories account for a wider range of such knowledge than was previously available, they are, in general, not simply different from, but superior to, the theories of the past even though they do not build upon them.

It is true that recent critics have also rejected the very distinction between *theoretical* and *experimental* knowledge upon which the latter interpretation rests. But they have found it very difficult not to replace it with parallel distinctions within their own interpretive frameworks. Thus, Kuhn himself says that scientists are reluctant to embrace a new paradigm unless, first, it seems to resolve some outstanding problem that can be met in no other way and, second, it promises[1]

> to preserve a relatively large part of the concrete problem-solving ability that has accrued to science through its predecessors. Novelty for its own sake is not a desideratum in the sciences as it is in so many other creative fields. As a result, though new paradigms seldom or never possess all the capabilities of their predecessors, they usually preserve a great deal of the most concrete parts of past achievement and they always permit additional concrete problem-solutions besides. . . . Both the list of problems solved by science and the precision of individual problem-solutions will grow and grow.

The interpretation we have been considering is, still, however, far from persuasive. For it leaves the fact of non-cumulative *theoretical* change to be dealt with. Science does not establish, fix, and conserve theories, but exposes them continually to maximal test; the theoretical agreements of one period are accordingly often, in fact, uprooted and superseded by conflicting agreements at a later time. And this fact seems, in itself, incompatible with the project of showing science to be maximally effective in fixing

[1] Ibid., 168–9 (also 2nd ed., 1970, 169–70). For further critical remarks on Kuhn see I. Scheffler, *Science and Subjectivity* (Indianapolis: Bobbs-Merrill Company, 1967), Chapter 4.

belief, in general. Perhaps, it may be conjectured, some such train of thought accounts for the first difficulty with the essay earlier mentioned, i.e., that the defence of the method of science seems to shift ground, moving from a consideration of effectiveness, to other reflections of various sorts.

These reflections seem to me to have this in common; they transfer attention from the stability of beliefs to that of methods, arguing that the method of science is *itself* firmer than the other methods discussed. Because it rests on the undoubted supposition of real things, because it is self-corrective, because it tests beliefs not by reference to human attitudes, intuitions, or institutions but rather by reference to those facts to which the beliefs in question purport to refer, scientific method is *itself* capable of standing firm through the change of specific beliefs. A challenge to a particular belief sanctioned by any of the other methods calls the method itself into question, because none of these methods is capable of allowing consistent correction of its own pronouncements. These methods are thus, one might say, brittle, incapable of absorbing changes without fracture. Or, changing the figure, they might be compared to a car without shock absorbers, in which shocks to the wheels are transmitted directly to the frame. The method of science, by contrast, achieves stability through flexibility. Rejecting pretensions to certainty, opening the testing process to the ideal community of all competent investigators, requiring continual correction to account for all available facts, the method is itself capable of absorbing change without upset.

This array of considerations indeed represents a shifting of ground in the essay, and it must be admitted that the essay does not therefore fulfil its promise. Nevertheless the defence of science it offers is of interest in its own right. Moreover, it represents an important emphasis on the *primacy of method* which is pervasive among pragmatic writers. As Gallie expresses the point:[1]

> A scientific thinker . . . is one who [knows] how to seek truth; and he makes his claims, not so much for the truth of this or that belief, as for the fact that his conclusions, as reached so far, conform to the standards and ideals of inquiry.

[1] W. B. Gallie, *Peirce and Pragmatism* (New York: Dover, 1966), 91.

It is method rather than doctrine that defines the community of science, and it is the stability of method in pursuit of the truth that holds the community together throughout doctrinal change. This is the general pragmatic response to change, later extended and ramified, especially in the writings of Dewey.

VII

THE PRAGMATIC MAXIM

Peirce's *pragmatism*, in particular, was certainly his most famous doctrine. 'But', as Murphey states, 'pragmatism was made famous by William James, not by Peirce; and it was made famous in 1898, not in 1878. Surprisingly little of Peirce's own writing prior to 1898 deals with this subject, and that which does shows that pragmatism was simply a part of a theory of inquiry which Peirce developed in the 1870's.'[1] The critical term 'pragmatism' does not appear in the paper 'How to Make Our Ideas Clear', although James misremembered it as having occurred there. The term was probably first used by Peirce in a paper he read to the Metaphysical Club in 1872. The so-called 'pragmatic maxim', however, does appear in 'How to Make Our Ideas Clear', and we turn now to a consideration of this paper.

'How to Make Our Ideas Clear' contains an attack on rationalist conceptions of meaning. We have already seen Peirce's rejection of rationalist cosmology and epistemology. Here he focuses on the traditional notions of *clarity* and *distinctness*, arguing that they have been made obsolete by the newer science, and proposing a new principle of his own as a method for the attainment of a higher grade of clarity.

Descartes, he says, discarded 'the practice of the schoolmen of looking to authority as the ultimate source of truth', replacing it by the *a priori* method, resting upon an appeal to self-consciousness as determining what was agreeable to reason. 'Since, evidently, not all ideas are true,' Descartes gave as his 'first condition of

[1] Murray G. Murphey, *The Development of Peirce's Philosophy* (Cambridge, Mass.: Harvard University Press, 1961), 156.

infallibility, that they must be clear', not troubling to distinguish between an idea seeming clear and really being so. Clarity was, however, not sufficient, since 'men, who seemed to be quite clear and positive' have held 'opposite opinions upon fundamental principles'. Thus Descartes proposed as a further condition that of distinctness, by which ideas are required 'to have nothing unclear about them'. Peirce here interprets Descartes as holding that the ideas in question 'must sustain the test of dialectical examination'.[1] Leibniz, in whose philosophy 'abstract definitions played a great part', saw that Descartes's method 'labored under the difficulty that we may seem to ourselves to have clear apprehensions of ideas which in truth are very hazy'. He proposed, therefore, 'to require an abstract definition of every important term'. In adopting the distinction of clear and distinct ideas, he characterized the quality of *distinctness* accordingly as 'the clear apprehension of everything contained in the definition'.[2]

Now it is indeed proper, says Peirce, to take familiarity with a notion (i.e., Cartesian 'clearness') as 'the first step toward clearness of apprehension',[3] and to take the notion's abstract definition as the second step. But neither step alone, nor both in combination, can be adequate, for the process of clarification may still be utterly removed from any action we might take with regard to the objects of the notion in question. But, says Peirce, 'the essence of belief is the establishment of a habit, and different beliefs are distinguished by the different modes of action to which they give rise'.[4] Beliefs establishing the same habit are identical no matter how they may otherwise differ, and beliefs establishing different habits are themselves different, no matter how similar in other respects.

Indeed, 'the whole function of thought is to produce habits of action', and thus, 'to develop its meaning, we have, therefore, simply to determine what habits it produces, for what a thing means is simply what habits it involves'.[5] Peirce thus presents his maxim, which he describes as 'the rule for attaining the third grade of clearness of apprehension', as follows: 'Consider what effects, which might conceivably have practical bearings, we conceive the object of our conception to have. Then, our conception

[1] *CP*, V.391; *W*, 115–16.
[2] *CP*, V.392; *W*, 116.
[3] *CP*, V.392; *W*, 117.
[4] *CP*, V.398; *W*, 121.
[5] *CP*, V.400; *W*, 123.

of these effects is the whole of our conception of the object.'[1] An *effect with practical bearings* is, more precisely, a sensible or perceptible consequence contingent on our practice or action. The proposal is now to sum up all such *action-contingent consequences* of the object. Our conception of these consequences is our very conception of the object.

Our conception of hardness, as represented by the adjective 'hard', is just our conception of all those sensible effects resulting from practical operations upon hard things. A hard thing is one that will, for example, 'not be scratched by many other substances',[2] will make a noise if struck, will offer perceptible resistance if pushed, etc. *Hardness* is exemplified by a variety of sensible effects connected in determinate ways with certain sorts of action taken toward things that are hard; the idea of hardness is nothing more than the idea of these practically contingent effects. 'The whole conception of this quality, as of every other, lies in its conceived effects.'[3] It is, thus, specifiable in a set of if-then propositions, each one setting forth some sensible occurrence as a result of some hypothetical operation on an object. An idea cannot, generally, be clarified by introspection, for there is, typically, no appropriate image to be found. Nor will an abstract definition help us in applying the idea correctly in practice. The idea is rather to be clarified by spelling out the connections between hypothetical actions and associated consequences, these connections themselves representing traits or habits of relevant objects: a hard object is one that *habitually* responds to specified actions in characteristic ways.

When we turn from the clarification of particular ideas (represented by *terms* such as 'hard') through if-then specifications (such as 'If x is rubbed against standard substance S, then x scratches S') to *whole statements* such as 'This stone is hard', we approach the level of belief. For belief is embodied not in particular ideas or terms but rather in whole statements or the propositions they may be taken to express. What does it mean to *believe* that this stone is hard? If a person has this belief, *he* has a certain habit of action with respect to the stone; he is set to act toward it in accordance with *its* supposed trait of hardness, in pursuit of his purposes.

---

[1] *CP*, V.402; *W*, 124.
[2] *CP*, V.403; *W*, 124.
[3] Ibid.

That is, he is prepared to act toward it in certain ways, should he wish to produce sensible effects. For example, should he wish to make a mark on some surface composed of the standard substance, S, he is set to use the stone as a marking instrument. The function of thought is, after all, as Peirce has told us, to produce habits of action and 'the identity of a habit depends on how it might lead us to act'.[1] This identity depends, in short,[2]

> on *when* and *how* it causes us to act. As for the *when,* every stimulus to action is derived from perception; as for the *how,* every purpose of action is to produce some sensible result. Thus, we come down to what is tangible and practical as the root of every real distinction of thought, no matter how subtle it may be; and there is no distinction of meaning so fine as to consist in anything but a possible difference of practice.

A *statement* therefore has meaning, one might say, just in so far as it is capable of expressing a belief, capable therefore of representing a habit of action relating perceptual stimuli and sensible results. To have meaning, in sum, it must embody conditional predictions testable by the senses.

It must be especially noted that Peirce's *pragmatism* is not a theory of *truth* but of *meaning*. Peirce allows that false as well as true beliefs have meaning. It is the processes of scientific investigation, he holds, that tend to weed out the false beliefs and bring scientists to converge on the true. Indeed, Peirce defines truth in terms of such ultimate and ideal convergence. The truth for him is an absolute and ideal limit of endless investigation: 'The opinion which is fated to be ultimately agreed to by all who investigate is what we mean by the truth, and the object represented in this opinion is the real.'[3] The *pragmatic* doctrine he offers us (as distinct from his definition of truth) is one that at best clarifies ideas worth investigating, whether they be in fact true or false. We shall have occasion to consider further Peirce's notion of truth in our subsequent discussion of James's views on this topic. Here we provide some brief critical remarks on the pragmatism of Peirce.

The pragmatic maxim anticipates the notion that has come to

---

[1] *CP*, V.400; *W*, 123.
[2] Ibid.
[3] *CP*, V.407; *W*, 133.

be known as 'operational definition', following P. W. Bridgman's treatment in his book of 1927, *The Logic of Modern Physics*.[1] The notion that statements, or beliefs, are to be construed as clear only in so far as predictive of observable consequences since 'our idea of anything *is* our idea of its sensible effects',[2] moreover fore-shadows positivistic attempts to formulate criteria of meaning-fulness based on verification or observational prediction.

Peirce's idea was certainly a pioneering conception, but it has not survived the process of logical clarification and intensive exami-nation of the past several decades. This process has revealed criti-cal weaknesses both in positivistic meaning criteria and in the concept of operational definition. Rather than review the develop-ments in detail, I refer the reader to two important papers by Professor C. G. Hempel on these points: 'A Logical Appraisal of Operationism', and 'Empiricist Criteria of Cognitive Significance: Problems and Changes', both included in his book, *Aspects of Scientific Explanation*.[3]

Here I will merely note some problems: first, the pragmatic maxim seems inapplicable to so-called theoretical terms. It is one thing to say that a mineral x is hard if, when a certain operation o is performed on it, some sensible consequence k ensues. It is quite another to say that an electron e has a certain property P if it produces a sensible response to an operation performed on it. For electrons cannot thus be singled out and operated upon. Nor can we say, for example, that a patient's super-ego is repressive, say, if it produces some sensible result when it is acted upon, since super-egos are not the sort of thing one can act upon at all.

Second, the notion of summing up all sensible effects condi-tional upon all hypothetical actions associated with a given notion is far from clear. How many of such conditional effects are we required to consider before supposing that we have clarified the notion sufficiently for practical purposes? And what logical inter-pretation shall we give to the if-then connective required to describe each conditional effect? To take it as the simple indicative conditional poses a variety of problems explored in the classic

[1] P. W. Bridgman, *The Logic of Modern Physics* (New York: Macmillan, 1927).
[2] *CP*, V.401; *W*, 124.
[3] Carl G. Hempel, *Aspects of Scientific Explanation* (New York: Free Press, 1965). See also my book, *The Anatomy of Inquiry* (New York: Alfred A. Knopf, 1963), pt II, sections 2, 3, 5, 6.

paper by Rudolf Carnap, 'Testability and Meaning'.[1] To take it rather as a subjunctive connective invites interpretation in terms of real possibilities and necessities that are themselves too obscure to serve in the clarification of other notions.

Third, the notion that meaningful statements are individually associated with observational predictions cannot be upheld. Purely existential statements, for example, make no predictions, nor do the universal conditional statements typically taken to represent scientific laws; additional premises are needed. Moreover, attempts to circumscribe *admissible* additional premises have uniformly failed to yield a satisfactory criterion. Finally, statements, generally, yield empirical predictions in a manner that is qualified by their relations to other statements. Thus C. G. Hempel concludes that[2]

> it is not correct to speak, as is often done, of the 'experiential meaning' of a term or a sentence in isolation. In the language of science, and for similar reasons even in pre-scientific discourse, a single statement usually has no experiential implications. A single sentence in a scientific theory does not, as a rule, entail any observation sentences; consequences asserting the occurrence of certain observable phenomena can be derived from it only by conjoining it with a set of other, subsidiary, hypotheses.

Two systems with exactly the same observational consequences cannot therefore, in general, be judged to be the same in significance. For they may differ in their observational yield under identical supplementation. There is a systematic and theoretical element in scientific theorizing that cannot be eliminated. Scientific systems, in sum, surely require linkages to observation, but these linkages relate to the whole network of theory; they do not tie each concept or statement individually to observation, nor do they exhaust the meaning of the systems in question. The attempt to absorb all knowledge into sensible experience thus seems to have failed.

Nevertheless, I believe that Peirce's ideas retain a certain lasting value: that beliefs are in fundamental ways tied to action and

[1] Rudolf Carnap, 'Testability and Meaning', *Philosophy of Science*, III (1936), 420–471; IV (1937), 2–40. See also Scheffler, op. cit., pt II, section 9.
[2] Hempel, op. cit., 112.

expectation expresses an insight that is important both in philosophy of science and in vital contexts of practice as well. Consider education, for example. The point here is that we are not simply striving for familiarity with ideas, or for verbal facility to be exhibited by giving proper definitions or correct answers to test questions. We are forming active systems of habit and expectation, to be displayed in an indefinite variety of applications. In teaching, the idea needs to be presented, therefore, as concretely related to the child's actions and expectations of consequences; such presentation requires the provision of opportunities for him to act in a purposive context. This train of thought, though Peirce did not spell it out himself, is an important root of the progressive educational theory associated with pragmatism.

We turn, in the next section, to a consideration of some of Peirce's explicit views on social topics, in particular, education and religion.

VIII

PEIRCE'S EDUCATIONAL AND RELIGIOUS IDEAS

It may be thought ironic that the educational writings of Peirce so heavily stress the rational and theoretical aspects of learning. Not only does this emphasis contradict the popular stereotype of pragmatism as a practical philosophy; it also conflicts with the theory of inquiry as originating in real and living doubt, and it seems, moreover, at odds with the general tendency of pragmatism to absorb the world into categories of action.

We saw earlier how Peirce himself qualified the theory of inquiry by including not only actual doubt but also feigned doubt, and how he allowed for the existence of a positive doubt-seeking motive. Moreover, despite his stress on relating ideas to action and his insistence on the observational consequences of hypotheses, we saw how he retained a certain epistemological stability through his concepts of truth as an ideal limit, and of the community of scientific investigators as unified, ideally, by the pursuit of truth in accord with a firm self-corrective method.

Peirce, it is clear, did not want to *eliminate* the idea of a real world, but rather to *interpret* it through categories appropriate to human thought and action. Thus, having explained reality as the object of opinion fated to be agreed on by all who investigate, he responds to the charge that his view 'makes the characters of the real depend on what is ultimately thought about them'. 'Reality', he says,[1]

[1] *CP*, V.408; *W*, 133.

is independent, not necessarily of thought in general, but only of what you or I or any finite number of men may think about it . . . though the object of the final opinion depends on what that opinion is, yet what that opinion is does not depend on what you or I or any man thinks.

In short, he interprets the world through the category of thought supplemented, however, by the notion of generality and the concept of a limit of investigative processes. In an important passage in 'What Pragmatism Is' (1905),[1] he criticizes the idea that[2]

what is relative to thought cannot be real. But why not, exactly? *Red* is relative to sight, but the fact that this or that is in that relation to vision that we call being red is not *itself* relative to sight; it is a real fact.

And he says further, in the same article:[3]

That which any true proposition asserts is *real*, in the sense of being as it is regardless of what you or I may think about it. Let this proposition be a general conditional proposition as to the future, and it is a real general such as is calculated really to influence human conduct; and such the pragmaticist holds to be the rational purport of every concept.

Interpreting *reality* in terms of such rational *purport*, he furthermore interprets *science* as a community defined by its general method and ideal purpose. Increasingly, he stresses the autonomy of its pursuits and, accordingly, the theoretical element of scientific research. The doubt-belief theory of inquiry becomes attenuated and itself subordinated to the disinterested motive of investigation for its own sake. In his 'Lessons from the History of Science' (*c*. 1896), Peirce thus writes,[4]

True science is distinctively the study of useless things. For the useful things will get studied without the aid of scientific men. To employ these rare minds on such work is like running a steam engine by burning diamonds.

[1] *Monist*, XV (April 1905), 161–81. See *CP*, V.411–37.
[2] *CP*, V.430; *W*, 198.
[3] *CP*, V.432; *W*, 199.
[4] *CP*, I.76.

In a review in *Science* (1900), Peirce attacks the exaltation of the practical:[1]

> Of the three verbs, to *be*, to *do*, and to *know*, the great majority of young men unhesitatingly regard the second as expressing the ultimate purpose and end of life. This is, as a matter of course, the idea of the practical man, who knows what he wants, and does not desire to want anything else.

Trustees of American colleges, he says, look askance upon the professor who devotes much energy to purely theoretical research, thinking it commendable rather for him 'to employ all the time he can possibly save in making money'. The English scholar, Karl Pearson, justified science in that it preserves 'the stability of society'. In fact, Peirce concedes his own guilt in furthering a utilitarian conception of science. 'In my youth', he says, 'I wrote some articles to uphold a doctrine I called Pragmatism, namely, that the meaning and essence of every conception lies in the application that is to be made of it.'[2]

All very well, he says, but *what is* the application? 'At that time I seem to have been inclined to subordinate the *conception* to the *act*, knowing to doing.' This is a mistake, for 'the only thing that is really desirable without a reason for being so, is to render ideas and things reasonable'.[3] This, in turn, is a matter of association and generalization, of assimilation and union. 'In the emotional sphere, this tendency towards union appears as Love; so that the Law of Love and the Law of Reason are quite at one.'[4]

Education needs a larger aim than welfare, whether individual or social; the only aim large enough to serve is the furtherance of the double law of Love and of Reason. American education, says Peirce, is directed toward the welfare of individual students, encouraging them to seek their own welfare as an exclusive aim, but 'whoever makes his own welfare his object will simply ruin it utterly'.[5] Welfare can occur only if it is not deliberately sought as an aim; it arises as a concomitant of the pursuit of other and larger aims.

[1] C. S. Peirce, review of *Clark University, 1889–1899: Decennial Celebration* (Worcester, Mass., 1899), in *Science*, n.s. XI (20 April 1900), pp. 620–2. See also *W*, 331–4.
[2] Ibid.
[3] Ibid.
[4] Ibid.
[5] Ibid.

To justify education by its capacity to increase income fosters a narrow view of purpose. 'What comes of such a conception of education and of life, for surely the purpose of education is not different from the purpose of life?'[1] 'Spiritual meagreness'[2] is only to be expected from a view that fails to provide persons with purposes that reach beyond their own advantage, in terms of which their own lives may be seen as 'meaningful', that is to say, as having significant consequences. Individual advantage is itself, Peirce seems to say, a product of a point of view that reaches beyond individual advantage; it is acquired only by surrendering it as a fixed point of reference. Just as the self is no pre-formed and absolutely known entity but develops out of life in a particular social context that reaches beyond it, so the self's spiritual advantage rests on a vision that embraces more than itself.

Certain institutions have, in fact, provided a larger context for education:[3]

> The great mediaeval universities, the modern German universities, the new science colleges of England, which did, and do, great things for their students personally, were never in the least founded for their students' individual advantage, but, on the contrary, because of the expectation that the truths that would be brought to light in such institutions would benefit the state.

Though providing a larger purpose for orienting individual lives, such a conception rests, however, on 'a low view of learning and science'. In a striking passage, Peirce denies that 'the searching out of the ideas that govern the universe has no other value than that it helps human animals to swarm and feed'. Rather, 'the only thing that makes the human race worth perpetuation is that thereby rational ideas may be developed, and the rationalization of things furthered'. He concludes with the statement that 'no other occupation of man is so purely and immediately directed to the one end that is alone intrinsically rational as scientific investigation'.[4]

Now this is certainly an extreme conclusion, and it does not

[1] Ibid.
[2] Ibid.
[3] Ibid.
[4] Ibid.

seem to flow even from Peirce's own premises. The general conception of the Law of Reason is here disconnected from the Law of Love, and restricted to its special embodiment in scientific investigation. A conception of education, and therefore of life, dominated by the primary aim of scientific investigation is a hierarchical and monopolistic conception. It unifies education, but only at the cost of exclusions that are intolerable. Where is the life of art, the cultivation of history and poetry, the formation of character, the pursuit of justice, the impatience with suffering and evil?

Peirce himself is not very consistent in his views. Elsewhere, he develops the idea that innovation requires *logic*, in the sense of a theory of methods.[1]

> When new paths have to be struck out, a spinal cord is not enough; a brain is needed, and that brain an organ of mind, and that mind perfected by a liberal education. And a liberal education – so far as its relation to the understanding goes – means *logic*.

But he here goes on to place logic within a matrix of *other* educational aims, rather than construing it as primary.[2]

> A young man wants a physical education and an aesthetic education, an education in the ways of the world and a moral education, and with all these logic has nothing in particular to do; but so far as he wants an intellectual education, it is precisely logic that he wants.

This is a more tolerable, pluralistic conception, but logic is now restricted to its function in the intellectual life and affords no *general* integration of the studies.

Despite the abstract formula that the Law of Reason and the Law of Love are one, Peirce thus does not succeed in offering a broad and unified conception of education. Either science dominates and the other areas are diminished or excluded, or else the other areas are acknowledged, but are not related by any over-

---

[1] *W*, 336–7; From the Johns Hopkins University Circulars (November 1882) as excerpted by Max H. Fisch and Jackson I. Cope, 'Peirce at the Johns Hopkins University', in Philip P. Wiener and Frederic H. Young, eds, *Studies in the Philosophy of C. S. Peirce* (Cambridge, Mass.: Harvard University Press, 1952), 289–90.

[2] Ibid.

arching conception to the intellectual pursuits. The conception of logic is indeed stretched beyond its traditional meaning, but it remains powerless, in Peirce's hands, to connect the intellect with other realms of human striving. It remained for James and Dewey to propose further solutions to the problem of integration by emphasizing, respectively, the ideal of pluralism coupled with the test of individual experience, and the concept of intelligence or critical thought as applicable in all realms, not only that of science.

Peirce sought a proper reconciliation of science and religion. He rejected both the denial of religious sentiment in the name of a mechanistic philosophy, and the positive evidence for miracles, ghosts and 'spiritualistic marvels'.[1] Though the possibility of a future life, as distinct from an immortal soul, cannot be ruled out as for ever beyond investigation, or denied dogmatically, especially in light of the newer evolutionary philosophy, no practical conclusion ought to be drawn from this possibility alone. In particular, no conclusion may be drawn 'that human happiness and human rights are of little account, that all our thoughts ought to be turned away from the things of this world'.[2]

The positive evidence for miracles and ghosts Peirce rejects as worthless, and he pokes fun at popular beliefs in ghosts:[3]

Granting all the ghost stories that ever were told, and the reality of all spiritual manifestation, what would they prove? These ghosts and spirits exhibit but a remnant of mind. Their stupidity is remarkable. They seem like the lower animals. . . . Then these spirits and apparitions are so painfully solemn. I fancy that, were I suddenly to find myself liberated from all the trials and responsibilities of this life, my probation over, and my destiny put beyond marring or making, I should feel as I do when I find myself on an ocean steamer, and know that for ten days no business can turn up, and nothing can happen. I should regard the situation as a stupendous frolic, should be at the summit of gayety, and should only be too glad to leave the vale of tears behind. Instead of that, these starveling souls come mooning back to their former haunts, to cry over spilled milk.

[1] *CP*, VI.549; *W*, 346.
[2] *CP*, VI.556; *W*, 350.
[3] *CP*, VI.550; *W*, 347.

What then is the relation, properly conceived, between science and religion? Science is not systematized knowledge, or even, in an ultimate sense, method, but a certain forward-looking spirit 'determined not to rest satisfied with existing opinions, but to press on to the real truth of nature'.[1] Religion in the individual is a sentiment, 'an obscure perception . . . of a something in the circumambient All'.[2] Such perception cannot, however, reside solely in the individual, for 'like every species of reality, it is essentially a social, a public affair'.[3]

It is the idea of a whole church, welding all its members together in one organic systemic perception of the Glory of the Highest – an idea having a growth from generation to generation and claiming a supremacy in the determination of all conduct, private and public.[4]

Science and religion move in different directions. Science moves toward increasing perfection, whereas religion tends to diminish in perfection, 'even as judged from its own standpoint'.

Like a plucked flower, its destiny is to wilt and fade. The vital sentiment that gave it birth loses gradually its pristine purity and strength, till some new creed treads it down. Thus it happens quite naturally that those who are animated with the spirit of science are for hurrying forward, while those who have the interests of religion at heart are apt to press back.[5]

The divergence does not call for praise or blame. 'You cannot', Peirce says, 'lay blame upon elemental forces.'[6] Instead of retreating after defeats on particular points of fact, or defending impossible denials of scientific advances, religionists should retain the essence of religion and hold fast as far as possible to the church, but relinquish timidity. They should be confident that the truth is one, and therefore that new knowledge can only alter the expression of faith 'but not the deep mystery expressed'.[7] Religion can-

[1] *CP*, VI.428; *W*, 350.
[2] *CP*, VI.429; *W*, 350–1.
[3] *CP*, VI.429; *W*, 351.
[4] Ibid.
[5] *CP*, VI.430; *W*, 351.
[6] *CP*, VI.432; *W*, 352.
[7] Ibid.

not spring from science but only from the religious sensibility; yet a more confident cultivation of such sensibility can be wedded to a scientific spirit of openness to new knowledge of nature.

Religion, for Peirce, begins in sentiment, but it requires a social organization, and eventually theology, whose purpose it is to settle the quarrels that arise when religion has become public and its initial perception has degenerated into abstract belief. However,[1]

> the ideas of theologians always appreciably differ from those of the universal church. They swamp religion in fallacious logical disputations . . . drawing tighter and tighter . . . the narrowing bounds of doctrine, with less and less attention to the living essence of religion.

Religion is not, however, mere belief. 'You might as well call society a belief, or politics a belief, or civilization a belief. Religion is a life. . . .'[2] In so far as the essence of the Christian faith can be expressed, it is love, and in so far as this can be further 'contracted to a rule of ethics, it is: Love God, and love your neighbor'.[3]

Peirce's counsel to religionists is to define their scope as broadly as possible, to re-emphasize the essential religious sensibility, and the ethical and spiritual life at the core of religion. At the same time, he counsels patience and tolerance to the scientifically minded who are presently excluded from the churches, and he is sceptical of the foundation of new scientific religions: 'Wait, if you can', he says to these people,[4]

> but if you cannot wait, why then Godspeed! Only, do not, in your turn, go and draw lines so as to exclude such as believe a little less – or, still worse, to exclude such as believe a little more – than yourselves. Doubtless, a lot of superstition clings to the historical churches; but superstition is the grime upon the venerable pavement of the sacred edifice, and he who would wash that pavement clean should be willing to get down on his knees to his work inside the church.

[1] *CP*, VI.438; *W*, 354.
[2] *CP*, VI.439; *W*, 354.
[3] *CP*, VI.441; *W*, 355.
[4] *CP*, VI.447; *W*, 357.

Peirce's counsel is thus one of reconciliation between science and the historic religions. He does not perhaps sufficiently recognize the positive function of theology: the fact that sentiment cannot subsist without rationalization and formulation. Moreover, despite his interpretation of religion as essentially backward-directed, he ends by suggesting a recapture of religious sentiment – a recapture seemingly ruled out by his own interpretation of 'its destiny . . . to wilt and fade'.[1] It might further be argued that any effort at a recapture of religious inspiration *must* attempt a reconsideration of doctrinal and historical questions; it cannot hope to succeed upon a basis of sentiment alone, or yet upon vague formulations of a law of love.

Still, Peirce's attitude on this topic is distinctive and important in its acceptance both of scientific and of religious institutions, and its striving for a wholeness of spirit in which man's respect for fact, love of his fellow man, and religious response to existence can live peaceably together. James's view is more individualistic and less institutional, and Dewey's view is that religious values require new embodiments in universal forms to replace the divisive embodiments of the past. Peirce hopes rather for a retention of the historic religions, with a progressive purification and universalization from within.

[1] *CP*, VI.430; *W*, 351.

PART TWO
WILLIAM JAMES

I

BIOGRAPHICAL COMMENTS

William James was born in 1842, the eldest of five children, of whom the others were Henry, Garth Wilkinson, Robertson, and Alice. His father, Henry James, Snr., was brought up in a Calvinist environment and at the age of twenty-four entered the Princeton Seminary to study for the ministry. However, he left a few years later and remained alienated from the church. He never followed any profession, perhaps partly because he was lame, having lost a leg when he was a boy. Having an independent income, he proceeded[1]

> without qualms of conscience to live on it, and for the next few years led the life of a gentleman of leisure, reading, travelling, and visiting and corresponding with friends, who included Emerson, Wendell Holmes, and other well-known men of the day. He married at the age of twenty-nine, and William, the first child, was born two years later.

Introduced, at the age of thirty-five, to the writings of Swedenborg, Henry James, Snr., was forcibly affected. 'From that time on, his mission in life was decided; he devoted himself wholeheartedly to the study of Swedenborg, and to the spread of his doctrines by lecturing, writing, and otherwise proselytizing.'[2] If he was a crank, he was, as Margaret Knight says, 'a crank in the best sense of the word; that is to say, he had the tolerance, and the enthusiasm for ideas, that go with high intelligence, though he

[1] Margaret Knight, *William James* (Harmondsworth: Penguin, 1950), 13. I have drawn upon this book for other points in this paragraph.
[2] Ibid., 14.

lacked the critical faculty that is the fruit of intellectual training.'[1] He was surely, however, a most unusual father and provided for his children a remarkable environment in which to develop. The reading, travel, study, and writing that he did were done together with, or in the sight of, his family. His children were[2]

all highly intelligent, high-spirited and argumentative; and he appears to have achieved the remarkable feat of bringing them up without ever telling them that father knew best. He was a firm believer in children's thinking for themselves, and forming their views in the give-and-take of intellectual combat; and his sons grew up quite unhampered by the notion that it is rude to contradict.

The family climate was warm and loving but also intellectual and argumentative, opinions being formed in free give and take, without dictation from above. 'The father would propound some provocative idea, and throw it into the midst of his brood in order that they might sharpen their teeth on it and, in their eagerness to refute him or one another, exercise themselves in the art of combative thinking.'[3] Both the intellectual climate and the friendly interchanges within the family circle are illustrated by Alice James's recollection of the effect on her of a casual remark of her brother's, when she was only eight. She writes:[4]

I remember so distinctly the first time I was conscious of a purely intellectual process. . . . We were turned into the garden to play . . . Harry suddenly exclaimed: 'This might certainly be called pleasure under difficulties!' The stir of my whole being in response to the exquisite, original form of his remark almost makes my heart beat now with the sisterly pride which was then awakened, and it came to me in a flash – the higher nature of this appeal to the mind, as compared to the rudimentary solicitations which usually produced my childish explosions of laughter, and I can also feel distinctly the sense of self-satisfaction in that I could not only

[1] Ibid.

[2] Ibid., 15.

[3] Ralph Barton Perry, *The Thought and Character of William James*, vol. I (Boston: Little, Brown, 1935), 172.

[4] *Alice James, Her Brothers – Her Journal* (ed. by Anna R. Burr) (New York: Dodd, Mead, 1934), 166–7.

perceive but appreciate this subtlety, as if I had acquired a new sense, a sense whereby to measure intellectual things, wit as distinguished from giggling, for example.

The family experience was clearly a most important formative influence on James; the affectionateness, good nature, and intellectual excitement of his family circle were characteristic of James's mind and character throughout his life.

William James's formal education was irregular and intermixed with travel. He attended schools in New York, Paris, Boulogne, Rhode Island, Geneva, and Bonn.[1] He started an art career, gave it up for chemistry, then shifted to biology, and eventually medicine, but he was not well enough to practise. For several years, he was afflicted with a severe neurotic depression – but this condition improved sufficiently so that he could assume the regular duties that came with his appointment in 1872 as instructor in physiology at Harvard. Eventually, his career led him from the sciences to philosophy, and he later became professor of philosophy at Harvard, but his early scientific training retained a definite importance in his later thought both on psychological and on philosophical topics.

We have seen earlier how he helped and encouraged Peirce. This attitude was characteristic. He was a generous person who inspired affection as well as respect, and he had a rare capacity for sympathetic dialogue with people of different temperaments and ways of life. Whereas Peirce was difficult, arrogant, remote, and austerely impersonal in his views, James was warm, outgoing, and fascinated by the individual and the personal in all things. Yet he was enough of a scientist by training and sympathy to find a strong appeal in Peirce's laboratory conception of thinking. Moreover, the stress on activity, on consequences, and on indeterminism found a willing response in James's energetic and open temperament.

He saw in pragmatism a way of unifying science and religion, since the test of all truth is in experience, and the religious experience of the individual person is surely a phenomenon that needs to be acknowledged as a fact, by all. Such reflections led him also to *pluralism* in a personal and moral sense, and not only a metaphysical sense. Metaphysically, he opposed the necessities of

[1] Knight, op. cit., 18; see also Perry, op. cit., vol. I, 177.

rationalism and mechanism as well as the 'block universe'[1] of the absolute idealists. But his pluralism had a personal side as well in the recognition of value in different inner lives and experiences, in different beliefs and ways of life. The test, for pragmatism, of any belief is what difference it makes in life, and on this test, a variety of outlooks pass. Thus, he declares:[2]

> Hands off: neither the whole of truth nor the whole of good is revealed to any single observer, although each observer gains a partial superiority of insight from the peculiar position in which he stands. . . . It is enough to ask of each of us that he should be faithful to his own opportunities and make the most of his own blessings, without presuming to regulate the rest of the vast field.

In general, it is the human, personal, and individual phenomena that appeal to James, and he opposes, both temperamentally and philosophically, whatever is abstract, formalistic, rationalistic, and doctrinaire.

James's *Principles of Psychology* (1890)[3] is a classic, forming a kind of bridge between the philosophical psychology of the nineteenth century and the scientific psychology of the twentieth. He deals freely with the philosophical issues permeating the subject, but always stresses the dependence of the mental life upon the physiological. He was instrumental in starting the career of experimental psychology in the United States, through setting up the psychological laboratory at Harvard, the first in America. He was himself, however, not an experimenter in his primary inclinations, and was much more at home with the theoretical and the subjective elements of the subject. In turning in his later years more and more to philosophy, he never, however, relinquished the psychological orientation and interests of his earlier work. In *Varieties of Religious*

[1] William James, *A Pluralistic Universe* (New York: Longmans, Green, 1912), 328. See also Perry, op. cit., vol. II, 591: 'The universe is not a block or an organism, but an all-navigable sea – a great neighborhood embracing lesser neighborhoods, in which accessibility is universal and intimacy proportional to propinquity.'

[2] William James, *Talks to Teachers on Psychology: and to Students on Some of Life's Ideals* (New York: Henry Holt, 1901), 264.

[3] William James, *The Principles of Psychology* (copyright 1890 by Henry Holt, copyright 1918 by Alice H. James) (New York: Dover, 1950, 2 vols. Reprinted by special arrangement with Henry Holt.).

Experience (1902),[1] both his psychological and his philosophical concerns are unified in application to the religious life, a descriptive account of religious phenomena being presented first, and a philosophical account of their significance concluding the book. His *Pragmatism* (1907)[2] offers a theory of truth which is itself interwoven with psychological considerations, and it is this fact which accounts for its distinctiveness as well as for much of the controversy it aroused. In discussing James's work, I propose to deal first with his theory of truth, and then with some of his psychological notions, emphasizing particularly his treatment of *habit* and *consciousness*.

[1] William James, *The Varieties of Religious Experience* (New York: Longmans, Green, 1902).
[2] William James, *Pragmatism* (New York: Longmans, Green, 1907, 1910).

II

PEIRCE AND JAMES ON TRUTH[1]

Peirce defined truth, we saw, as 'the opinion which is fated to be ultimately agreed to by all who investigate'.

> Different minds may set out with the most antagonistic views, but the progress of investigation carries them by a force outside of themselves to one and the same conclusion. This activity of thought by which we are carried, not where we wish, but to a foreordained goal, is like the operation of destiny.[2]

This notion of truth is an ideal and absolute one: the truth is not relative to time, person, or circumstance; it is the fixed limit toward which inquiry tends. As Peirce says, 'the opinion which would finally result from investigation does not depend on how anybody may actually think'.[3]

To the objection that there are indefinitely many real facts of history long lost and for ever beyond the reach of further investigation, Peirce replies that 'it is unphilosophical to suppose that, with regard to any given question . . ., investigation would not bring forth a solution of it, if it were carried far enough'.[4] It is, indeed, he says, impossible to be sure that facts of any given sort will not be revealed by continuing science, for science has already

---

[1] In this and the next two sections, I have drawn upon, and elaborated, the treatment which was given in my *Conditions of Knowledge* (Chicago: Scott, Foresman, 1965), 39–54.

[2] *CP*, V.407; *W*, 133.

[3] *CP*, V.408; *W*, 134.

[4] *CP*, V.409; *W*, 134.

brought to light numerous facts previously thought impossible to know.

This reply still falls short, it must be noted, of a positive guarantee that all facts *will* indeed be unearthed by limitless investigation. It rests, in any case, as Peirce admits, on 'remote considerations' seemingly at odds with his own principle that 'only practical distinctions have a meaning'.[1] To the latter point, Peirce replies in two ways: (1) He concedes that possible facts never brought to light make no real difference to us, but argues that such possible facts have only verbal import and do not affect meanings: 'That there are gems at the bottom of the sea, flowers in the untraveled desert, etc., are propositions which, like that about a diamond being hard when it is not pressed, concern much more the arrangement of our language than they do the meaning of our ideas.'[2] This reply is rather weak, since the distinction on which it rests is utterly unclear; critics might, moreover, protest that any account of truth is inadequate which holds it to be an indifferent matter whether there are gems at the bottom of the sea, or whether a diamond not pressed is hard. The verbal interpretation of possible facts is, in any event, one that Peirce later rejected in favour of a realistic concept of possibility. (Such a concept would allow that possible facts after all affect meanings despite Peirce's concession that they make very little practical difference; his realism thus collided with his practicalism.)

(2) His second reply seems to be just that, whether dependent on 'remote considerations' or not, his account of truth is consonant with a clear apprehension of the object and procedures of science. He seems to suggest that only if we think of truth as a fixed ideal of scientific method can we make sense of the fact that scientific controversies are often settled in the course of time, apparently under the control of impersonal and objective factors. Peirce does not, at any rate, attempt to clarify the concept of truth by the direct application of his own pragmatic maxim.

It may be argued that Peirce's notion of truth is thus not consonant with his pragmatism. There are, in any case, *independent* questions to be raised about his account of truth. The notion of truth as a 'foreordained goal'[3] can hardly be taken seriously. Cer-

---

[1] *CP*, V.409; *W*, 135.
[2] Ibid.
[3] *CP*, V.407; *W*, 133.

tainly, there have always been disagreements in science as elsewhere; how could it possibly be known that fate decrees an ultimate settlement? Peirce himself allows that 'Our perversity and
that of others may indefinitely postpone the settlement of opinion;
it might even conceivably cause an arbitrary proposition to be
universally accepted as long as the human race should last. Yet',
he continues,[1]

> even that would not change the nature of the belief, which
> alone could be the result of investigation carried sufficiently
> far; and if, after the extinction of our race, another should
> arise with faculties and disposition for investigation, that true
> opinion must be the one which they would ultimately come
> to. 'Truth crushed to earth shall rise again.' . . .

What, however, gives Peirce the assurance that settlement must
ultimately fix upon the truth in every case? It is surely not logically
contradictory to suppose that it never does, even on the assumption of endless investigation. His reference to 'investigation carried sufficiently far' of course gives him the option of denying, so
long as settlement upon the truth has not yet been achieved, that
investigation has been sufficient. But then, the assertion: that
agreement upon the truth must come after sufficient investigation,
is *empty*, since it reduces to the claim that such agreement must be
the result of investigation that is sufficient to secure it.

Peirce is impressed with the control of scientific assertions by
objective criteria, and it is this, I have suggested, that drives him
to interpret truth as independent of what any particular man may
think. On the other hand, he wants to reduce everything to what
is accessible to thought. He thus construes truth as the agreed
object of 'thought in general'[2] – of endless investigation by the
community of science. Yet what, in this construction, rules out the
possibility that perfect agreement *is* reached but fastens on a false-
hood, and is never reversed? If, for instance, an erroneous account
of some particular historical event long past has been propagated
and become entrenched, never to be revised until the end of time,
must it be *true*, and must it therefore represent *reality*?

Peirce argues that we cannot be sure that such an opinion will
not be revised, but, equally, he cannot be sure that it *will*. Indeed, it

[1] *CP*, V.408; *W*, 133–4.
[2] *CP*, V.408; *W*, 133.

seems to fly in the face of all probability to *assume* that it will, in every case. And to say that it *would*, if investigation were 'carried far enough'[1] is, in the absence of an independent criterion for 'far enough', to reduce the claim to triviality. To admit, on the other hand, that it is *conceivable* that there might be facts *not* revealed by investigation, or that there might be purported facts *erroneously* fixed by investigation, is to acknowledge that investigation itself (even investigation *in general*) is not coincident with truth – that truth requires independent interpretation.

We may interpret James's theory of truth as an attempt to clarify the idea of truth by application of Peirce's pragmatic maxim, an application that Peirce himself, as we have seen, did not explicitly make. The ironic result of this attempt was that James, using Peirce's maxim, produced a theory of truth that diverges radically from Peirce's own view. Whereas Peirce offers an ideal and absolute conception of truth, James formulates a practical and relative interpretation.

Addressing himself, in the spirit of the pragmatic maxim, to clarification of the general term 'true', James must specify action-contingent consequences associated with beliefs or propositions properly called 'true'. Accordingly, he needs to specify a relevant *operation* or action with respect to beliefs or propositions, and to indicate also a relevant class of *sensible effects* or consequences associated with this operation whenever it is applied to beliefs that are true.[2] The operation he chooses is that of *acting on* the belief, his general idea being that if, and only if, a belief is *true* will it yield *sensibly satisfactory results in experience* when thus acted upon. Truth is, in short, to be seen as relating sensibly satisfactory consequences with the actions undertaken in banking upon given beliefs. It is not, in particular, a matter of relating experiences to a reality *external* to experience, but rather a matter of the relations which *certain* experiences bear to *others*. It is thus always accessible to us as acting and perceiving beings.

Moreover, truth so conceived can be seen to be *good*, for the relation of action to satisfactory outcomes is clearly involved in the achievement of any of our purposes through deliberate effort. Contrary to the intellectualists' so-called copy theory of truth, James thus considers his own theory to satisfy two desiderata:

[1] *CP*, V.409; *W*, 134.
[2] See Morton White, *The Age of Analysis* (New York: Mentor, 1955), 154–60.

(1) to make judgments of truth accessible, (2) to show why truth is good. ' "Truth" in our ideas and beliefs means the same thing that it means in science', says James.[1]

> It means . . . nothing but this, *that ideas (which themselves are but parts of our experience) become true just in so far as they help us to get into satisfactory relation with other parts of our experience.*

What sorts of things, specifically, fall under the rubric of satisfactory results? James's account is rather vague. In a typical passage, he writes:[2]

> Any idea upon which we can ride, so to speak; any idea that will carry us prosperously from any one part of our experience to any other part, linking things satisfactorily, working securely, simplifying, saving labor; is true for just so much, true in so far forth, true *instrumentally.*

James's theory aroused a storm of controversy. We may divide the main points of criticism into two groups: (1) Those dealing with the notion of satisfaction, and (2) those dealing with the relativity or mutability of truth. We shall consider both sorts of criticism, taking first those that hinge on *satisfaction.*

[1] William James, *Pragmatism* (New York: Longmans, Green, 1907, 1910), 58.
[2] Ibid.

III

JAMES'S NOTION OF SATISFACTION

James's references to satisfaction seem to allow for a broad as well as a narrow interpretation. On the narrow interpretation, a belief functions satisfactorily when *it* is satisfied or confirmed by experience. On the broad interpretation, it is not simply a matter of whether the belief is satisfied, i.e., confirmed, but also a matter of whether the believer derives satisfaction consequent upon his believing the proposition in question. Satisfactory function, that is, includes also such satisfying effects of belief as, for example, pleasant or comfortable states of mind, constructive attitudes toward life, and healthy traits of character.

Several of James's passages seem to presuppose this broad notion of satisfaction. Let us consider, for example, his extended discussion of absolute idealism, the philosophy which postulates an Absolute Mind as 'the rational presupposition of all particulars of fact'.[1] This Mind, idealism's substitute for God, is a 'pantheistic deity working *in* things rather than above them'. 'Old fashioned theism', says James, 'was bad enough, with its notion of God as an exalted monarch, made up of a lot of unintelligible or preposterous "attributes"; but, so long as it held strongly by the argument from design, it kept some touch with concrete realities.'[2] Once design was displaced by Darwinism, the older dualistic theism way to the immanent deity constituted by the Absolute Mind of idealism. This conception, says James, is far too

[1] William James, *Pragmatism* (New York: Longmans, Green, 1907, 1910), 71.
[2] Ibid., 70.

intellectualistic to appeal to the fact-loving temperament. It is 'supremely indifferent to what the particular facts in our world actually are. Be they what they may, the Absolute will father them.'[1]

Yet this remoteness from fact cannot be, for *pragmatism*, a decisive argument against the Absolute.[2]

> Pragmatism, devoted though she be to facts, has no such materialistic bias as ordinary empiricism labors under. . . . *If theological ideas prove to have a value for concrete life, they will be true, for pragmatism, in the sense of being good for so much.*

And indeed the conception of the Absolute does have the 'capacity to yield religious comfort to a most respectable class of minds'.[3] Despite its remoteness from fact, therefore, the pragmatist must acknowledge that 'so far as it affords such comfort, it surely is not sterile; it has that amount of value; it performs a concrete function'.[4] 'As a good pragmatist', concludes James, 'I myself ought to call the Absolute true "in so far forth" then; and I unhesitatingly now do so.'[5] Here the satisfaction or value of true ideas clearly includes the religious comfort of the believer; James thus requires the *broad* interpretation earlier mentioned.

What is the particular sort of comfort afforded by belief in the Absolute? It is the comfort of knowing that, in an ultimate sense, 'finite evil is "overruled" already',[6] so that we may[7]

> without sin, dismiss our fear and drop the worry of our finite responsibility . . . we have a right ever and anon to take a moral holiday, to let the world wag in its own way, feeling that its issues are in better hands than ours and are none of our business.

If this is the 'cash value'[8] of belief in the Absolute, 'who can

[1] Ibid., 71.
[2] Ibid., 73.
[3] Ibid., 71.
[4] Ibid., 73.
[5] Ibid.
[6] Ibid.
[7] Ibid., 74.
[8] Ibid.

possibly deny the truth of it? To deny it would be to insist that men should never relax, and that holidays are never in order.'[1]

However, James goes on to criticize belief in the Absolute nevertheless, because it conflicts with other beliefs having greater 'vital benefits'.[2] A belief, he insists, cannot be judged true simply in virtue of the satisfaction it affords *in itself*; it must also fail to be overridden by conflicting beliefs with *greater* capacity to satisfy.[3]

> In other words, the greatest enemy of any one of our truths may be the rest of our truths. Truths have once for all this desperate instinct of self-preservation and of desire to extinguish whatever contradicts them. My belief in the Absolute, based on the good it does me, must run the gauntlet of all my other beliefs. Grant that it may be true in giving me a moral holiday. Nevertheless, as I conceive, – and let me speak now confidentially, as it were, and merely in my own private person, – it clashes with other truths of mine whose benefits I hate to give up on its account. It happens to be associated with a kind of logic of which I am the enemy, I find that it entangles me in metaphysical paradoxes that are inacceptable, etc., etc. But as I have enough trouble in life already without adding the trouble of carrying these intellectual inconsistencies, I personally just give up the Absolute. I just *take* my moral holidays; or else as a professional philosopher, I try to justify them by some other principle.
>
> If I could restrict my notion of the Absolute to its bare holiday-giving value, it wouldn't clash with my other truths. But we can not easily thus restrict our hypotheses.

The value afforded by belief in the Absolute is thus not, in itself, a *decisive* count in its favour; it does not show that we ought to adopt this belief. The value of other beliefs needs to be considered as well. In general, James says:[4]

> If there be any life that it is really better we should lead, and if there be any idea which, if believed in, would help us to lead that life, then it would be really *better for us* to believe in

[1] Ibid., 75.
[2] Ibid., 76.
[3] Ibid., 78–9.
[4] Ibid., 76–7.

that idea, *unless, indeed, belief in it incidentally clashed with other greater vital benefits.*

'What would be better for us to believe'! This sounds very like a definition of truth.

James, as is clear from these passages, surely is *not* guilty of allowing the pleasantness or the comfort of a belief to override all other considerations. He is furious with critics who impute such a view to him:[1]

> These pragmatists destroy all objective standards, critics say, and put foolishness and wisdom on one level! A favorite formula for describing Mr. Schiller's doctrines and mine is that we are persons who think that by saying whatever you find it pleasant to say and calling it truth you fulfil every pragmatistic requirement. . . . The unwillingness of some of our critics to read any but the silliest of possible meanings into our statements is as discreditable to their imaginations as anything I know in recent philosophic history. Schiller says the true is that which 'works'. Thereupon he is treated as one who limits verification to the lowest material utilities. Dewey says truth is what gives 'satisfaction'. He is treated as one who believes in calling everything true which, if it were true, would be pleasant.

James, indeed, rightly rejects criticisms to the effect that the pragmatist calls 'everything true which, if it were true, would be pleasant'.[2] But it seems undeniable nevertheless that he takes pleasantness or comfort as *one* evidence of truth. It is this that remains subject to legitimate criticism, in my opinion, since the effects of a belief on the believer are altogether irrelevant to the question whether or not the belief is true. That a belief comforts the believer is no count at all in favour of its truth, and that a belief is unpleasant to contemplate is no count against its truth. What counts at all is whether things appear likely, on the evidence, to be as the belief asserts them to be, and clearly this condition is logically independent of the psychological effects of accepting the belief. If truth is, as James says, 'one species of good',[3] this

[1] Ibid., 233–4.
[2] Ibid., 234.
[3] Ibid., 75.

particular good (or satisfaction) needs to be narrowly circumscribed. The *narrow* interpretation of *satisfaction* in James's theory is addressed, indeed, not to psychological consequences of belief-acceptance that are satisfactory in the sense of being pleasant, but rather to logical consequences of the accepted belief that are satisfactory in the sense of being borne out by experience.

The latter idea forms the basis of a less objectionable version of James's theory of truth; the satisfactory character of a true belief consists in its *predictive adequacy*. If a given belief is true, then, and only then, if you act on this belief, forming your expectations or predictions in accordance with it, experience will *satisfy these expectations or predictions*, it being irrelevant whether or not *you are satisfied also*. The satisfaction of a prediction by experience represents verification of the belief upon which this prediction rests. Truth, in short, is a function of particular verifications, and the value of true beliefs lies in their preparing us to face our future experience, whether pleasant or unpleasant.[1]

> Truth for us is simply a collective name for verification-processes, just as health, wealth, strength, etc., are names for other processes connected with life, and also pursued because it pays to pursue them. Truth is *made*, just as health, wealth and strength are made, in the course of experience.

[1] Ibid., 218.

IV

JAMES AND THE MUTABILITY
OF TRUTH

The formulation of James's theory in terms of verification-processes escapes the criticism that psychological satisfaction is taken as an index of truth. In the notion that 'truth is made ... in the course of experience', we find, however, a fundamental *relativism* affecting this narrower version of James's theory. This relativism occasions further difficulties which we shall here consider.

The relativism in question is not merely an incidental by-product of James's theory. James is concerned explicitly to deny the rationalist view that 'the quality [of truth] ... is timeless',[1] insisting rather that truth appears in the historic process as a concomitant or resultant of verification. Thus, he writes, '*ideas (which themselves are but parts of our experience) become true just in so far as they help us to get into satisfactory relation with other parts of our experience.*'[2] In another passage, he expresses his point still more directly, as follows: 'The truth of an idea is not a stagnant property inherent in it. Truth *happens* to an idea. It *becomes* true, is *made* true by events. Its verity *is* in fact an event, a process: the process namely of its verifying itself, its veri-*fication*.'[3]

It is conceivable that James's notion of truth *as a process* is to be interpreted not only as making truth relative to time, but also

[1] William James, *Pragmatism* (New York: Longmans, Green, 1907, 1910), 219.
[2] Ibid., 58.
[3] Ibid., 201.

as construing truth to be a variable property – capable of changes in degree. For such a strong interpretation of James, the truth of an idea *consists* in its verifications: the more verifications, the truer the idea. Such a strong interpretation would, in any event, be very difficult to maintain; it is certainly clear that it would lead to absurd consequences in parallel cases of clarification by the pragmatic maxim. For example, we would need to say that the hardness of a diamond *consists* in the positive outcomes of hardness tests to which it has been subjected: the more such outcomes, the harder the diamond. Now Peirce, indeed, appears willing to accept some such consequence in 'How to Make Our Ideas Clear'. He asks, 'What prevents us from saying that all hard bodies remain perfectly soft until they are touched, when their hardness increases with the pressure until they are scratched.'[1] In reply, he declares that such a view would be not false but merely different from present modes of speech.

Peirce, however, later abandoned this view, as we have already seen. It is in any case untenable, for it destroys the distinction between (1) a genuine increase in hardness by ordinary standards – say the hardening of a fresh egg when boiled – and (2) an increasing confidence in an object's constant hardness with repeated positive tests. We could, on such a view, get as hard a substance as we liked, simply by repeated positive testing; we could increase our intelligence without limit by repeated, and identical, positive outcomes on intelligence tests. Such a view, in short, confuses the *property itself* with the *strength of the belief* that the property obtains. The latter certainly increases with positive outcomes of relevant tests, but the property itself does not therefore also, correspondingly, increase.

We do not, however, need to adopt this strong interpretation of James's view of truth as a process. We may renounce the idea that truth *consists* in, and increases with the number of, its verifications. For a more moderate interpretation, we keep simply the notion that 'truth happens to an idea':[2] that is, an idea may at one time be true, at another time not, depending on whether or not, up to the time in question, the idea has been verified, and verified without exception. An idea may thus *acquire* truth with its first verification

---

[1] *CP*, V.403; *W*, 125.
[2] James, op. cit., 201.

and *retain* such truth (without any change of degree) throughout a further period of continued verification or, at any rate, non-falsification, finally to lose truth with its first falsification.

A general notion of this sort has been proposed by many thinkers in recent times: we are to construe truth not as an absolute property of ideas but rather as relative to time and person, for it is to be correlated with verification or confirmation, which are themselves relative to time and person. A major motivation for this view is to bring truth into line with the spirit and practice of science, the supposition being that an absolute notion of truth leads to dogmatism. As James puts it,[1]

> the great assumption of the intellectualists is that truth means essentially an inert static relation. When you've got your true idea of anything, there's an end of the matter. You're in possession; you *know*; you have fulfilled your thinking destiny. . . . Epistemologically you are in stable equilibrium.

James's theory of truth as *relative* is thus counterposed to the view of truth as *absolute*, since the absolute view is thought to justify dogmatism. But this latter assumption seems to be just a mistake. There is a difference between absolute truth and the conviction of certainty in one's claims to the truth. It is one thing to believe that truth is an absolute, i.e., time-independent and person-independent property of ideas or beliefs; it is quite another to suppose that we can ever be certain that we have the truth. Accordingly, it is logically possible to deny *certainty* and yet to uphold an *absolute* theory of truth. The spirit and practice of science are indeed opposed to dogmatism, but dogmatism rests on a conviction of certainty (or indubitable intuition), not absolute truth. The denial of certainty is not relativistic truth but fallibilism, and we have already seen how Peirce combined his doctrine of fallibilism, inspired by science, with a notion of truth as an ideal and absolute limit of scientific investigation. He believed, in other words, that the truth is a non-relative property of beliefs, but that none of us is ever in a position to say, 'I'm in possession! There's an end of the matter.'

The truth of a statement must, of course, be clearly distinguished

[1] Ibid., 200.

from its being taken, at a given time, to be true or estimated as true, just as the hardness of a substance needs to be distinguished from its being taken, at a given time, to be hard, or estimated as hard. Clearly, we have, at any given time, ideas or propositions we estimate as true or take to be true. Clearly, also, we may at other times take these same propositions to be not true but false. Estimation of truth thus alters in the course of our experience, but it does not follow that truth itself is altered or alterable.

James, it seems to me, is best interpreted as concerned to attack the spirit of dogmatism – the conviction of certainty that closes the mind to new experiences. In this concern, his position is admirable; he is, however, mistaken in formulating his view as an attack on absolute truth. In criticizing dogmatic attitudes, he brilliantly describes the processes by which our truth-estimations develop and change with new experience, but he is wrong in thinking he has shown that the truth itself thus changes. In these opinions, I am, in effect, siding with Peirce, who deplored James's notion of the 'mutability of truth' as a 'seed of death' that has been allowed to infect pragmatism, 'a philosophy so instinct with life'.[1]

It is worth noting several independent arguments against relativizing truth through assimilating it to concepts of active processes such as verification or confirmation.[2] We typically suppose a statement to be either true or false, in accord with the principle of excluded middle. But some statements are neither confirmed nor disconfirmed for given persons at given times. We cannot now, for example, confirm or disconfirm Caesar's having had breakfast the day he crossed the Rubicon. Yet we must acknowledge that he either did or did not, and, accordingly, that it is either true that he did or true that he did not, even though we do not now know which it is.

We also suppose, in accord with the law of non-contradiction, that no statement can be both true and false. Yet some statements clearly are confirmed for some persons in some circumstances, and not for others in the same or other circumstances. Imagine, for example, that I have a toothache but am sufficiently skilled in hiding my feelings from my family to avoid giving them any

---

[1] *CP*, VI.485; *W*, 379.
[2] In some of these comments, I draw upon my review of Morton White, 'Toward Reunion in Philosophy', in *Harvard Educational Review*, XXVII (1957), 156–8.

inkling of my suffering. They will then, unless they have independent countervailing evidence, have good reasons to deny that I have a toothache – they *ought*, in fact, to deny it. On the other hand, I will have excellent, and painful, grounds for affirming that I do have a toothache. Yet it cannot be both true and false that I do.

Consider, now, the case of a *change* in the degree of confirmation of an idea, over time. If a previously well-confirmed scientific theory is now decisively disconfirmed by new evidence, we do not describe it as having first been true and as having now become false. We say, rather, that it had been taken as true but is now judged to be false. Otherwise, we should be driven to say that nature itself changes concomitantly with our changing theories, and, moreover, that the latter do not ever really conflict: so long as Newtonian theory was predictively satisfactory, it was *true*, that is, nature was *in fact* Newtonian. With the breakdown of Newtonianism, nature ceased its Newtonian ways and has since become Einsteinian. Certainly, it must be granted that nature may change, but what reason is there to suppose that it changes obediently every time a new physical theory prevails? What reason is there to believe, moreover, that our theories are *never* mistaken and never in conflict?

Since each theory purports to describe not merely large regions of nature but what is *always* and *everywhere* the case, it is logically absurd to hold that, of two theories ascribing incompatible properties to physical events or processes, *first* one and *then* the other is true. Historical examples are even more striking. It used to be thought that Galileo dropped iron balls from the leaning tower of Pisa. Nowadays, it is held by historians that this story is a myth. Now we cannot suppose that it was for a time true that Galileo did drop iron balls from the tower of Pisa, and that then it became true that he never did. Either he did at some time or he never did; the truth in this matter is not mutable, although, of course, our *opinions* as to what the truth is *are* surely subject to change.[1]

James himself seems less than consistent on these matters. He wants to say, on the one hand, that earlier theories *were* true within their 'borders of experience'[2] and that earlier processes were

---

[1] See A. Koyré, 'Galilée et l'expérience de Pise', *Annales de l'université de Paris* (1937), 441–53; and Herbert Butterfield, *The Origins of Modern Science* (New York: Macmillan, 1960), 81–2.

[2] James, op. cit., 223.

'truth-processes for the actors in them',[1] though not for us. Yet, on the other hand, he also says that what our retrospective judgments assert about the past *was* true, despite earlier thinkers, shedding a 'backward light'[2] on the past. He even admits that the views of earlier thinkers are false 'absolutely' (he puts quotation marks around the word),[3] since the borders of their experience might conceivably have been transcended by them, even though in fact they were not. Indeed, I believe that all James succeeds in showing is that what is *taken to be true* changes from time to time with the progress of investigation. Even he seems to acknowledge, however, that whatever is *taken to be true* is taken to be true *absolutely*, so that our present judgments, casting a backward light on the past, may genuinely conflict with the judgments of earlier theorists. Even seems thus to recognize difficulties in our *taking* the same idea to be *now true now false*, whereas there are *no* difficulties in *now taking* an idea to be true and *then taking* it to be false. Variability, in sum, characterizes estimation of the truth, not truth itself.

It is important to distinguish the absoluteness of truth from the fixity of natural processes, for these two ideas are quite independent. Truth is an attribute of statements, beliefs, propositions, or ideas, not an attribute of things, processes, or events, generally. To say that truth is absolute is to say that *whatever* true statements or ideas affirm is unqualifiedly in fact the case; no further requirement is made that true statements must affirm only natural constancies or fixities. The facts of natural change, whatever they may be, render their true descriptions true absolutely.

Spatial as well as temporal qualifications of all sorts apply to things describable by true statements, but this does not imply that the truth itself must be similarly qualified. If it rained in Mexico City on 7 April 1934, the sentence 'It rained in Mexico City on 7 April 1934' is not just true in Mexico City; neither is it just true on 7 April 1934. It is simply true. In so far, then, as a relativistic doctrine of truth is motivated by the desire to stress the fluidity of history and the pervasiveness of natural change, the same purpose can perfectly well (and with enormously less logical strain) be accomplished by an absolute theory of truth.

[1] Ibid., 224.
[2] Ibid., 223–4.
[3] Ibid., 223.

Such a theory, systematically developed in recent times by the logician Alfred Tarski,[1] has convinced most contemporary analytic philosophers that an absolute conception of truth is logically coherent, that it is independent of the relative concept of confirmation and that it is, moreover, perfectly consistent with scientific attitudes.

[1] Alfred Tarski, 'The Semantic Conception of Truth', *Philosophy and Phenomenological Research* (1944); reprinted in Herbert Feigl and Wilfrid Sellars, *Readings in Philosophical Analysis* (New York: Appleton-Century-Crofts, 1949), 52–84. See also Rudolf Carnap, 'Truth and Confirmation', in Feigl and Sellars, op. cit., 119–27.

V

JAMES'S PSYCHOLOGICAL VIEWS: GENERAL REMARKS

James's psychological views may be introduced by contrasting British associationist conceptions with American functionalism, in which James was a dominant figure, and which was, in general, closely allied to the pragmatic trend in philosophy. Before this contrast can be made, we need to return again to Descartes as our starting point.

We have seen Descartes's attempt to construct all of knowledge upon the indubitable base of self-consciousness available to the individual mind. This *rationalistic* approach is rejected by the British *empiricist* school which denies that the mind has innate and indubitable ideas to begin with. On the contrary, the mind is at birth a blank slate upon which experience writes. Through experience it becomes furnished with ideas which eventually represent for it, in diverse ways, the various objects of its environment. Through its powers of comparison, classification and association, the mind is capable of building up, from the simple ideas of sense received from without, the complex structures of adult knowledge. The study of the mind may be conceived as tracing the specific processes by which simple sensory ideas are associated into wholes, ordered in groups, and set into the general relations by which we form our expectations and manage our practical affairs.

Empiricist theories of the mind, interpreted primarily as psychologies rather than as theories of knowledge, have been subjected to a variety of plausible criticisms: for one thing, our mental organization is not exclusively associative and synthetic in its development; it is also discriminative and analytic. We perceive wholes as well as elements. For another, the absolute simplicity of the sensory elements presupposed by empiricism is difficult to take seriously, as is the correlated idea of general mental powers. Simplicity is a relative, not an absolute notion; it hinges on pre-supposed concepts and categories of analysis. Our knowledge is embodied in such concepts and categories; it is couched in language not derivable from the data of sense but imposed upon them. These concepts and categories are related to action and motivation. They arise and function in organisms with determinate biological characteristics. They are also cultural and historical products, rather than an affair of the individual mind merely. The mind should not only be analysed into its individually constitutive elements but also related to its biological matrix and social context; moreover, it should be seen in the perspective of action.

Functional psychology, taking such criticisms of associationism seriously, provided a view with relevant counter-emphases: it stressed the notions of *dynamism*, *utility*, and *organism*. James Angell's presidential address to the American Psychological Association in 1906 discussed 'The Province of Functional Psychology',[1] and it presented three characterizations:[2]

1) Functional psychology is the 'psychology of mental operations in contrast to the psychology of mental elements'. In E. G. Boring's words, 'Structural psychology deals with psychology's *what*, but functional psychology, said Angell, adds the *how* and *why*. . . . *Why* means either a purpose, which is item 2 below, or a cause, which would be neural and item 3 below.'

2) Functional psychology is the 'psychology of the fundamental utilities of consciousness', in which mind is to be seen as 'primarily engaged in mediating between the environment and the needs of the organism'. As Boring put it, 'The function of consciousness is "accommodation to the novel", since

[1] James R. Angell, 'The Province of Functional Psychology', *Psychological Review*, 14 (1907), 61–91. My treatment is based on Edwin G. Boring, *A History of Experimental Psychology* (New York: Appleton-Century-Crofts, 1950), 557.
[2] Ibid.

consciousness wanes in the face of an habitual situation. . . .
Habit rules for the familiar, but let the environment present
a novel situation and "in steps consciousness" to take
charge.'

3) The broadest view of functional psychology is that it is all
of 'psychophysics', in Boring's words: 'the psychology of
the total mind-body organism. Such a view goes far beyond
the conscious states, bringing in the well-habituated, half-
unconscious acts as of service to the organism.'

Functionalism, in short, reflected the influence of evolutionary
modes of thought and, in applying them to psychology, recast the
setting of classical philosophies of mind, introducing, in a critical
and pervasive manner, biological, social, and purposive considerations.

We have already seen the strong influence of biology on pragmatism as a theory of knowledge and inquiry. The biological
influence also unifies the dominant psychological emphases in
James: the physical context is seen as defining the fundamental
problem for an organism that requires fulfilment of characteristic
needs and desires in order to survive. The whole organism,
characterized by a range of cognitive and emotive capacities, must
adapt to this situation. These capacities are developed and altered
in specific ways as functions whose job it is to meet the problem
set by the environment. 'Mental life', says James, 'is primarily
teleological; that is to say, that our various ways of feeling and
thinking have grown to be what they are because of their utility
in shaping our reactions on the outer world.'[1] This is a far cry
from the rationalist conception of the self-contained individual
mind with its intuitive certainty of existence, as well as from the
empiricist conception of the mind as blank register of simple
qualities supplied by experience, to be processed in fixed and
standard ways.

In *The Principles of Psychology* (1890), James treats states of consciousness as entities, adopting for the purposes of psychology a
'methodological dualism' of mind and body.[2] This position was a

---

[1] William James, *Psychology: Briefer Course* (New York: Henry Holt, 1900), 4.
[2] See Charles Morris, *The Pragmatic Movement in American Philosophy* (New York:
George Braziller, 1970), 123–5.

transitional one for James who later answered 'No' to the title question of his 1904 article, 'Does Consciousness Exist?',[1] arguing there that 'thoughts in the concrete are made of the same stuff as things are',[2] the distinction of thought and thing being a functional contrast within experience. In the earlier *Principles*, however, he accepts the working hypothesis of physiological psychology that all mental states are effects of brain states. Accordingly, he continues to speak of *mental states* as special distinguishable entities, although he strives to connect them causally with bodily states.

Mental states are for James, however, not simply causal offshoots of bodily states, without significance for the organism's life problems. James, in other words, is not an 'epiphenomenalist' as was Santayana, for whom the mental life is a dazzling display produced by physical causes but itself without effect on those causes, somewhat like the colourful spray of sparks produced by the knife-grinder's wheel.[3] For consciousness has, after all, evolved, hence it probably has utility, and James locates this utility in the process of choice. Consciousness, choosing on the basis of pleasures and pains, provides, as a matter of empirical fact, a service that tends to promote survival. 'Pleasures [being] . . . generally associated with beneficial, [and] pains with detrimental, experiences', it happens that 'what seems best to consciousness is really best for the creature',[4] on the average and in the long run.

There is no *necessary* connection, to be sure, between our sensations of pleasure and our prospects of organic benefit, but since such a connection largely holds in fact, what is pleasurable for us is in general good for our survival and well-being. The selection of pleasurable conscious states thus helps, in influencing the selection of corresponding neural patterns, to steer the organism toward what is beneficial for its survival. At the same time, the dependence of mental life upon the physiological implies a certain realistic limitation upon the powers of choice: neural patterns are

---

[1] William James, 'Does Consciousness Exist?', *Journal of Philosophy*, I (1904), 477–91; reprinted in William James, *Essays in Radical Empiricism* (New York: Longmans, Green, 1912).

[2] Ibid., 37.

[3] George Santayana, *The Life of Reason*, vol. 1: *Reason in Common Sense* (New York: Collier, Macmillan, 1906), 213: 'A bodily feat, like nutrition or reproduction is celebrated by a festival in the mind, and consciousness is a sort of ritual solemnising by prayer, jubilation, or mourning, the chief episodes in the body's fortunes.'

[4] James, *Psychology: Briefer Course*, 103.

structural facts, and choices become crystallized in stable neural structures which are resistant to change. Accordingly, succeeding choices operate within increasingly stringent limitations. We shall explore this theme further in examining James's views of habit.

VI

JAMES'S TREATMENT OF HABIT

Several of James's basic ideas converge in his treatment of habit. His teleological emphasis leads him to think of habit-formation, as well as of specific habits, in terms of their functions in dealing with the environment. His appreciation of the selective role of consciousness leads him to consider the possibilities of altering habits through choice. Finally, his recognition of the physiological substructure of habit leads him to see the limitations on such choice in the learning and unlearning of habits. *Habit* is thus a key notion in James's psychology. Though it has a clear physical basis, it is formed through the functioning of the organism, partly subject to, and simultaneously limiting, conscious choice, hence strongly conditioning the ethical quality of life. James's concept of habit, accordingly, links body and mind, and relates choice, action, and character.

That habit is manifested in physical structure implies, for James, that it is not simply a product of deliberate choice, that is to say, it is not subject to alteration simply by the will. Moral resolve and moral exhortation cannot, in themselves, directly influence habit, since habit has a structural basis in the nervous system, representing a 'new pathway of discharge formed in the brain, by which certain incoming currents ever after tend to escape'.[1]

Sensory currents pour in and are discharged through the nerves controlling movement. The intervening paths once formed become more readily used and, in this manner, stable patterns are developed. The habit pathway links perceptible stimuli with motor effects, and can therefore be influenced by resolutions only

[1] William James, *Psychology: Briefer Course* (New York: Henry Holt, 1900), 134.

when the latter result in actions affecting the motor disposition of sensory stimulation in given circumstances. 'It is not in the moment of their forming but in the moment of their producing *motor effects*, that resolves and aspirations communicate the new "set" to the brain.'[1]

The function of habit, for James, is to economize and simplify our actions. Man's behaviour is not rigidly determined by instinct. His behaviour, unlike that of animals, is largely learned. If there were no such mechanism as habit to economize the effort required for learned performance, men would 'be in a sorry plight'.[2] Storing the fruits of past experience so as to economize effort and simplify action, habit reduces the need for conscious supervision. 'Habit', says James, 'diminishes the conscious attention with which our acts are performed.'[3] This leaves consciousness free to deal with perplexing and still unformed situations requiring our attention.

The stability of habit has social as well as personal significance. This stability is most highly exemplified in 'trained domestic animals . . . undoubtingly, unhesitatingly doing from minute to minute the duties they have been taught, and giving no sign that the possibility of an alternative ever suggests itself to their mind'. The same sort of stability is evident also in the lives of human beings. 'Men grown old in prison have asked to be readmitted after being once set free.'[4]

> Habit is thus the enormous fly-wheel of society, its most precious conservative agent. . . . It alone prevents the hardest and most repulsive walks of life from being deserted by those brought up to tread therein. It keeps the fisherman and the deck-hand at sea through the winter; it holds the miner in his darkness, and nails the countryman to his log-cabin and his lonely farm through all the months of snow.[5]

These remarks on the social aspects of habit seem curiously restricted in perspective. They suggest, misleadingly, that social stability is a matter of mere personal habituation. But, surely, it is

[1] William James, *The Principles of Psychology* (New York: Dover, 1950) (*PP*), vol. I, 124.
[2] Ibid., 113.
[3] Ibid., 114.
[4] Ibid., 120–1.
[5] Ibid., 121.

not typically the case that the miner, for example, has simply become so used to mining that he can hardly conceive any alternatives or desire another life. James, indeed, proceeds to elaborate his remarks so as to give a more realistic account of the matter. Habit, he says, selectively crystallizes our capabilities in line with early influences and choices so that, whether or not we may want to change our situation in adulthood, the time is very often past for relearning. We are caught, as it were, by the consequences of our early habit-formation.[1]

> [Habit] dooms us all to fight out the battle of life upon the lines of our nurture or our early choice, and to make the best of a pursuit that disagrees, because there is no other for which we are fitted, and it is too late to begin again.

The miner, in other words, may not simply have become *accustomed* to mining; his lot may have been fixed by the stabilization of his capacities through nurture and early choice and, much as he may now wish to alter his life, the possibilities of his doing so may be closed off because it is too late.

James thus recognizes a stabilizing effect of habit which is more than simply a matter of *getting used* to a particular way of life. It has rather to do with the loss of personal plasticity. Still, he seems to fall short of attaining a genuinely *social* perspective. For the notion that possibilities are open or closed to men not simply as a function of increasing personal rigidity but as a function of social organization is one that James never seems to envisage. In the passage we are considering, he makes the remark that '[habit] keeps different social strata from mixing',[2] but this single comment seems far too weak to do justice to the social dimension. That the miner's early nurture is itself conditioned by social structure, and that, even were it not too late for him to begin again, he would find his options limited by the prevailing organization of his society, are considerations that James does not raise in his discussion. It remained for Mead and for Dewey to expand the personal concept of habit to encompass social custom. It remained for Dewey, in particular, to broaden the notion of habit-formation so as to embrace also social reconstruction, and to take the social

[1] Ibid.
[2] Ibid.

customs defining each person's range of possibilities as themselves subject to intelligent criticism and reform.

James, by contrast, having noted the loss of plasticity and consequent diminution of the scope of personal choice, reverts immediately to illustrations of simple habituation to demonstrate the inertia of habit:[1]

> Already at the age of twenty-five you see the professional mannerism settling down on the young commercial traveller, on the young doctor, on the young minister, on the young counsellor-at-law. You see the little lines of cleavage running through the character, the tricks of thought, the prejudices, the ways of the 'shop', in a word, from which the man can by-and-by no more escape than his coat-sleeve can suddenly fall into a new set of folds. On the whole, it is best he should not escape. It is well for the world that in most of us, by the age of thirty, the character has set like plaster, and will never soften again.

James is concerned, then, not with social reform, but with personal character stabilization, which is a universal process in every society and upon which every system of morality depends. It is not that he opposes social reform; it is rather that he does not deal with the question, focusing his attention mainly on the 'ethical [and pedagogical] implications of the law of habit'.[2]

Education, in particular, should 'make our nervous system our ally instead of our enemy', capitalizing upon the precious early time of plasticity to form useful traits of character before it is too late.[3]

> For this we must make automatic and habitual, as early as possible, as many useful actions as we can. . . . The more of the details of our daily life we can hand over to the effortless custody of automatism, the more our higher powers of mind will be set free for their own proper work.

For habit-formation, James offers several useful maxims: first, we must 'launch ourselves with as strong and decided an initiative

[1] Ibid.
[2] Ibid., 120.
[3] Ibid., 122.

as possible', using our resolve to set up environmental aids that will stably support our new direction when initiative weakens.[1]

> Accumulate all the possible circumstances which shall re-enforce the right motives; put yourself assiduously in conditions that encourage the new way; make engagements incompatible with the old; take a public pledge, if the case allows; in short, envelop your resolution with every aid you know. This will give your new beginning such a momentum that the temptation to break down will not occur as soon as it otherwise might; and every day during which a breakdown is postponed adds to the chances of its not occurring at all.

A second maxim emphasizes that continuity of training is of the highest importance. 'Never suffer an exception to occur till the new habit is securely rooted in your life.'[2] The third maxim offered by James emphasizes the *action* rather than just the resolve: 'Seize the very first possible opportunity to act on every resolution you make, and on every emotional prompting you may experience in the direction of the habits you aspire to gain.'[3] Character is a matter of will and will is[4]

> an aggregate of tendencies to act in a firm and prompt and definite way upon all the principal emergencies of life. . . . Every time a resolve or a fine glow of feeling evaporates without bearing practical fruit is worse than a chance lost; it works so as positively to hinder future resolutions and emotions from taking the normal path of discharge.

Failure to act itself becomes part of the character. Sentiment may give the illusion of having improved our situation, while leaving everything as it was, indeed hindering further efforts at improvement. Here, formulated for the individual case, is the key idea underlying Dewey's later insistence on connecting social ideas with social reconstruction, for if social ideas are isolated, they give a fine glow of self-satisfaction, while reinforcing the initial social conditions requiring alleviation.

[1] Ibid., 123.
[2] Ibid.
[3] Ibid., 124.
[4] Ibid., 125.

For his final maxim, James offers this advice:[1]

Keep the faculty of effort alive in you by a little gratuitous exercise every day. That is, be systematically ascetic or heroic in little unnecessary points, do every day or two something for no other reason than that you would rather not do it, so that when the hour of dire need draws nigh, it may find you not unnerved and untrained to stand the test.

Physiology, James concludes, is the ally of ethics, since it tells us:[2]

We are spinning our own fates, good or evil, and never to be undone. . . . Nothing we ever do is, in strict scientific literalness, wiped out. Of course, this has its good side as well as its bad one. As we become permanent drunkards by so many separate drinks, so we become saints in the moral, and authorities and experts in the practical and scientific spheres, by so many separate acts and hours of work.

James's chapter on habit has been described by Margaret Knight as 'the most famous Chapter of the *Principles,* and one of the most effective lay sermons that can ever have been delivered in a lecture-room'. She remarks further that it 'has special value today, as an antidote to the current misconception that psychology depreciates the will, and encourages a weak-kneed and fatalistic acceptance of one's own deficiencies'.[3] There is certainly a good deal of useful practical wisdom in James's recommendations, and the application of these and other of the ideas of the *Principles* to education, as outlined in James's *Talks to Teachers,*[4] remains today of great interest.

I want here, however, to note one critical point regarding James's conception of a basic contrast between habit and consciousness. The conception he presents is that the latter is spontaneous and innovative while the former is automatic and unconscious,

---

[1] Ibid., 126.
[2] Ibid., 127.
[3] Margaret Knight, *William James* (Harmondsworth: Penguin, 1950), 73.
[4] William James, *Talks to Teachers on Psychology: and to Students on Some of Life's Ideals* (New York: Henry Holt, 1901).

storing learning so that the mind may be freed for newer challenges. 'The more of the details of our daily life we can hand over to the effortless custody of automatism, the more our higher powers of mind will be set free for their own proper work.'[1]

This contrast seems to me over-simplified in allocating learned performance and intelligence to separate compartments. Some species of learned performance are indeed automatized through repetition, others are not. Gilbert Ryle stresses this important point in introducing his notion of 'intelligent capacities'; these capacities are built up by training, rather than drill, and they never dispense with judgment:[2]

> The recruit learns to slope arms by repeatedly going through just the same motions by numbers. The child learns the alphabet and the multiplication tables in the same way. The practices are not learned until the pupil's responses to his cues are automatic, until he can 'do them in his sleep', as it is revealingly put. Training, on the other hand, though it embodies plenty of sheer drill, does not consist of drill. It involves the stimulation by criticism and example of the pupil's own judgment. He learns how to do things thinking what he is doing, so that every operation performed is itself a new lesson to him how to perform better. The soldier who was merely drilled to slope arms correctly has to be trained to be proficient in marksmanship and map-reading. Drill dispenses with intelligence, training develops it. We do not expect the soldier to be able to read maps 'in his sleep'.

The critical point is that in certain performances, habit and intelligence are fused through practice, so that experience teaches, but not through automatization. This point is very important for all processes of education, and especially for education in the professions and in the arts. The point is made also by Dewey:[3]

> The artist is a masterful technician. The technique or mechanism is fused with thought and feeling. The

---

[1] *PP*, 122.

[2] Gilbert Ryle, *The Concept of Mind* (London: Hutchinson, 1949), 42–3.

[3] John Dewey, *Human Nature and Conduct* (New York: Modern Library, 1922, 1930), 71.

'mechanical' performer permits the mechanism to dictate the performance. It is absurd to say that the latter exhibits habit and the former not. We are confronted with two kinds of habit, intelligent and routine.

VII

JAMES'S VIEW OF THOUGHT

James sets out in chapter IX of the *Principles* (entitled 'The Stream of Thought') to 'begin [the] study of the mind from within'.[1] What should be the starting point of such study? To begin, as most have done, with sensations 'as the simplest mental facts, and proceed synthetically, constructing each higher stage from those below it' is to give up 'the empirical method of investigation'.[2]

> No one ever had a simple sensation by itself. Consciousness, from our natal day, is of a teeming multiplicity of objects and relations, and what we call simple sensations are results of discriminative attention, pushed often to a very high degree. . . . The only thing which psychology has a right to postulate at the outset is the fact of thinking itself, and that must first be taken up and analyzed. If sensations then prove to be amongst the elements of the thinking, we shall be no worse off as respects them than if we had taken them for granted at the start.

James proceeds, accordingly, to assert that 'the first fact for us, then, as psychologists, is that thinking of some sort goes on', explaining that the word 'thinking' is to be understood as referring to 'every form of consciousness indiscriminately'. Indeed, he remarks that if English allowed the expression 'it thinks' (as it does 'it rains') the fact would be statable most simply and with the

[1] *PP*, 224.
[2] Ibid.

'minimum of assumption'. Since the former expression is not available, 'we must simply say that *thought goes on*'.[1]

James proceeds next to list 'five characters' of the process of thought, which he proposes to discuss in a general way in the chapter. He formulates the five characters in the following statements, to each of which I here append a short name, in brackets, for easy reference:[2]

(1) 'Every thought tends to be part of a personal consciousness.' [This is a principle of *personality*.]

(2) 'Within each personal consciousness thought is always changing.' [This is a principle of *change*.]

(3) 'Within each personal consciousness thought is sensibly continuous.' [This is a principle of *continuity*.]

(4) 'It always appears to deal with objects independent of itself.' [This is a principle of *intentionality*.]

(5) 'It is interested in some parts of these objects to the exclusion of others, and welcomes or rejects – *chooses* from among them, in a word – all the while.' [This is a principle of *selectivity*.]

We shall here consider certain aspects of James's discussion of each of these five principles.

1 PERSONALITY: 'EVERY THOUGHT TENDS TO BE PART OF A PERSONAL CONSCIOUSNESS'

The facts underlying this principle of James are facts pertaining to the clustering of thoughts. No thought is utterly isolated and independent nor do all thoughts cohere into a single whole. Thoughts cluster together into packages, and there are many such packages.[3]

> In this room – this lecture-room, say – there are a multitude of thoughts, yours and mine, some of which cohere mutually, and some not. They are as little each-for-itself and reciprocally independent as they are all-belonging-together.

[1] Ibid., 224–5.
[2] See ibid., 225.
[3] Ibid., 225–6.

They are neither: no one of them is separate, but each belongs with certain others and with none beside. My thought belongs with my other thoughts, and your thought with your other thoughts. . . . The only states of consciousness that we naturally deal with are found in personal consciousness, minds, selves, concrete particular I's and you's.

James further says:[1]

It seems as if the elementary psychic fact were not *thought* or *this thought* or *that thought*, but *my thought*, every thought being *owned*. . . . Everyone will recognize this to be true, so long as the existence of *something* corresponding to the term 'personal mind' is all that is insisted on, without any particular view of its nature being implied. On these terms the personal self rather than the thought might be treated as the immediate datum in psychology. The universal conscious fact is not 'feeling and thoughts exist', but 'I think' and 'I feel'.

Now these remarks appear to be manifestly contradictory to James's earlier assertion of the impersonality of psychology's initial datum. There he said that the first fact for psychologists might best be expressed by the words 'it thinks', were English to allow such an expression. Here he says the immediate datum is *not* 'feeling and thoughts exist' but 'I think' and 'I feel'. Is the 'first fact' for psychology then at odds with James's principle of personality?

It is perhaps barely conceivable that James is here suggesting the latter principle as an *alternative* 'first fact' for psychology, conceded to be as well founded as his original impersonal formulation. This seems unlikely, however, for the latter formulation is given without hint of alternatives, and the principle of personality, along with the other four principles, is assigned a clearly subordinate status in relation to the 'first fact'. If not alternatives, then are the 'first fact' and the principle simply in contradiction?

It is, indeed, hard to reconcile the two, since the 'first fact', which does *not* imply the existence of personal selves, is intended to state the situation with *minimum assumption*, whereas the principle of personality, which *does* assert the existence of personal

---

[1] Ibid., 226.

selves, takes the latter as *immediate data*. But if the minimum assumption needed to state the psychological situation with which we begin requires *no* supposition of *selves*, the assertion of selves can hardly (it may be argued) be a report of *immediate* data: it clearly goes beyond what is needed to describe these data. Thus 'I think', in particular, cannot be supposed to report 'the immediate datum in psychology'.

Perhaps James intends to say that 'personal consciousness' does not require a reference that transcends the realm of thoughts; such consciousness consists in thoughts clustered in certain ways. Thus, assuming only the existence of thoughts as our minimal units, and employing the notion of some appropriate clustering relation, we might then understand personal selves as consisting wholly of certain sets or sums of thoughts suitably clustered. Personal selves would then be 'immediate' only in the sense that they were 'constructible' out of *minimal immediate* units (i.e., thoughts), not in the sense that they were themselves among the elements 'minimally' assumed.

If this is James's intention, however, it is not clear why he criticizes the analogous strategy of beginning with *sensations*, and constructing 'higher' stages out of these by a synthetic procedure, as an abandonment of the empirical method of investigation. He says, 'No one ever had a simple sensation by itself.'[1] But equally, no one ever had a simple thought by itself. It is interesting to note that James's 'first fact', which says 'thinking (or thought) goes on',[2] does not individuate thoughts at all, but that, in discussing the principle of personality, he passes, without warning, to treating thoughts as individuated elements, speaking of 'thoughts', 'each thought', 'other thoughts', etc. Surely, such individuation is no less hazardous for thoughts than it is for sensations. If individuation and construction are to be permitted in the case of thoughts, why not elsewhere? One may, of course, evaluate alternative programmes of construction differently, in the light of their specific successes and failures. But it is not fair to deplore the method of 'synthetic' construction as such, when it is applied to sensations, while allowing it free rein in application to thoughts.

But James, it may be argued, intends something different in saying that 'the personal self *rather than* the thought might be treated

[1] Ibid., 224.
[2] Ibid., 224-5.

as the immediate datum in psychology'.[1] For he is here *contrasting* the personal self with the thought, and this contrast is not given any basis – indeed, it is thwarted – in the interpretation we have just considered. For this interpretation construes personal selves to be immediate since constructible out of minimal immediate units, i.e., thoughts. But it thereby implies that thoughts are no less immediate than selves.

Suppose, then, that the intended point has to do with the *temporal* dimension. We suppose, as before, that thoughts are taken as our minimal units, and that selves are 'constructible' out of these units, so that they do not add to our assumed stock of elements. Now, however, we give the concept of 'immediacy' a temporal interpretation. We do *not*, as before, take thoughts as immediate, since they can be reached only through a process of discriminative analysis that takes time. By contrast, selves *are* immediate in that they are temporally prior – they appear first in the life of the mind. This new interpretation *does* support the required contrast between the self, as immediate, and the thought as non-immediate. Moreover, it preserves the main advantage of the prior interpretation: thoughts alone are required as assumed minimal elements, selves being constructible out of these.

It remains puzzling, however, with this interpretation no less than with the earlier one, why James criticizes the analogous procedure when the minimal units are sensations rather than thoughts. If thoughts can be taken as minimal units for the purpose of theoretical construction without implying that they are temporally prior to selves constituted of thoughts, why cannot the same be said of sensations? Why, that is, cannot sensations be taken as minimal units for theoretical construction even though they lack temporal priority, even though, as James says, 'what we call simple sensations are results of discriminative attention, pushed often to a very high degree'?[2] Why, in the case of sensations alone, does James consider the 'synthetic' procedure to be an abandonment of the empirical method of investigation?

Could James have held that selves, as thought-clusters, arise in the mind earlier than objects, as sensation-clusters, and thus have greater immediacy? Could he have argued that this absolute

[1] Ibid., 226.
[2] Ibid., 224.

priority allows a synthetic procedure, without misleading temporal connotations, only in the former case? Such an argument would hardly be persuasive even were the supposed priority granted. James, moreover, himself denies such priority. He remarks that 'consciousness, from our natal day, is of a teeming multiplicity of objects and relations',[1] suggesting that, so far as *absolute* priority is concerned, objects and relations must be given preference. Indeed, in his later discussion of the principle of intentionality, he says explicitly, 'The consciousness of objects must come first.'[2]

James's various comments on the topics we have been considering thus seem to me exceedingly problematic. In general, it seems to me that the 'synthetic' procedure of analysis and construction is consonant with the empirical method, and that such method is compatible with the choice of an indefinite variety of analytical units. James may be understood, in any event, to be taking thoughts as his minimal units and considering personal consciousnesses to be constructed out of these. Personal selfhood is a matter of the organization and coherence of thoughts, rather than an object or property that transcends thought. The 'mental procession' is 'itself the very "original" of the notion of personality'.[3]

Viewed simply in this way, James's doctrine is appealing, but it also raises questions. For example, it may be asked how the organization of thoughts is to be understood exactly. Moreover, it may be questioned whether empirical psychology can develop adequate explanations if it does not go beyond concepts of personality as clusters of thoughts and freely postulate theoretical entities and mechanisms underlying the play of mental phenomena. The matter cannot be settled by *a priori* reasoning, but the probabilities, based on the example of available attempts at psychological explanation, seem to point to a negative answer.

---

[1] Ibid.
[2] Ibid., 273.
[3] Ibid., 227.

2 CHANGE: 'WITHIN EACH PERSONAL CONSCIOUSNESS THOUGHT IS ALWAYS CHANGING'

James does *not* mean 'necessarily'[1] that no single state of mind has any duration – that it *must* be instantaneous, since thought is in constant flux. He remarks that 'even if true, that would be hard to establish'.[2] He allows, thus, that a single state of mind may indeed endure, may, that is, have 'spread' in physical time. Or, put otherwise, phases of the mental life that are distinguished by different positions in physical time may still belong together as making up a single state of mind. In saying that thought is constantly changing, he refers more particularly to change taking place 'in sensible intervals of time'.[3] His point is, then, that no two states of mind, which are temporally different by *sensible* criteria, can be the same. He insists that 'no state once gone can recur and be identical with what it was before'.[4] James quotes Shadworth Hodgson's statement: 'I may shut my eyes and keep perfectly still, and try not to contribute anything of my own will; but whether I think, or do not think, whether I perceive external things or not, I always have a succession of different feelings.'[5]

James is, here as before, concerned to attack the empiricist theory of ideas. Previously, he attacked its synthetic procedure and its emphasis on sensations. Now he attacks the effort to find *constant elements* amid the flow of consciousness. 'The celebrated "theory of *ideas*" ', he says,[6]

> admitting the great difference among each other of what may be called concrete conditions of mind, seeks to show how this is all the resultant effect of variations in the *combination* of certain simple elements of consciousness that always remain the same. These mental atoms or molecules are what Locke called 'simple ideas'. Some of Locke's successors made out that the only simple ideas were the sensations strictly so

---

[1] Ibid., 229.
[2] Ibid.
[3] Ibid., 230.
[4] Ibid.
[5] Ibid. The passage from Hodgson is from his *The Philosophy of Reflection*, vol. I (London: Longmans, Green, 1878), 248.
[6] *PP*, 230.

called. Which ideas the simple ones may be does not, however, now concern us. It is enough that certain philosophers
have thought they could see under the dissolving-view-
appearance of the mind elementary facts of *any* sort that
remained unchanged amid the flow.

In opposition to this view, James defends the doctrine that 'no
two "ideas" are ever exactly the same'.[1] The constancy that we
find is a constancy of the object rather than the idea.[2]

> What is got twice is the same object. We hear the same *note*
> over and over again; we see the same *quality* of green, or
> smell the same objective perfume, or experience the same
> *species* of pain. The realities, concrete and abstract, physical
> and ideal, whose permanent existence we believe in, seem to
> be constantly coming up again before our thought, and lead
> us, in our carelessness, to suppose that our 'ideas' of them
> are the same ideas. . . . The grass out of the window now
> looks to me of the same green in the sun as in the shade, and
> yet a painter would have to paint one part of it dark brown,
> another part bright yellow, to give its real sensational effect.
> We take no heed, as a rule, of the different way in which the
> same things look and sound and smell at different distances
> and under different circumstances. The sameness of the *things*
> is what we are concerned to ascertain; and any sensations that
> assure us of that will probably be considered in a rough way
> to be the same with each other.

Such considerations are reinforced by the dependence of sensations upon cerebral action. 'For an identical sensation to recur
it would have to occur the second time *in an unmodified* brain.'[3] But
this, says James, is physiologically impossible. Moreover, 'Every
brain-state is partly determined by the nature of [the] entire past
succession. . . . It is out of the question, then, that any total
brain-state should identically recur.'[4] James concludes: '*A per-
manently existing "idea" or "Vorstellung" which makes its appearance
before the footlights of consciousness at periodical intervals, is as mythological*

---

[1] Ibid., 235.
[2] Ibid., 231.
[3] Ibid., 232.
[4] Ibid., 234.

an entity as the Jack of Spades.[1] Consciousness flows; only the totality of objects of consciousness – the world of realities – is characterized by constancy. When we read the latter constancy back into the mind, it is understandable that we must get a distorted picture.

James's emphasis here is certainly well taken. The dominant concerns of men with the objective features of their environment lead typically to a parallel, but false, objectification of consciousness. We need to study consciousness without presupposing that it is 'structurally' parallel to the physical environment. The question may, nevertheless, be raised as to whether James's view is not formulated too strongly.

Take first the doctrine that no two states of mind, of which one is sensibly earlier than the other, can be identical. We may assume that by 'identity' is meant something short of *literal or numerical* identity, for otherwise the doctrine would be trivial since we have supposed two states, one earlier than the other. The claim is then, perhaps, that no sensibly later state can be *qualitatively* identical with any earlier state (under some suitable interpretation of 'qualitative identity'). But if the two states in question are *sensibly* differentiable by their temporal features, it follows that they are not qualitatively identical; again the claim seems trivial. Suppose the claim is, then, that states which are sensibly distinguishable in respect of time must *also* be, in every case, sensibly distinguishable in respect of some other characteristic than time. Given two adjacent states, that is, one cannot be aware of them as *merely* temporally different, for there will always be some further difference between them in consciousness. This claim is not trivial, but it is hard to see why James is so sure of it. I cannot see that it is either self-evident or empirically so well established as to be virtually beyond question.

Take now James's denial of constancy in the world of *ideas*, as distinct from the world of *objects*. James here appears to be propounding two theses rather than one, but he seems not to notice the difference between them. One thesis is that there are no 'elementary facts of *any* sort that remain . . . unchanged amid the flow';[2] that 'no two "ideas" are ever exactly the same'.[3] The

---

[1] Ibid., 236.
[2] Ibid., 230.
[3] Ibid., 235.

second thesis is that there is no *constant dependence* of ideas upon physical circumstances:[1]

> Are not the sensations we get from the same object, for example, always the same? Does not the same grass give us the same feeling of green, the same sky the same feeling of blue, and do we not get the same olfactory sensation no matter how many times we put our nose to the same flask of cologne? It seems a piece of metaphysical sophistry to suggest that we do not; and yet a close attention to the matter shows that *there is no proof that the same bodily sensation is ever got by us twice.*

Now a denial of *constant physical dependencies* of ideas is not the same as a denial of *qualitative constancies* altogether. The denial of constant physical dependencies may readily be granted, but the denial of all qualitative constancy whatever is difficult to conceive, let alone to accept. Certainly we tend uncritically to think that grass looks green, whether in the sun or the shade, and certainly 'a painter would have to paint one part of it dark brown, another part bright yellow, to give its real sensational effect'.[2] But the painter is here presumed to be able to identify such *sensational effects*, e.g., various instances of 'dark brown' or 'bright yellow' and, *a fortiori*, the phenomenal contrast between such instances. The 'physical' green of the grass is, to be sure, compatible with 'phenomenal' colour variation, but the latter variation is itself describable by means of a relevant analytical vocabulary of general terms. It is even describable in terms of phenomenal elements, e.g., *qualia*, as in Nelson Goodman's *Structure of Appearance*.[3]

Phenomenal properties are, I suggest, treated in contradictory fashion by James, who takes them sometimes as objects, sometimes as ideas. We may distinguish *physical* green from *phenomenal* green, and both of these from the *idea of* phenomenal green. Assume that there are phenomenal constancies not dependent on physical circumstances, for example, that the painter may use two bits of pigment conventionally representing phenomenal green to depict, respectively, a physically blue object and a physically purple object. What does James say to this case? On the one hand,

[1] Ibid., 231.
[2] Ibid.
[3] Nelson Goodman, *The Structure of Appearance* (Indianapolis: Bobbs-Merrill, 1951, 1966 (2nd ed.)).

we may suppose him to say that such phenomenal constancy is a constancy of the (abstract) *object*: 'we see the same *quality* of green'.[1] Such constancy does not, he says, affect the principle of change in application to *ideas*: i.e., an idea of (phenomenal) green is never identical with another such idea. We must not be led, 'in our carelessness, to suppose that our "ideas" of [such realities as the quality of green or a given species of pain] are the same ideas'.[2]

On the other hand, summing up his rejection of psychological atomism, he says that a permanent 'idea' making 'its appearance before the footlights of consciousness at periodical intervals, is as mythological an entity as the Jack of Spades'.[3] Here, his wholesale rejection presumably includes the phenomenal property itself, in line with his first thesis, noted above, that there are no 'elementary facts of *any* sort that remain . . . unchanged amid the flow'.[4] For if phenomenal properties are to be allowed to recur before the footlights of consciousness, it is not at all evident how atomism has been rebutted. Thus, phenomenal properties are here denied constancy altogether.

James, it seems, takes 'idea' sometimes as embracing putative phenomenal objects, sometimes as excluding them. To include them within the scope of the principle of change would, as I have argued, be very difficult. James accordingly tends to objectify them, speaking of them as (abstract) objects or realities. On the other hand, to exclude them, and thus to allow phenomenal constancies, would mean giving up the strong thesis that there are no 'elementary facts of any sort that remain unchanged amid the flow'.[5] It would, in effect, mean surrendering the wholesale rejection of atomism and the attack on sensations.[6] One might, of course, still maintain the principle of change in application to the *idea* of a phenomenal property, holding, for example, that no two *ideas of* phenomenal green can be qualitatively identical. But the basis for the latter doctrine would now be weakened, for it would no longer be supported by the analogy of the painter. Nor would it, I suggest, be strongly supported by introspection, if indeed such a

---

[1] *PP*, 231.
[2] Ibid.
[3] Ibid., 236.
[4] Ibid., 230.
[5] Ibid.
[6] Ibid.

thing as an *idea of phenomenal green* can be presumed clear and steady enough to be introspected at all.

Consider, finally, the argument for change from constant modification of brain-states. Does it follow from such modification that sensations cannot recur? The answer would seem to be negative, for even if no two brain-states are, as wholes, physically indistinguishable, it does not follow that there are no parallel parts that are indistinguishable. James indeed notes:[1]

> It need of course not follow, because a total brain-state does not recur, that no *point* of the brain can ever be twice in the same condition. That would be as improbable a consequence as that in the sea a wave-crest should never come twice at the same point of space. What can hardly come twice is an identical *combination* of wave-forms all with their crests and hollows reoccupying identical places.

The latter argument is based on probabilities only, and it does not, in any case, deny that points or parts may recur in qualitatively identical manner. It must therefore be denied that James has succeeded in showing that 'For an identical sensation to recur it would have to occur the second time in an *unmodified brain*'.[2]

3 CONTINUITY: 'WITHIN EACH PERSONAL CONSCIOUSNESS THOUGHT IS SENSIBLY CONTINUOUS'

Continuity for James means continuity of consciousness across time-gaps, and qualitative continuity at all times in consciousness. Unfelt time-gaps of course pose no obstacle to continuity *in consciousness*, but James means more than this. After waking from sleep, we may know we have been unconscious, but the parts of our consciousness remain 'inwardly connected and belonging together'.[3] Community of self is supported by memory, and 'Remembrance is like direct feeling; its object is suffused with a warmth and intimacy to which no object of mere conception ever attains . . . community of self is what the time-gap cannot break in

[1] Ibid., 235n.
[2] Ibid., 232.
[3] Ibid., 238.

twain.'[1] Consciousness is 'nothing jointed; it flows. A "river" or a "stream" are the metaphors by which it is most naturally described. *In talking of it hereafter, let us call it the stream of thought, of consciousness, or of subjective life.'*[2]

Qualitative continuity in *thought* is supported by the recognition that apparent abrupt breaks are breaks in the objects of thought rather than in thought itself.[3]

> A silence may be broken by a thunder-clap, and we may be so stunned and confused for a moment by the shock as to give no instant account to ourselves of what has happened. But that very confusion is a mental state, and a state that passes us straight over from the silence to the sound. The transition between the thought of one object and the thought of another is no more a break in the *thought* than a joint in a bamboo is a break in the wood. It is a part of the *consciousness* as much as a joint is a part of the *bamboo*.

Moreover: 'Into the awareness of the thunder itself the awareness of the previous silence creeps and continues; for what we hear when the thunder crashes is not thunder *pure*, but thunder-breaking-upon-silence-and-contrasting-with-it'.[4]

James's arguments here, while appealing, seem to me to establish less than what he intends. Certainly the 'transition between the thought of one object and the thought of another' may involve no 'break in the thought'.[5] It does not, however, follow that adjacent or transitional thoughts are *qualitatively continuous* simply from the fact that the sequence is unbroken. Similarly, the consciousness of a given moment may indeed be *conditioned* by temporally prior awarenesses. It does not, however, follow that it is therefore qualitatively continuous with them.

James, emphasizing the flow of thought, stresses the importance of feelings of transition and relation. Sensationalists, he says, have denied the existence of such feelings, juxtaposing substantive sensations 'like dominoes',[6] whereas intellectualists, on the other

[1] Ibid., 239.
[2] Ibid.
[3] Ibid., 240.
[4] Ibid.
[5] Ibid.
[6] Ibid., 245.

hand, have put our knowledge of relations into the realm of thought rather than sensibility. It is not, however, clear how James, in interposing *feelings of transition* between substantive sensations, avoids juxtaposing these transition-feelings with sensations like so many further dominoes.

Nevertheless, James's treatment is most certainly important in expanding the realm of conscious contents beyond the usual catalogue of sensational elements. The treatment of attitudes ('Wait!' 'Hark!' 'Look!'), of gaps, of feelings of tendency, of vagueness,[1] is of the utmost significance in fostering a more realistic conception of the conscious life:[2]

> The traditional psychology talks like one who should say a river consists of nothing but pailsful, spoonsful, quarterpotsful, barrelsful and other moulded forms of water. Even were the pails and the pots all actually standing in the stream, still betwe them the free water would continue to flow. It is just this free water of consciousness that psychologists resolutely overlook.

4 INTENTIONALITY: 'IT ALWAYS APPEARS TO DEAL WITH OBJECTS INDEPENDENT OF ITSELF'

Human thought is directed to objects independent of itself: 'that is, it is cognitive, or possesses the function of knowing'. A mind that is 'conscious of its own cognitive function plays . . . "the psychologist" upon itself. It not only knows the things that appear before it; it knows that it knows them.'[3] Such a condition is the typical adult state, but it is not primitive, for 'consciousness of objects must come first'.[4] In the development of a sense of objects, 'sameness' plays a special role, for James. 'The judgment that *my* thought has the same object as *his* thought is what makes the psychologist call my thought cognitive of an outer reality.'[5] Moreover, the judgment that my past thought and my present one are of the same object 'is what makes *me* take the object out of either

[1] Ibid., 250–4.
[2] Ibid., 255.
[3] Ibid., 272–3.
[4] Ibid., 273.
[5] Ibid., 272.

and project it by a sort of triangulation into an independent position, from which it may *appear* to both. *Sameness* in a multiplicity of objective appearances is thus the basis of our belief in realities outside of thought.'[1] We have here an elaboration of the Peircean theme of cognition being directed in the first instance outward, and also a development of the social construction of objects, harking back to Peirce and foreshadowing a dominant theme in Mead.

5 SELECTIVITY: 'IT IS INTERESTED IN SOME PARTS OF THESE OBJECTS TO THE EXCLUSION OF OTHERS'

'Accentuation and Emphasis are present in every perception we have',[2] says James, and he proceeds to give a remarkable sketch of the selective processes of consciousness. The senses are themselves organs of selection, and the sensations they yield are further reduced by the selectivity of attention. Notice is given only to sensations that serve as signs of things, but these things are themselves defined by interest. In itself, 'apart from my interest, a particular dust-wreath on a windy day is just as much of an individual thing, and just as much or as little deserves an individual name, as my own body does'.[3]

Of the various sensations got from a thing, the mind chooses some to stand for the thing most truly, taking the rest as appearances 'modified by the conditions of the moment'.[4] Of 'present sensations, we notice mainly such as are significant of absent ones; and out of all the absent associates which these suggest, we again pick out a very few to stand for the objective reality *par excellence*'.[5]

Moreover, habitual forms of attention condition the rest of thought for they carve out the objects with which a man is concerned.[6]

A man's empirical thought depends on the things he has experienced, but what these shall be is to a large extent

[1] Ibid.
[2] Ibid., 284.
[3] Ibid., 285.
[4] Ibid.
[5] Ibid., 286.
[6] Ibid.

determined by his habits of attention. A thing may be present
to him a thousand times, but if he persistently fails to notice
it, it cannot be said to enter into his experience. We are all
seeing flies, moths, and beetles by the thousand, but to whom,
save an entomologist, do they say anything distinct? On the
other hand, a thing met only once in a lifetime may leave an
indelible experience in the memory.

In connecting objects already individuated, selection is further
evident, in reasoning processes, in aesthetic creation, and in the
realm of ethics, where choice reigns supreme.[1] In sum:[2]

The highest and most elaborated mental products are filtered
from the data chosen by the faculty next beneath, out of the
mass offered by the faculty below that, which mass in turn
was sifted from a still larger amount of yet simpler material,
and so on . . . the world of each of us, howsoever different
our several views of it may be, all lay embedded in the
primordial chaos of sensations, which gave the mere *matter* to
the thought of all of us indifferently. We may, if we like, by
our reasonings unwind things back to that black and jointless
continuity of space and moving clouds of swarming atoms
which science calls the only real world. But all the while the
world *we* feel and live in will be that which our ancestors and
we, by slowly cumulative strokes of choice, have extricated
out of this, like sculptors, by simply rejecting certain portions
of the given stuff. Other sculptors, other statues from the
same stone! Other minds, other worlds from the same
monotonous and inexpressive chaos! My world is but one in
a million alike embedded, alike real to those who may abstract
them. How different must be the worlds in the consciousness
of ant, cuttle-fish, or crab!

James goes on to modify this view somewhat by remarking
that there is a substantial commonality within the human race as
to what objects and aspects are selected and accentuated. He says
nothing, however, about social and cultural aspects of selection,
and it remained for Mead and Dewey, among the pragmatists, to

[1] Ibid., 287.
[2] Ibid., 288–9.

emphasize these matters. The general interpretation they offer rests on the following considerations: if experience is conditioned by habits of attention, and these habits are in turn related to social custom, then experience itself is, at least in part, a product of society – of culture at large and of specific culture patterns associated, for example, with class and vocation. The modification of experience is, then, a matter of education, and of social reform with which education is continuous.

James's educational views are spelled out in detail in *Talks To Teachers*.[1] Here I shall note just a few points related to the topic of 'interest'. If consciousness is thoroughly selective, interest must be of supreme importance in education. Each child is an individual person with a selective and purposive mental life. We cannot, as teachers, just put things before children to learn. We need rather to strive to attach them to interest, in such a way as to evoke action through the child's effort. We must begin with native interests and offer objects attached to these. The effort required of the child in pursuit of his interests will then take over and provide hard training.[2]

> ... what becomes interesting enough to be attended to is not thereby attended to *without effort*. Effort always has to go on, derived interest, for the most part, not awakening attention that is *easy*, however spontaneous it may now have to be called. ... The teacher, therefore, need never concern himself about *inventing* occasions where effort must be called into play. Let him still awaken whatever sources of interest in the subject he can by stirring up connections between it and the pupil's nature, whether in the line of theoretic curiosity, of personal interest, or of pugnacious impulse. The laws of mind will then bring enough pulses of effort into play to keep the pupil exercised in the direction of the subject. There is, in fact, no greater school of effort than the steady struggle to attend to immediately repulsive or difficult objects of thought which have grown to interest us through their association as means, with some remote ideal end.

[1] William James, *Talks to Teachers on Psychology: and to Students on Some of Life's Ideals* (New York: Henry Holt, 1901). This book is based on lectures to Cambridge teachers, which James delivered at the invitation of the Harvard Corporation in 1892.
[2] Ibid., 110–11.

PART THREE
GEORGE
HERBERT MEAD

I

BIOGRAPHICAL COMMENTS

If Peirce's point of departure was the laboratory, and James's focus was the life of the individual person, Mead's inspiration was *social*. He was a philosopher, but also a social psychologist – indeed he played a leading role in the formation of the latter subject, and he developed a distinctively social version of familiar pragmatic themes.

Mead was born in 1863 in South Hadley, Massachusetts; his father was pastor of the local congregation.[1] When George Mead was seven, his family moved to Oberlin, Ohio, where his father became professor of homiletics at the Oberlin Theological Seminary. Having completed his early schooling, the young man entered Oberlin College and graduated in 1883, with a primary interest in classics. Mead worked for four years after graduation, teaching school, tutoring, and surveying. He then continued his studies at Harvard in 1887 and 1888, working primarily with Josiah Royce and William James, and developing his main concern with philosophical and psychological topics. Extending his study of these subjects for three years at Berlin and Leipzig, he ended his graduate work at Berlin to accept a teaching position at the University of Michigan in 1891.

It was at Michigan that Mead and Dewey met and became close friends. When Dewey left Michigan for the University of Chicago in 1894, he brought Mead along as a colleague. Mead remained at Chicago until his death in 1931, exercising a strong influence,

[1] For information in this paragraph, I am indebted to H. S. Thayer, *Meaning and Action: a Critical History of Pragmatism* (Indianapolis: Bobbs-Merrill, 1968), 76.

through his teaching, on students of the social sciences as well as students of philosophy.[1]

Although he is less well known than any of his fellow pragmatists, and though he never succeeded in setting down his thoughts in volume form – his books being created from edited lecture notes of his students – his thinking had an important effect on the development of pragmatic philosophy. In a paper written for the memorial service for Mead held in 1931, Dewey said of him, 'His mind was deeply original – in my contacts and my judgment the most original mind in philosophy in the America of the last generation. . . . I dislike to think what my own thinking might have been were it not for the seminal ideas which I derived from him.'[2]

It is worth noting briefly the character of the 'Chicago School', of which Dewey was the leader and Mead a major figure. The phrase 'Chicago School' was used by James in referring to pragmatist thinkers at Chicago.[3]

> In a letter of October 17, 1903, written to John Dewey, James refers to 'your School (I mean your philosophic school) at the University of Chicago'; and 'The Chicago School' is the title of James's 1904 review of *Studies in Logical Theory* by Dewey and his collaborators which had appeared in 1903. Charles Peirce also used the phrase 'the Chicago School' in his 1904 review of the same book in *The Nation*. . . . Dewey, Mead, Moore, and Tufts, together with Edward Scribner Ames, constitute the Chicago school of pragmatist philosophers . . . there were a number of other persons who collaborated in *Studies in Logical Theory* and, later, in *Creative Intelligence*. But in a distinctive sense Dewey, Mead, Moore, Tufts and Ames were the 'Chicago School', and Dewey was its acknowledged leader.

The Chicago spirit was, however, associated with a wider group of thinkers, and the intellectual tendency it exemplified was fundamentally social: it stressed the social dimension of human action,

---

[1] See Charles Morris, *The Pragmatic Movement in American Philosophy* (New York: George Braziller, 1970), 187–8.

[2] John Dewey, 'George Herbert Mead', *Journal of Philosophy*, XXVIII (1931), 310–11. See also Morris, op. cit., 187.

[3] Ibid., 175.

and denied that it could be reduced to the merely biological or physiological adaptation of man to his environment. Moreover, in line with the evolutionary spirit that held sway by the end of the last century, Chicago thinkers attempted to analyse this social dimension genetically, and to see it as a new factor in human evolution itself, making a distinctive contribution to the quality of human selfhood and experience. W. I. Thomas thus traced the evolution of the various civilized interests out of primitive drives directed toward food and sex. Albion Small's 'dynamic' sociology 'conceived the science of society as an integral part of social "growth" or reform'. James Tufts applied an evolutionary method to ethics. But it was Mead who 'made the most detailed and systematic contribution to [the] theory of the social formation of the self by his analysis of language and symbolic processes'.[1] Starting from Wilhelm Wundt's theory of gesture, he attempted to construct a radical view of mind and self as developing out of society, rather than the reverse. In our discussion of Mead, we shall concentrate on this fundamental aspect of his work, as represented in his *Mind, Self and Society*.[2]

[1] Herbert W. Schneider, *A History of American Philosophy* (New York: Columbia University Press, 1946), 391. I have drawn upon Schneider for points in this paragraph.
[2] George H. Mead, *Mind, Self and Society: from the Standpoint of a Social Behaviorist* (edited, with Introduction, by Charles W. Morris) (University of Chicago Press, 1934) (*MSS*).

II

MEAD'S SOCIAL BEHAVIOURISM

We saw earlier how James tried to connect body and mind through his physiological-moral concept of habit, and how he incorporated interest and activity into his general notion of consciousness. Yet he did, in the *Principles*, continue to treat conscious states as separate entities. Moreover, he did not put much emphasis on the social context as a developmental factor shaping the mind. Mead went further in both respects: he construed mind as a special patterning of behaviour rather than a complex of special entities. Further, he viewed this patterning as growing out of social interaction.

Mead was thus a behaviourist, but, in the phrase of Charles W. Morris, the editor of *Mind, Self and Society*, a *social behaviourist*.[1] For he was critical of the behaviourism of John B. Watson in that it failed to do justice to the social character of symbolic functioning while, at the same time, it ruled out the private, i.e., the realm of observations of ourselves that are not shareable by others. Moreover, it over-emphasized the influence of the environment, ignoring the acquisition of symbolism by which a person may come to influence himself and modify his own further behaviour through the forecasting and control of consequences.

Symbolism is oversimplified by Watson, in Mead's opinion:[2]

Though Watson talks much about language, the essence of language as found in a certain type of social interplay has escaped entirely, and hidden itself under the skin. And even

[1] Charles W. Morris, Introduction to *MSS*, xvi.
[2] Ibid., xvi.

there it hides in the movements of the vocal cords, or in the responses substituted for vocal responses, and is finally lost entirely among implicit responses. In contrast, for Mead language is an objective phenomenon of interaction within a social group, a complication of the gesture situation, and even when internalized to constitute the inner forum of the individual's mind, it remains social – a way of arousing in the individual by his own gestures the attitudes and roles of others implicated in a common social activity.

Symbolism, for Mead, enables new forms of modification of behaviour, but such modification is not reducible to processes of conditioning by external stimuli. The notion that the behaviour of the organism is utterly dependent upon the physical stimuli of its environment was, in general, repugnant to Mead. In agreement with Dewey's 1896 paper 'The Reflex Arc Concept in Psychology',[1] Mead stresses the correlative character of the very concepts of stimulus and response. The rise of symbolism increases the organism's capacities for activity and control of the environment. As Morris puts it:[2]

Aspects of the world become parts of the psychological environment, become stimuli, only in so far as they effect the further release of an ongoing impulse. Thus, the sensitivity and activity of the organism determine its effective environment as genuinely as the physical environment affects the sensitivity of the form. The resulting view does more justice to the dynamic and aggressive aspects of behavior than does Watsonism, which gives the impression of regarding the organism as a puppet, whose wires are pulled by the physical environment. Thus, in the case of reflective thinking, which Watson treats quite on a par with the conditioning of the rat, Mead is able to give a penetrating analysis of such reflection in terms of the self-conditioning of the organism to future stimuli in virtue of being able to indicate to itself through symbols the consequences of certain types of response to such stimuli. This account is able to explain the

[1] John Dewey, 'The Reflex Arc Concept in Psychology', *Psychological Review*, III 1896), 357–70.
[2] Morris, Introduction to *MSS*, xvii–xviii.

behavior of Watson in conditioning the rat, and not merely the resulting behavior of the conditioned rat.

As to the private, Mead insists that it must be acknowledged as a fact; correspondingly, there must be a role for introspection, which is wrongly denied by Watson's behaviourism. 'Watson', says Mead,[1]

> insists that objectively observable behavior completely and exclusively constitutes the field of scientific psychology, individual and social. He pushes aside as erroneous the idea of 'mind' or 'consciousness' and attempts to reduce all 'mental' phenomena to conditioned reflexes and similar physiological mechanisms – in short, to purely behavioristic terms. This attempt, of course, is misguided and unsuccessful. . . .

In sum, Mead was a behaviourist, not in ruling out the realm of the private, or in thinking of human learning as shaped primarily by the physical environment, or yet in depreciating human capacities for rational self-control, but rather in taking *social conduct* to be the primary factor in terms of which mind and self are to be explained.

His approach in effect represents a new orientation to the mind-body problem. Instead of starting with individual minds as given and then trying to fit them into both the physical and the social worlds, he starts with the latter worlds as given, and proposes to show how individual minds are formed within them. Instead of explaining society as an aggregation of individual minds, he proposes to explain the individual mind as an absorption into the individual of the process of social communication.

His method is to offer a hypothetical genetic picture of how such absorption might have taken place, a theory outlining conceivable mechanisms through which the mind and self might have developed. Mead's method poses problems of interpretation: how is his genetic account to be understood? Can it be taken seriously as a literal historical survey? Surely, it is too speculative for that. Perhaps it is best read as an interpretation of the *function* of symbolic processes in human life as we know it today. In this respect, it invites comparison with the social contract theory, taken as an

[1] Ibid., 10.

interpretation of contemporary civil society rather than as an account of the origins of such society. Embodied in such interpretations are, of course, empirical hypotheses about relevant mechanisms or lawlike relations among various phenomena. Mead's interpretation of the functions of symbolism, in particular, embraces constituent hypotheses as to the mechanisms through which symbolism operates and the capacities it makes possible; and such hypotheses may be understood as subject, in principle, to the tests of empirical investigation.

III

MEAD ON MIND, SELF, AND SOCIETY

What, then, is Mead's genetic account? It provides a description of four phases or stages of development. In *stage one,* he imagines a group of organisms, with minimal physiological capacities, engaged in some activity within the same area, in such a way that a rudimentary form of 'signalling' interaction develops. These organisms are, of course, to be assumed to lack developed minds or language. Nevertheless, in becoming jointly involved in some task, they tend *involuntarily* to modify one another's behaviour. Certain aspects of each organism's action in pursuit of the task in question come, involuntarily, to influence the other organisms to respond in certain ways. Such aspects constitute *gestures.*

The emphasis on gesture seems to have originated in Mead's study of the German psychologist, Wilhelm Wundt (1832–1920).[1]

> Wundt saw the gesture in a social context where Darwin, in his book on *The Expression of the Emotions in Man and Animals,* had treated gesture in a purely individualistic context. For Wundt a gesture intended communication of meaning; for Darwin it was merely self-expression. Mead, however, went farther than Wundt in thinking of the gesture in social terms. He traced the whole development of genuine communication in language from gestures.

Mead presents the dog-fight as a favourite example: the snarl is

---

[1] Joseph L. Blau, *Men and Movements in American Philosophy* (New York: Prentice-Hall, 1952), 263.

a *concomitant* of the dog's combative stance, not a *symbol*. Yet it serves to stimulate the other dog to combativeness, or to heighten its initial combative tendencies. Moreover, the final stage of the first dog's act is modified by the response of the second dog to its initial snarl; and similarly for the second dog. The snarl is thus a gesture, and the dog-fight a *'conversation of gestures'*,[1] but there are here no *significant*, that is to say *symbolic*, gestures at all. The snarl has a minimal sign-meaning, but it has no intent or idea behind it. We may also take a co-operative act as an example, rather than a case of combat: imagine two organisms trying to push a boulder away from a cave entrance. Here the involuntary motions, sounds, or alterations of breathing or pressure of each organism may serve to influence the other to adjust its own efforts in certain ways. Again, we have a *conversation of gestures*.

Mead makes two points concerning this first stage: (1) that it sees the rise of a rudimentary meaning, and (2) that it does not yet possess significant meaning. We shall comment on these two points in turn. (1) He characterizes the rudimentary meaning as:[2]

> found in the threefold relationship of gesture to adjustive response and to the resultant of the given social act. Response on the part of the second organism to the gesture of the first is the interpretation – and brings out the meaning – of that gesture, as indicating the resultant of the social act which it initiates, and in which both organisms are thus involved. This threefold or triadic relation between gesture, adjustive response, and resultant of the social act which the gesture initiates is the basis of meaning. . . .

The response evoked by a gesture modifies its future course; the gesture thus takes on new consequences as a result of social interaction. It has acquired a rudimentary meaning from which symbolic meaning may later emerge.[3]

> Just as in fencing the parry is an interpretation of the thrust, so, in the social act, the adjustive response of one organism to the gesture of another is the interpretation of that gesture by that organism – it is the meaning of that gesture.

[1] See, for example *MSS*, 63.
[2] Ibid., 80.
[3] Ibid., 78–9.

At the level of self-consciousness such a gesture becomes a symbol, a significant symbol. But the interpretation of gestures is not, basically, a process going on in a mind as such, or one necessarily involving a mind; it is an external, overt, physical, or physiological process going on in the actual field of social experience. Meaning can be described . . . in terms of symbols or language at its highest . . . stage of development . . . but language simply lifts out of the social process a situation which is logically or implicitly there already. The language symbol is simply a significant or conscious gesture.

(2) The rudimentary meaning of the conversation of gestures is, however, not yet *significant*, for the meaning involved is not *shared*. In responding to a given gesture and thus interpreting 'or bringing out a meaning for' the gesturing organism, the responding organism 'is not at the same time indicating or bringing out the same thing or meaning to or for himself . . .'.[1] In a fuller explanation of this point, Mead ascribes to meanings in the *full* sense the two characteristics of *participation* and *communicability*.[2]

Meaning can arise only in so far as some phase of the act which the individual is arousing in the other can be aroused in himself. There is always to this extent participation. And the result of this participation is communicability; i.e., the individual can indicate to himself what he indicates to others. There is communication without significance where the gesture of the individuals call out the response in the other without calling out or tending to call out the same response in the individual himself.

The *second stage* in Mead's scheme is reached when each organism indeed grasps the meaning of his own gestures. He does not merely involuntarily influence the other, but is attitudinally responsive to his own gesture in a way that is similar to the active response of the other. He is able to call forth in himself the response that his gesture is likely to produce in others and, moreover, to use such foreknowledge to control his own conduct. Here we have *significant gesture* or *symbolism*.

[1] Ibid., 81.
[2] Ibid., n. 15.

The organism may now be said to appreciate how his act affects the other: he does not merely produce his act but 'sees' it also from the other side – from the perspective of the receiver. In consequence, he is, at this stage, normally treated as communicating what he wants to communicate. He is now 'minded', that is to say, capable of taking an objective view of his own acts, and monitoring his behaviour in the light of their anticipated consequences as seen from the perspective of others who may be affected by them.[1] The gesture he now makes has meaning, not in the minimal sense that it contributes to the modification of the resultant social act, but in the further sense that there is an *idea* behind it – a shared form of response.[2]

> In one case the observer sees that the attitude of the dog means attack, but he does not say that it means a conscious determination to attack on the part of the dog. However, if somebody shakes his fist in your face you assume that he has not only a hostile attitude but that he has some idea behind it. You assume that it means not only a possible attack, but that the individual has an idea in his experience.
>
> When, now, that gesture means this idea behind it and it arouses that idea in the other individual, then we have a significant symbol. In the case of the dog-fight we have a gesture which calls out appropriate response; in the present case we have a symbol which answers to a meaning in the experience of the first individual and which also calls out that meaning in the second individual. Where the gesture reaches that situation it has become what we call 'language.' It is now a significant symbol and it signifies a certain meaning.

How does a symbol acquire a common meaning? It must produce the same response in producer as in hearer. In the producer, the response is implicit, in the hearer explicit, but it is the same response that is involved. This identity of response makes thinking and social communication possible:[3]

> . . . every gesture comes within a given social group or community to stand for a particular act or response, namely,

[1] See Blau, op. cit., 264–5.
[2] *MSS*, 45–6.
[3] Ibid., 47.

the act or response which it calls forth explicitly in the
individual to whom it is addressed, and implicitly in the
individual who makes it; and this particular act or response
for which it stands is its meaning as a significant symbol. . . .
The internalization in our experience of the external con-
versations of gestures which we carry on with other
individuals in the social process is the essence of thinking;
and the gestures thus internalized are significant symbols
because they have the same meanings for all individual
members of the given society or social group, i.e., they
respectively arouse the same attitudes in the individuals
making them that they arouse in the individuals responding
to them: otherwise the individual could not internalize them
or be conscious of them and their meanings.

In the process of developing common meanings, Mead emphasizes the paramount role of the *vocal* gesture, since the vocal
gesture is heard by the producer as well as the organism to which
it is addressed. By contrast, the facial gesture is seen by the
organism addressed, but not also by the producer. In the case of
the vocal gesture in particular, the producer stands to his own
gesture also as receiver, and thus responds, even if only implicitly,
as he would were the vocal gesture to be made by another
organism.[1]

> We cannot see ourselves when our face assumes a certain
> expression. If we hear ourselves speak we are more apt to
> pay attention. One hears himself when he is irritated using a
> tone that is of an irritable quality, and so catches himself. But
> in the facial expression of irritation the stimulus is not one
> that calls out an expression in the individual which it calls
> out in the other. One is more apt to catch himself up and
> control himself in the vocal gesture than in the expression of
> the countenance.

The actor may, of course, simulate this situation with facial ex-
pressions by using a mirror.[2]

> If we exclude vocal gestures, it is only by the use of the
> mirror that one could reach the position where he responds

[1] Ibid., 65.
[2] Ibid., 66.

to his own gestures as other people respond. But the vocal gesture is one which does give one this capacity for answering to one's own stimulus as another would answer.

Vocalization does not, however, always have the same force, as Mead makes clear. The tendency to respond as another would to one's own vocal gesture 'may be a very slight tendency – the lion does not appreciably frighten itself by its roar'.[1] Analogously, 'exclamatory sounds'[2] in human speech do not call forth identical responses in both hearer and producer. However, meanings in symbolic speech always have this shared character.[3]

> We are not consciously frightened when we speak angrily to someone else, but the meaning of what we say is always present to us when we speak. The response in the individual to an exclamatory cry which is of the same sort as that in the other does not play any important part in the conduct of the form. The response of the lion to its roar is of very little importance in the response of the form itself, but our response to the meaning of what we say is constantly attached to our conversation. We must be constantly responding to the gesture we make if we are to carry on successful vocal conversation. The meaning of what we are saying is the tendency to respond to it.

With mind, the organism acquires a certain responsibility for its gestures, since it, in effect, 'sees' how its gestures affect others and can modify its own behaviour in the light of this realization. The organism now takes the other's point of view into itself, with respect to its own gestures, since these have now acquired a common, socially objective meaning. He shares others' responses to his own gestures. The essence of mind, for Mead, is this capacity to see our own acts from the perspective of another.

A further, *third stage* is reached when the particularity of the other in a social act is transcended, and the minded organism becomes the object of its own reflection, aware of itself from the standpoint of a 'generalized other'.[4] In this stage, the organism

---

[1] Ibid., 63–4.
[2] Ibid., 66.
[3] Ibid., 66–7.
[4] Ibid., 154. See also Blau, op. cit., 265.

has become a *self*. The significance of this stage may be seen in the contrast Mead makes between *play* and *games*. In play, the child takes on different special roles, 'plays at being a mother, at being a teacher, at being a policeman . . .'.[1] In an organized game where a number of participants are involved,[2]

> the child taking one rôle must be ready to take the rôle of everyone else. If he gets in a ball nine he must have the responses of each position involved in his own position. He must know what everyone else is going to do in order to carry out his own play. He has to take all of these rôles. They do not all have to be present in consciousness at the same time, but at some moments he has to have three or four individuals present in his own attitude, such as the one who is going to throw the ball, the one who is going to catch it, and so on. These responses must be, in some degree, present in his own make-up. In the game, then, there is a set of responses of such others so organized that the attitude of one calls out the appropriate attitudes of the other.

The game, Mead seems to say, is a *structure* of roles which the child needs to internalize in order to participate properly. He is not simply taking some other point of view toward his action, but is learning to judge his act by reference to the abstract and structured perspective of the rules and roles of the game. To have internalized such a perspective is to have developed a self – to have come to take one's act as subject to appraisal in the light of an abstract set of social expectations or rules, i.e., a *generalized other*. It is, in effect, to have learned to see oneself as incumbent of a role in some social structure providing standards for describing and judging one's particular performance. The process might be characterized as the development of a conscience, which defines one's aspirations and identity as an agent, that is to say, a self. One now regularly takes an impartial and general standpoint in observing and evaluating one's own conduct.

Mead again uses the baseball example to explain and elaborate these points:[3]

[1] *MSS*, 150.
[2] Ibid., 151.
[3] Ibid., 153–4.

The fundamental difference between the game and play is that in the [former] the child must have the attitude of all the others involved in that game. The attitudes of the other players which the participant assumes organize into a sort of unit, and it is that organization which controls the response of the individual. . . . Each one of his own acts is determined by his assumption of the action of the others who are playing the game. What he does is controlled by his being everyone else on that team, at least in so far as those attitudes affect his own particular response. We get then an 'other' which is an organization of the attitudes of those involved in the same process.

The organized community or social group which gives to the individual his unity of self may be called 'the generalized other'. The attitude of the generalized other is the attitude of the whole community.

Moreover, for self 'in the fullest sense' to develop, the attitude of the generalized other must be taken, not just toward one's own or others' particular acts, but also toward the common social activity in which all are implicated.[1]

The seemingly paradoxical result (analogous in certain fundamental respects to Peirce's treatment of the topic) is that the acquisition of selfhood depends on attaining an abstract position outside the self. Such a position, affording the self no privileged locus in the world, is itself impersonal. It is at once the standpoint of reason and of the social process.[2]

How can an individual get outside himself (experientially) in such a way as to become an object to himself? This is the essential psychological problem of selfhood or of self-consciousness; and its solution is to be found by referring to the process of social conduct or activity in which the given person or individual is implicated. The apparatus of reason would not be complete unless it swept itself into its own analysis of the field of experience; or unless the individual brought himself into the same experiential field as that of the other individual selves in relation to whom he acts in any given social situation. Reason cannot become impersonal

[1] Ibid., 154-5.
[2] Ibid., 138.

unless it takes an objective, non-affective attitude toward itself; otherwise we have just consciousness, not *self-consciousness*. And it is necessary to rational conduct that the individual should thus take an objective, impersonal attitude toward himself, that he should become an object to himself. For the individual organism is obviously an essential and important fact or constituent element of the empirical situation in which it acts; and without taking objective account of itself as such, it cannot act intelligently, or rationally.

To attain the required objective standpoint, the individual cannot rely on *direct* experience. On the contrary, he[1]

experiences himself as such, not directly, but only indirectly, from the particular standpoints of other individual members of the same social group, or from the generalized standpoint of the social group as a whole to which he belongs. For he enters his own experience as a self or individual, not directly or immediately, not by becoming a subject to himself, but only in so far as he first becomes an object to himself just as other individuals are objects to him or in his experience; and he becomes an object to himself only by taking the attitudes of other individuals toward himself within a social environment or context of experience and behavior in which both he and they are involved.

This process of objectification of standpoint is dependent on, or at one with, the internalization of communication, a process that also enables the development of self-control.[2]

That process . . . of responding to one's self as another responds to it, taking part in one's own conversation with others, being aware of what one is saying and using that awareness of what one is saying to determine what one is going to say thereafter – that is a process with which we are all familiar. We are continually following up our own address to other persons by an understanding of what we are saying, and using that understanding in the direction of our continued

[1] Ibid.
[2] Ibid., 140–1.

speech. . . . One starts to say something, we will presume an unpleasant something, but when he starts to say it he realizes it is cruel. The effect on himself of what he is saying checks him; there is here a conversation of gestures between the individual and himself. We mean by significant speech that the action is one that affects the individual himself, and that the effect upon the individual himself is part of the intelligent carrying-out of the conversation with others.

In thinking, one separates out this internal phase and converses with oneself, although potentially this conversation is addressed equally to others.[1]

One separates the significance of what he is saying to others from the actual speech and gets it ready before saying it. He thinks it out, and perhaps writes it in the form of a book; but it is still a part of social intercourse in which one is addressing other persons and at the same time addressing one's self, and in which one controls the address to other persons by the response made to one's own gesture. . . . I know of no other form of behavior than the linguistic in which the individual is an object to himself, and, so far as I can see, the individual is not a self in the reflexive sense unless he is an object to himself. It is this fact that gives a critical importance to communication, since this is a type of behavior in which the individual does so respond to himself.

As the generalized other comes to influence the conduct of members of a whole group, we have, finally, a *fourth stage*, that of a community of selves, in a distinctively human sense. This new development arises continuously out of the social process, but constitutes an emergent level of human organization, influencing society in new ways. Nor does this fourth stage constitute a totally rigid situation, for selfhood involves not only the (shared) social identity, which Mead calls the 'me', but also the spontaneous and active aspects of the individual, which he calls the 'I'. The 'I' reacts upon the 'me' and therefore upon the socialization process itself, continually altering it. It is the constant reaction of the organism to its socialized selfhood.[2]

[1] Ibid., 142.
[2] See ibid., 175.

The 'I', then, in this relation of the 'I' and the 'me', is something that is, so to speak, responding to a social situation which is within the experience of the individual. It is the answer which the individual makes to the attitude which others take toward him when he assumes an attitude toward them. Now, the attitudes he is taking toward them are present in his own experience, but his response to them will contain a novel element. The 'I' gives the sense of freedom, of initiative. . . . We are aware of ourselves, and of what the situation is, but exactly how we will act never gets into experience until after the action takes place. . . . Taken together [the 'I' and the 'me'] constitute a personality as it appears in social experience. The self is essentially a social process going on with these two distinguishable phases. If it did not have these two phases there could not be conscious responsibility, and there would be nothing novel in experience.[1]

[1] Ibid., 177–8.

IV

MEAD AND THE MIND-BODY PROBLEM

We turn now to an evaluation of Mead's theory. Does his account indeed offer a solution to the mind-body problem? It might be argued that it does not, since his theory smuggles in mental contents at the very beginning. His first stage, after all, assumes animals capable of perceiving, attending, and striving to do various things. Such capacities are clearly mental capacities; therefore, in presupposing them from the start, Mead violates the conditions of the problem at issue. Indeed, the basic terms he employs as explanatory, i.e., 'conduct', 'act', 'attitude', are themselves *intentional* and thus presumably mentalistic. They cannot well be expected to yield an explanation of mental characteristics. Of course, if there were, in Mead's account, a further attempt to reduce all ostensibly mentalistic notions to those of *physical movement*, the situation might be judged differently. But there is no such attempt.

Mead, in fact, explicitly includes mental elements in his explanatory picture. 'We all have hands and speech, and are all, as social beings, identical, intelligent beings. We all have what we term "consciousness" and we all live in a world of things.'[1] He further acknowledges the individual's phenomenal experiences:[2]

Our environment exists in a certain sense as hypotheses. 'The wall is over there', means 'We have certain visual experiences

[1] *MSS*, 237.
[2] Ibid., 247.

167

which promise to us certain contacts of hardness, roughness, coolness.' . . . We are occasionally subject to illusions, and then we realize that the world that exists about us does exist in a hypothetical fashion.

As against the dominance of environmental stimuli over the organism, Mead stresses the active and selective screen of attention:[1]

> The human animal is an attentive animal, and his attention may be given to stimuli that are relatively faint. One can pick out sounds at a distance. Our whole intelligent process seems to lie in the attention which is selective of certain types of stimuli. Other stimuli which are bombarding the system are in some fashion shunted off. . . . The organism goes out and determines what it is going to respond to, and organizes that world. . . . You look for a book in a library and you carry a sort of mental image of the back of the book; you render yourself sensitive to a certain image of a friend you are going to meet.

Finally, Mead is critical of Watson for ignoring the 'inner experience of the individual'.[2] Conditioning can explain up to a point, says Mead, but[3]

> There remain contents, such as those of imagery, which are more resistant to such analysis. What shall we say of responses that do not answer to any given experience? We can say, of course, that they are the results of past experiences. But take the contents themselves, the actual visual imagery that one has: it has outline; it has color; it has values; and other characters which are isolated with more difficulty. Such experience is one which plays a part, and a very large part, in our perception, our conduct; and yet it is an experience which can be revealed only by introspection. . . . Watson insists that objectively observable behavior completely and exclusively constitutes the field of scientific psychology, individual and social. He pushes aside as erroneous the idea of 'mind' or 'consciousness', and attempts to reduce all

[1] Ibid., 25–6.
[2] Ibid., 7.
[3] Ibid., 9–10.

'mental' phenomena to conditioned reflexes and similar physiological mechanisms – in short, to purely behavioristic terms. This attempt, of course, is misguided and unsuccessful, for the existence as such of mind or consciousness, in some sense or other, must be admitted – the denial of it leads inevitably to obvious absurdities.

Now, if Mead insists on such mental features as we have enumerated and if he, moreover, builds mental capacities into the very first stage of his developmental theory, how can he be said to have contributed to the solution of the mind-body problem? In what respects can a theory such as he offers possibly be thought even to promise an explanation of the mental characteristics of organisms? To consider these questions, we shall turn first to Mead's general remarks on explanation. Following our consideration of his ideas on explanation, we shall return to an examination of his stage theory.

V

MEAD ON EXPLANATION

Having criticized Watson, as we have seen, on the ground that it is absurd to deny the existence of consciousness, Mead proceeds to introduce a critical distinction between *reduction* and *explanation*, as follows:[1]

> But though it is impossible to *reduce* mind or consciousness to purely behavioristic terms – in the sense of thus explaining it away and denying its existence as such entirely – yet it is not impossible to *explain* it in these terms, and to do so without explaining it away, or denying its existence as such, in the least. Watson apparently assumes that to deny the existence of mind or consciousness as a psychical stuff, substance, or entity is to deny its existence altogether, and that a naturalistic or behavioristic account of it as such is out of the question. But, on the contrary, we may deny its existence as a psychical entity without denying its existence in some other sense at all; and if we then conceive it functionally, and as a natural rather than a transcendental phenomenon, it becomes possible to deal with it in behavioristic terms. . . . Mental behavior is not reducible to non-mental behavior. But mental behavior or phenomena can be explained in terms of non-mental behavior or phenomena, as arising out of, and as resulting from complications in, the latter.

Mead here asserts that mind is explainable by, though not reducible to, non-mental phenomena. He also asserts that one may deny

[1] *MSS*, 10–11.

the existence of mind as a psychical entity without denying its existence as such, allowing, in particular, that it may be given a functional interpretation. The passage gives rise, however, to several puzzling questions.

A functional interpretation, we may imagine, would not presuppose any but physical elements, and would translate all mentalist talk into vocabulary referring solely to such elements – characterizing their qualities, relations, and functions. Such an interpretation, if successful, might well be thought to 'deny' the existence of mind as psychical stuff: it would show, at any rate, that we can say what we want to say 'about the mind' without presupposing any but physical elements and without going beyond our primitive physicalistic vocabulary. However, such an interpretation would, by the same token, constitute a genuine reduction – a thorough-going elimination of the theoretical need for postulating non-physical elements or employing a primitive mentalistic vocabulary. But Mead, upholding functionalism, denies reduction.

He wants to deny the existence of mind as psychical stuff but not to deny it as a function or set of functions. Yet to construe it functionally is to reduce it. Suppose, then, that he takes functional interpretation to require a departure from 'purely behavioristic terms'.[1] To reduce mental talk to functional talk is thus to eliminate mental substance and mentalistic conceptions, but it is not yet to reach the rock bottom of 'pure behaviorism'. To construe the mind as a set of dispositions and latencies may, that is to say, not be mentalistic, but it is still not utterly physicalistic: it does not reduce the mind to observable characteristics of physical elements. For dispositions are themselves not observable properties or happenings.

Such an interpretation of Mead, while appealing, has its own difficulties. First of all, Mead criticizes Watson as attempting to reduce mental phenomena to purely behaviouristic terms. But can 'conditioned reflexes and similar physiological mechanisms'[2] themselves be understood as non-dispositional, that is, as observable properties of physical objects? Is Mead's objection to Watson, then, merely that his own interpretation of what he was doing was inaccurate – that it should not have been described as a denial, or

[1] Ibid., 10.
[2] Ibid.

behaviouristic reduction, of the mind? Or is it that the particular Watsonian mechanisms were inadequate? The objection seems to run deeper than these possibilities would suggest.

Furthermore, Mead insists that mental phenomena, though not reducible, are explainable in behaviouristic terms, as arising out of behaviouristic phenomena. That is to say, he imagines that *unreduced* mental dispositions can be correlated with, or causally related to, antecedent physical phenomena, and in this sense explained by them. But the possibility of such explanation in no way depends upon functionalism. Unreduced psychic entities may theoretically also, in the same way, be causally explained by correlation with physical conditions. The suggestion that functional interpretation is required in order to make causal explanation possible is simply false.

To sum up, Mead puts forth two ideas on explanation but does not distinguish them clearly or relate them appropriately. One idea is that unreduced mental features may yet be causally explained by reference to non-mental phenomena. This idea is compatible with retention of the notion of psychic entities. The other idea is that all psychic entities are to be analysed as functions of physical behaviour, arising under special conditions. This latter idea seeks to eliminate all reference to mental entities through functional translation.

When we turn to Mead's practice, we find that he employs both ideas. On the one hand, he tries frequently to give functional analyses of mental concepts in terms of attitudes or readinesses for response, in a manner reminiscent of Peirce's dispositional accounts of meaning. Thus he speaks of an idea of an object as involving a general attitude representing alternative responses to it.[1]

> A person who is familiar with a horse approaches it as one who is going to ride it. He moves toward the proper side and is ready to swing himself into the saddle. . . . But the horse is not simply something that must be ridden. It is an animal that must eat, that belongs to somebody. . . . The individual is ready to do a whole series of things with reference to the horse, and that readiness is involved in any one of the many

[1] Ibid., 12.

phases of the various acts. . . . We can find in that sense in
the beginning of the act just those characters which we
associate to 'horse' as an idea, or if you like, as a concept.

On the other hand, Mead certainly speaks of phenomenal experiences, of the contents of imagery, and of illusions, without
offering functional accounts in every case. But he does suggest
that causal accounts are in any event possible, in which such
mental contents or experiences are correlated with phenomena of
other sorts.[1]

> The particular color or odor that any one of us experiences
> is a private affair. It differs from the experience of other
> individuals, and yet there is the common object to which it
> refers. It is the same light, the same rose, that is involved in
> these experiences. What we try to do is to follow these
> common stimuli in through the nervous system of each of
> these individuals. We aim to get the statement in universal
> terms which will answer to those particular conditions. . . .
> If one says that his experience of an object is made up of
> different sensations and then undertakes to state the conditions
> under which those sensations take place, he may say that he
> is stating those conditions in terms of his own experience. But
> they are conditions which are common to all . . . we take
> these common characters of experience and find in terms of
> them those experiences which are peculiar to the different
> individuals.

The suggestion here is that phenomenal experiences *peculiar* to
the individual are to be accepted as such, but put into causal, or
other, connection with environmental phenomena, in such a way
that the principles of connection are shareable and explanatory for
all. This is a kind of 'objective relativism'[2] which does not require
a total functional analysis of mental contents or elements.

Of course, Mead does not want to postulate a hard and fast
division of mental and physical languages at the outset, to accom-
modate the individual experiences and the environmental conditions between which correlation is sought. He wants rather 'to

---

[1] Ibid., 33–4.
[2] See, e.g., Charles Morris, *The Pragmatic Movement in American Philosophy* (New
York: George Braziller, 1970), 128ff.

carry out the correlation' stating 'both fields in as common a language as possible'. In fact, he says, 'behaviorism is simply a movement in that direction'.[1] He allows, however, presumably, that mental and physical languages may remain partly independent. Moreover, the correlation he seeks does *not depend* upon a functional analysis of all mental contents. Unreduced references to the individual's experiences are perfectly compatible with the psychological programme he advocates.

It must be admitted that Mead was himself not very clear on these points. One may, however, propose the following conception as outlining a consistent explanatory programme suggested by his treatment: functional analyses of mental phenomena are to be encouraged; postulated explanatory functions are, further, to be studied in their relations to other elements and to generating conditions of various sorts. Where functional interpretation fails, mental elements may be acknowledged, and they are equally to be studied in their relations, causal and otherwise, to various elements and, in particular, to generating circumstances. Functional reduction where possible, causal connection and genetic correlation in any case – that is the basic aim. Such a programme of course offers no solution, in itself, to the mind-body problem, but it seems, at any rate, a reasonable plan for contemporary investigations of the mind, neither behaviouristic in the narrow sense, nor opposed to the development of functional, causal, and correlational hypotheses wherever possible. With this programme in mind, we may return to our consideration of Mead's theory of stages and inquire, in particular, into its explanatory force.

[1] *MSS*, 40.

VI

MEAD'S STAGE THEORY AS
EXPLANATORY

Since Mead smuggles mental features into the first stage of his developmental theory, has he then succeeded in explaining the mind in terms of social factors, as he set out to do? It would seem that he has certainly not *fully* done so. For the mental features he attributes to the organisms in his first stage have not themselves been functionally analysed, nor have they been causally explained or otherwise correlated with generating non-mental circumstances. On the other hand, it does not follow from this fact that his theory therefore explains nothing. For it may plausibly be argued that there is still an enormous distance between Mead's first stage, with its admittedly mental features, and his latter stages, in which mindedness, selfhood, and community emerge. If, that is to say, Mead's genetic theory does not trace the latter phenomena all the way back to utterly non-mental beginnings, it may still be significant in carrying the development back over the large stretch from community to the rudimentary first stage he describes.

To what extent, however, is Mead's account *explanatory*, over the distance it sets itself to cover? We mentioned the social contract theory earlier, as offering an interpretation of civil society rather than an explanation of its origin. Certainly, it may be suggested, Mead's theory can be taken as similarly offering an *interpretation* of mind, self, and community as resting upon symbolic processes: if we perform an experiment in imagination, paring away from our adult community the common norms represented by the abstract framework of the generalized other, the concepts of self severally developed by its members, the language and empirical concepts defining their world, and the role reversals involved in symbolic communication and sympathy, we have reached the level of the animals in Mead's first stage. Conversely, then, see how our familiar human community is made possible by the rise of symbolic processes, themselves enabling the development of rational thought, definition of self, conceptualization of objects, actions, and structured social roles, achievement of planning and self-control, and identification with a generalized other.

Such an *interpretation* is possible and plausible even if no *explanation* is available for the emergence of the various stages in Mead's account. It, in effect, suggests a variety of conditions taken as necessary for the development of human society. At the very least, it must be said that Mead offers a persuasive interpretation along these lines and that his detailed treatment illuminates various aspects of human life. Does he provide, however, an explanation of the rise of the various stages? Does he show, for each stage, how it may be explained 'as arising out of, and as resulting from complications in',[1] earlier stages? Granted, for example, that the rudimentary gestures of his first stage were succeeded by the rise of significant symbolism, do we have, in Mead's account, a plausible explanation as to *how* such symbolism arose, or might have arisen? Let us assume that Mead is correct in describing the contrast between mere gestures and genuine symbols:[2]

> When [a] gesture means this idea behind it and it arouses that idea in the other individual, then we have a significant symbol. In the case of the dog-fight we have a gesture which calls out appropriate response; in the present case we have a symbol which answers to a meaning in the experience of the first individual and which also calls out that meaning in the second individual. Where the gesture reaches that situation it has become what we call 'language'. It is now a significant symbol and it signifies a certain meaning.

The critical question is how the genuine symbol has arisen, by

[1] *MSS*, 10.
[2] Ibid., 45–6.

what mechanisms or through what special circumstances the transition from gesture to symbol has taken place. This question has, I believe, no satisfactory answer in Mead's account. We are given a plausible sequence of stages, but no explanation of the movement from stage to stage.

VII

MEAD'S ANALYSIS OF SYMBOLISM

The special role of symbolic processes in Mead's theory requires special comment. In particular, it may be suggested that, even if his stage theory fails as an explanation of the mind in terms of social factors, he nevertheless offers an explanation of symbolism that is worthy of independent consideration. He provides, that is, a behaviouristic analysis of symbolism that constitutes a reduction not of mind as such, but of *meaning*, in terms of *response*.

This purported reduction is, however, not very convincing. For the reduction is not solely to *overt* responses but appeals to *implicit* responses as well. Mead thus writes:[1]

> In this way every gesture comes within a given social group or community to stand for a particular act or response, namely, the act or response which it calls forth explicitly in the individual to whom it is addressed, and implicitly in the individual who makes it; and this particular act or response for which it stands is its meaning as a significant symbol.

But *implicit* responses are as far from overt behaviour as *ideas*. Indeed, in some of his formulations, Mead uses the latter term: 'When, now, that gesture means this idea behind it and it arouses that idea in the other individual, then we have a significant symbol.'[2] Mead is certainly convincing in emphasizing that symbolism

[1] *MSS*, 47.
[2] Ibid., 45.

implies some element of commonality, ordinarily referred to as a shared meaning or idea. The point here is that no genuine behaviouristic reduction of this ordinary notion is achieved if 'response' is so stretched as to include implicit responses, which are no clearer, from a behaviouristic point of view, than ideas themselves. We have simply a change to a new terminology.

Mead's insistence on the importance of vocal gesture in the development of symbolism is certainly interesting and suggestive. Does it, however, explain the common meaning attaching to the vocal symbol? The basic idea is that 'in the case of the vocal gesture the form hears its own stimulus just as when this is used by other forms, so it tends to respond also to its own stimulus as it responds to the stimulus of other forms'.[1] Moreover, 'what is peculiar to [significant symbols] is that the individual responds to his own stimulus in the same way as other people respond'.[2] The contrast with facial gesture is emphasized by Mead: 'We cannot see ourselves when our face assumes a certain expression.'[3] Only the actor overcomes this natural asymmetry with respect to facial expression:[4]

> If we exclude vocal gestures, it is only by the use of the mirror that one could reach the position where he responds to his own gestures as other people respond. But the vocal gesture is one which does give one this capacity for answering to one's own stimulus as another would answer.

Now let us grant that a speaker perceives his own utterance as he perceives that of another, and as it is perceived by others. The utterance is, in these respects, 'symmetrically' related to the variant perspectives of speaker and hearer. More precisely, its perceived character is independent, for any speaker, of whether it is produced by himself or others, and independent, further, of variation in speakers. It may be abstracted, as a perceived object, from its variant personal context and considered, so to speak, as a public entity.

By contrast, the facial gesture is not thus symmetrical. A person

[1] Ibid., 65.
[2] Ibid., 67.
[3] Ibid., 65.
[4] Ibid., 66.

does not (without mirrors) perceive his own facial expression as he perceives that of another, nor does he perceive it as it is perceived by others. The perceived character of a given facial expression is not constant with variation in persons; for any person, moreover, its character depends upon whether he is its producer or not. The facial expression is not, as is the utterance, a shared or 'public' object.

If we grant this contrast of Mead's, have we explained the *shared meaning* of a significant vocal gesture? It is clear that we have not. We have rather, at best, explained the public character of the vocal gesture; we have accounted for the common recognition of the gesture as an object. Such 'objectification' of the vocal gesture may indeed, as Mead suggests, render it especially appropriate to serve as a *vehicle* of shared meaning. It does not itself *comprise* such shared meaning. Nor does the fact that *shared perception* contributes to the objectification of the vocal gesture show that *shared response to* the gesture makes up its meaning: it does not follow that, as Mead says, 'The meaning of what we are saying is the tendency to respond to it.'[1]

The shared perception of a vocal gesture is one thing; its consequent suitability as a meaning-vehicle may be conceded. That its meaning must be identified with the shared responses it evokes is a further claim, and it requires independent support. Unfortunately, it is a claim that is far from convincing. Mead himself notes the existence of divergent responses to utterances of certain sorts. He writes:[2]

> We are not consciously frightened when we speak angrily to someone else, but the meaning of what we say is always present to us when we speak. The response in the individual to an exclamatory cry which is of the same sort as that in the other does not play any important part in the conduct of the form. The response of the lion to its roar is of very little importance in the response of the form itself, but our response to the meaning of what we say is constantly attached to our conversation. We must be constantly responding to the gesture we make if we are to carry on successful vocal conversation.

[1] Ibid., 67.
[2] Ibid., 66–7.

Mead here contrasts exclamatory utterance, in which shared responses are insignificant to conduct, with conversational (presumably, symbolic) utterance, in which sharing of responses is essential. Yet he faces the problem that even in symbolic utterance, which *is* characterized by a common meaning, the actual responses to the utterance may, in fact, *not* be shared. Mead presumably wants to assimilate speaking angrily to the case of exclamatory utterance. But anger may be conveyed calmly and the effect of a mildly stated attribution of fault or lapse may be devastating. The symbolic content of an angry utterance may be separated from the warmth with which it is uttered and it may still have divergent effects. Symbolic utterance may thus, it would seem, resemble exclamatory utterance and the lion's roar. The lion does not frighten itself by its roar, but neither do we generally frighten ourselves when we symbolically convey anger to another. How, then, is the common meaning of such angry utterance to be understood in terms of shared response?

Two replies are suggested by the passage we have just cited. At the beginning of the passage, Mead says, 'The meaning of what we says is always present to us.' Since he holds that 'the meaning of what we are saying is the tendency to respond to it', the suggestion is that, despite the divergence of the *actual* responses to the angry utterance, there is a shared *tendency* that is here involved. Is the claim, then, that the tendency to be frightened is always present to us when we speak angrily? Does 'present to us' mean, implausibly, that we are *aware* of this tendency? Does it mean, rather, that we have the tendency, but are not aware of it? What then is the force of 'present to us'? Moreover, what clarification of meaning have we achieved if we have identified it, not with shared responses, but with shared tendencies to respond, of which the parties may themselves be unaware? And why is this sort of sharing of tendency not attributable to exclamatory utterances as well?

A second reply is suggested toward the end of the cited passage in which Mead no longer speaks of response to the *utterance*, but rather of response to its *meaning*: 'our response to the meaning of what we say is constantly attached to our conversation'. If we translate *meaning* here by *tendency to respond*, in accord with Mead's official doctrine, we get: 'Our response to the tendency to respond to what we say is constantly attached to our conversation.' This result is, if not meaningless, surely very difficult to render intelligible.

Since the tendencies may themselves be unconscious, we need to consider overt responses to these, which are not evident in fact, or else implicit responses to the tendencies in question, i.e., implicit responses to implicit responses. The purported clarification of meaning has surely disappeared into the mists.

If, on the contrary, we do not translate *meaning* by *tendency to respond*, but let it stand, then we have no analysis or reduction of meaning at all. For the concept of meaning is still employed. We have not eliminated it *in favour of* the concept of response; we have only *added* the notion of response, so that we consider responses to *meanings* as well as responses to *utterances*. Rather than clarifying the problem of meaning, this proposal seems only to add further perplexities.

The divergence of responses to symbolic utterances deserves a further comment. There may be numerous candidates for sharing among the responses of others to an utterance. Certain of these candidates are, prima facie, more likely than others, but without a special principle of selection, the concept of shared response alone fails to discriminate among them. Mead fastens upon a persuasive example when he discusses the bully and the coward:[1]

> If there is any truth to the old axiom that the bully is always the coward, it will be found to rest on the fact that one arouses in himself that attitude of fear which his bullying attitude arouses in another, so that when put into a particular situation which calls his bluff, his own attitude is found to be that of the others. If one's own attitude of giving way to the bullying attitude of others is one that arouses the bullying attitude, he has in that degree aroused the attitude of bullying in himself.

The bully's tendency to cower when bullied is aroused by his own bullying; the coward's giving way strengthens his own tendency to bully in other circumstances. If these assertions are indeed empirically true, it is not at all clear that the relations among these *attitudes* can be extended to the case of *symbolic speech* in general. Bullying, as an attitude, is directed toward producing a cowering response and succeeds or fails as the cowering occurs or does not. Mead illustrates the point also by the case of imperatives:[2]

[1] Ibid., 66.
[2] Ibid., 67.

You ask somebody to bring a visitor a chair. You arouse the tendency to get the chair in the other, but if he is slow to act you get the chair yourself. The response to the vocal gesture is the doing of a certain thing, and you arouse that same tendency in yourself.

Imperatives are also directed toward producing a certain response and succeed or fail as the response complies or does not.

But the case of attitudes and of imperatives cannot generally be taken as paradigms of symbolic speech, for symbolic utterances do not direct themselves toward producing responses of specified sorts, nor are the responses they in fact evoke uniform. Even symbolic utterances with evaluational or emotional content are not uniform in this regard. One person may be overwhelmed by a remark expressing a mildly negative evaluation of performance, for example; another may be angered, and yet another may hardly be touched. Is one or another of these responses to be taken as the meaning of the remark, or all? Is the tendency to one, or to all, strengthened in the producer of the remark? The decisive consideration, however, concerns statements with no direct emotional or attitudinal content at all: what, for example, are the shared responses constituting the meaning of the Pythagorean theorem, or of the statement that Sacramento is the capital of California?

Mead is rightly impressed with the common meanings that symbolism expresses. He must, however, be judged to have failed in interpreting such common meanings in terms of responses. I conclude that Mead's account offers neither a satisfactory explanation of mind nor an adequate behaviouristic analysis of symbolism. Nevertheless, he does, I believe, provide an interpretation of the role of symbolic processes in human life, of the ways in which, through a common language, we are enabled to enter into the perspectives of others, engage in rational thinking, develop a picture of the physical and social worlds within which we define our own selves and control our actions, and formulate abstract normative structures for the guidance of social endeavour.

His interpretation, it should be noted, is social rather than moral. What he describes is the general process of socialization into human society; but moral differences of profound significance separate human communities, all with their generalized others and common symbolic processes. From a moral point of view, development is not merely a matter of acquiring some generalized other, but of choosing between competing generalized others and competing ideals of selfhood which they serve to define. In the complex society in which our children grow up today, education can hardly be conceived purely in terms of socialization into a community which can itself be taken for granted. The problem of education presents itself rather, in large part, as the urgent and continuing need to decide among various structures of social norms that are all available as potential guides of development. We shall see in Dewey an explicit effort to go beyond the description of socialization toward a moral and practical conception of education and social reconstruction.

PART FOUR
JOHN DEWEY

I

BIOGRAPHICAL COMMENTS

In general influence and breadth of scope, Dewey was the giant of the pragmatists. He unified Peirce's laboratory concerns, James's psychological interests, and the social orientation of Mead; moreover, he applied his system of thought to the practical 'problems of men'. The latter phrase, the title of one of his books,[1] is symbolic of Dewey's basic attitude toward philosophy – that its main role is not to solve the problems of philosophers but rather to deal with the problems of men. Yet he fully appreciated the place of ideas in the development as well as the solution of the latter problems. He did not, therefore, reject the concern with classical philosophical issues. Rather, he sought always to see these issues in the widest context set by the social, moral, and intellectual questions of the age.

His own writings cover an enormous area, ranging over traditional philosophical divisions such as metaphysics, epistemology, logics, ethics, and aesthetics, as well as such applied fields as philosophy of science and philosophy of education. Moreover, several of his books are addressed to the interpretation of social concepts and problems, and his pen never ceased its flow of comment on public issues of the day. From the early decade, 1894–1904, when he chaired the combined Departments of Philosophy, Psychology, and Education at the University of Chicago and founded and directed the University Laboratory School,[2] to the later years, in which he headed the Commission of Inquiry into Stalin's Moscow

[1] John Dewey, *Problems of Men* (New York: Philosophical Library, 1946).
[2] See Arthur G. Wirth, *John Dewey as Educator* (New York: John Wiley, 1966).

trials,[1] and joined in protesting Bertrand Russell's dismissal from City College in New York because of his views on sex,[2] Dewey was actively engaged in a variety of causes that he judged to affect the prospects of intelligence and liberty.

James T. Farrell, in a fascinating memoir, has recounted the story of Dewey's involvement in the Commission of Inquiry.[3] Regarding the Russell case, I quote here from a letter of 16 May 1940 that Dewey wrote to William Ernest Hocking of the Harvard philosophy department, who had expressed his opinion that the issue to be joined was that of academic freedom of appointments rather than free speech. Dewey's letter, a copy of which he sent to Russell, is reprinted in Russell's *Autobiography*.[4] Dewey agreed with Hocking that the legal issue was one of academic freedom, but argued that the educational issue was much wider and should not be surrendered by default, once it had been raised by the public. He began by confessing himself disturbed by Hocking's view and wrote:[5]

If men are going to be kept out of American colleges because they express unconventional, unorthodox or even unwise views . . . on political, economic, social, or moral matters, expressing those views in publications addressed to the general public, I am heartily glad my own teaching days have come to an end. There will always be some kept prostitutes in any institution; there are always [the] more timid by temperament who take to teaching as a kind of protected calling. If the courts, under outside group pressures, are going to be allowed, without protest from college teachers, to confine college faculties to teachers of these two types, the outlook is dark indeed. If I express myself strongly it is because I feel strongly on this issue. While I am extremely

<hr/>

[1] See *The Case of Leon Trotsky: Report of Hearings on the Charges Made against Him in the Moscow Trials*, by the Preliminary Commission of Inquiry, John Dewey, Chairman (New York, London: Harper, 1937); and see also *Not Guilty: Report of the Commission of Inquiry into the Charges Made against Leon Trotsky in the Moscow Trials* (New York, London: Harper, 1938).

[2] John Dewey and Horace M. Kallen, eds, *The Bertrand Russell Case* (New York: Viking, 1941).

[3] James T. Farrell, 'Dewey in Mexico', in Sidney Hook, ed., *John Dewey: Philosopher of Science and Freedom* (New York: Dial, 1950), 351–77.

[4] *The Autobiography of Bertrand Russell: 1914–1944* (Boston: Little, Brown, 1968).

[5] Ibid., 359–60.

sorry for the thoroughly disagreeable position in which the
Russells have been personally plunged, I can't but be grateful
in view of the number of men of lesser stature who have been
made to suffer, that his case is of such importance as to
attract wide attention and protest. . . . I am grateful for the
service Russell renders the teaching body and educational
interests in general by taking up the challenge – accordingly
I am going to take the liberty of sending a copy of this letter
to Russell.

Unlike the blunt style of this letter, Dewey's academic writing
is difficult and fine-textured. Despite his heavy engagement in
public issues, he continued to think deeply and to publish original
works on theoretical problems throughout his long life. An indication of Dewey's vitality may be given by the fact that his most
technical book, *Logic: the Theory of Inquiry*,[1] appeared when he was
seventy-nine years of age. Another indication is afforded by the
fact that, coming to the field of art late in his career, he gave the
William James lectures at Harvard on this topic in 1931, when he
was seventy-two; the resulting *Art as Experience*,[2] acclaimed by
many as his finest work, is generally considered a major contribution to aesthetics.

There is, however, little doubt that his main influence has been
in the field of education. Unlike most philosophers, Dewey did not
consider education a separate realm to which a theorist ought
occasionally to devote some time, as a matter of moral obligation
or citizenship. Nor did he think of it as a field of application for
philosophical ideas worked out independently. On the contrary,
education represented for him the life of ideas in the formation of
men's habits of mind; the central test of any philosophy, he believed, is to be sought in the way it bears on the formation of such
habits, and so on the intellectual and moral quality of our common
life. In *Democracy and Education*, which appeared in 1916, and which
continued for many years, as he said, to offer the best presentation
of his general philosophy, he makes these points strongly:[3]

If we are willing to conceive education as the process of

---

[1] John Dewey, *Logic: the Theory of Inquiry* (New York: Henry Holt, 1938).
[2] John Dewey, *Art as Experience* (New York: Minton, Balch, 1934).
[3] John Dewey, *Democracy and Education* (New York: Macmillan (original date 1916),
1961), 328–9.

forming fundamental dispositions, intellectual and emotional, toward nature and fellow men, philosophy may even be defined *as the general theory of education*. Unless a philosophy is to remain symbolic – or verbal – or a sentimental indulgence for a few, or else mere arbitrary dogma, its auditing of past experience and its program of values must take effect in conduct. Public agitation, propaganda, legislative and administrative action are effective in producing the change of disposition which a philosophy indicates as desirable, but only in the degree in which they are educative – that is to say, in the degree in which they modify mental and moral attitudes. And at the best, such methods are compromised by the fact that they are used with those whose habits are already largely set, while education of youth has a fairer and freer field of operation. On the other side, the business of schooling tends to become a routine empirical affair unless its aims and methods are animated by such a broad and sympathetic survey of its place in contemporary life as it is the business of philosophy to provide.

Dewey's work in education has certainly been controversial, although it is fair to say that his major ideas have been neither closely studied nor properly understood by the general public. Arthur Wirth calls him 'the most controversial figure in twentieth-century American education'. Wirth writes of Dewey:[1]

> At the turn of the century, he was a leader in the criticism of traditional schooling. Sixty years later educational ideas associated with him were under heavy attack. He has suffered from uncritical adulation as well as unwarranted vituperation. In recent years [Wirth writes in 1966], it became the mode in the popular press to identify progressive education with loose, superficial educational practice and to label Dewey as its author. . . . After a period of unusually raucous commentary in the 1950's and early 1960's, we may be ready to seek a more rational appraisal of John Dewey's contributions to American education. 'Future thought in America must go beyond Dewey . . ., though it is difficult to see how it can

[1] Wirth, op. cit., vii. The last sentence is quoted from Robert J. Roth, S.J., *John Dewey and Self-Realization* (Englewood Cliffs, N.J.: Prentice-Hall, 1962), 144.

avoid going through him.'

In his long life, Dewey saw, and responded to, enormous social changes in America.[1]

He was born in 1859, at 186 South Willard Street, Burlington, Vermont, during the administration of James Buchanan. The Burlington of his boyhood might have been a model for Thornton Wilder's *Our Town*. He died in his apartment on Fifth Avenue, New York City, in June, 1952, in the month when Dwight David Eisenhower was making the moves that would win him the presidency. In the intervening decades, America was transformed from a country of farms, small towns, and an open frontier into a nation of factories, sprawling metropolises, and continental super-highways. After growing to manhood in the quiet environs of Burlington, Dewey spent his mature, productive years in Chicago and New York – our largest cities. . . . More was involved than a change in geography. . . . The fundamental transition was from intimate, tradition-oriented communities to the massive complexities of impersonal societies ruled by law and intellectual abstractions. A prescientific view of the world was giving way before the exciting and deeply disturbing insights and consequences of modern science. . . . He rejected a stance of wistful nostalgia and accepted the onrush of change as a challenge to human thought and imagination. . . . One of his responses was the conviction that children entering this new world needed to be prepared by a reformed kind of educational experience that would equip them for an effective, and fulfilling, go at life.

Dewey's academic history is briefly told. He attended the University of Vermont and later the Johns Hopkins University, where he came under the influence of Hegelianism through his teacher, G. S. Morris. It was at Hopkins that he developed the fundamental attachment to the notion of 'organic relationship of subject and object, intelligence and the world',[2] that was to remain a

---

[1] Wirth, op. cit., ix–x.
[2] Richard J. Bernstein, *John Dewey* (New York: Washington Square Press, 1966), 14. The comment is one made by Dewey about Morris. See Robert Mark Wenley, *The Life and Work of George Sylvester Morris* (New York: Macmillan, 1917), 316.

characteristic feature of his philosophy. He taught at the universities of Michigan, Minnesota, and Chicago and, from 1904 to his retirement in 1930, at Columbia University in New York City.

Dewey's early personal development was marked by a great transformation in outlook that is not easy to explain. As Richard J. Bernstein has written:[1]

> There is little in Dewey's youth in Vermont that distinguished him from his contemporaries. His upbringing was conventional, he was religiously devout, and he seems to have accepted the values of his environment rather than rebelled against them. Yet by the end of the nineteenth century, he had become the intellectual spokesman for social reform. Lewis Feuer poses the problem succinctly when he asks, 'What were these forces which helped to transform a callow Vermont boy, rooted in G.O.P. soil, Congregationalist, conventional, and devout, into the experimental philosopher of the nineties, agnostic, socialistic, and forever questioning?'

John Dewey's father was a farmer who had given up farming and become a grocer in Burlington. The young Dewey was unusually shy.[2]

> Even when Dewey reached high school, there was still some doubt about whether he would go on to college. During these early years, the only personality traits that distinguished Dewey from the other boys growing up in the New England town were his shyness and reticence. . . . Dewey's intellectual development was gradual: only during his last two years at college was there evidence of a decisive turning point in his intellectual life. Until then there was no reason to expect that Dewey would have done anything except participate in the New England way of life that he had found so congenial. During his last years at college, he developed an interest in philosophic speculation as well as in the broader political and social issues of the day.

When he graduated from college in 1879, he taught for some

---

[1] Bernstein, op. cit., 24. The question at the end of the cited passage is from Lewis S. Feuer, 'John Dewey and the Back-to-the-People Movement in American Thought', *Journal of the History of Ideas*, XX (1959), 545.

[2] Bernstein, op. cit., 24–5.

years at high school, first in Oil City, Pennsylvania and then at Charlotte, Vermont. During his spare time, he continued his philosophical studies, and wrote an article 'The Metaphysical Assumptions of Materialism', which he sent to W. T. Harris, editor of the *Journal of Speculative Philosophy*.[1] The letter Dewey sent with the manuscript read as follows:[2]

Oil City, Pennsylvania
1 May, 1881

Editor of *Journal of Speculative Philosophy*

Dear Sir:

Enclosed you will find a short article on the 'Metaphysical Assumptions of Materialism', which I should be glad if you could make use of, in your *Review*. If you cannot, if you will be so kind as to inform me, stamps will be sent for its return.

I suppose you must be troubled with many inquiries of this sort, yet if it would not be too much to ask, I should be glad to know your opinion on it, if you make no use of it. An opinion as to whether you considered it to show ability enough of any kind to warrant my putting much of my time on that sort of subject would be thankfully received, and, as I am a young man in doubt as to how to employ my reading hours, might be of much advantage. I do not wish to ask too much of your time and attention however.

Very truly yours,
John Dewey

Harris accepted the paper and encouraged the young Dewey. He continued his philosophical studies and decided to apply to the Johns Hopkins graduate school. He was turned down twice in his requests for financial aid and finally decided to borrow $500 from an aunt to see him through the start of his graduate career. He was accepted at Hopkins and was well received by his instructors there. When he was considered for a teaching fellowship for his second year of graduate work, President Gilman of Hopkins wrote to M. H. Buckham, president of the University of Vermont,

---

[1] The paper was published in the *Journal of Speculative Philosophy*, XVI (1882), 208–13.
[2] Letter quoted in George Dykhuizen, 'John Dewey: the Vermont Years', *Journal of the History of Ideas*, XX (1959), 537. See also Bernstein, op. cit., 26–7.

and one of Dewey's former teachers. Buckham responded with the following letter, which gives a picture of the early Dewey:[1]

Burlington, Vermont
April 3, 1883

President Gilman:

My Dear Sir:—

John Dewey has a logical, thorough-going, absolutely independent mind. He is sound and sweet all through – is true and loyal in matters of religion, and without any crotchets, or drawback of any kind, so far as I know. He is very reticent, as you see, – probably lacks a due amount of self-assertion. This is the only question that would arise in the minds of those who know him – whether he has the amount of dogmatism that a teacher ought to have. I am inclined to think that the confidence in him implied in an appointment would reinforce his own confidence in himself and go far toward overcoming the defect.

I will ask Mr. Torrey to give you his judgment.

Very truly yours,
M. H. Buckham

It is, as Bernstein remarks, 'a bit ironical that Dewey, who was soon to fight all forms of dogmatism in education, should be charged with lacking the "amount of dogmatism that a teacher ought to have" '.[2] The process of Dewey's transformation from a shy youth to an outstanding philosopher and spokesman of reform was a gradual one. We shall not here attempt to recount the details of that process.[3] It is interesting to note, however, that the transformation did not alter the basic character of Dewey's personality. In Bernstein's words,[4]

[1] Quoted in Dykhuizen, op. cit., 542.

[2] Bernstein, op. cit., 28.

[3] See Bernstein, Feuer, and Dykhuizen, op. cit.; also John Dewey, 'From Absolutism to Experimentalism', in G. P. Adams and W. P. Montague, eds, *Contemporary American Philosophy: Personal Statements*, vol. II (New York: Macmillan, 1930), 13–27; also Jane M. Dewey, ed., 'Biography of John Dewey', in P. A. Schilpp, ed., *The Philosophy of John Dewey* (Evanston and Chicago: Northwestern University Press, 1939), 3–45.

[4] Bernstein, op. cit., 28–9.

Dewey was always modest, a bit shy, respectful of others. . . .
The enormous influence that he exerted on others did not
stem from an overwhelming personality or a glittering
rhetorical ability. It was the power of his ideas, the integrity
of his conviction, and the genuineness of the searching quality
of his mind, that were so impressive.

As Sidney Hook wrote of him when Dewey was eighty years old,[1]

The Vermont and the New England of Dewey's boyhood
and youth are gone. But he still carries with him the traces
of its social environment, not as memories but as habits, deep
preferences, and an ingrained democratic bias. They show
themselves in his simplicity of manner, his basic courtesy,
freedom from every variety of snobbism, and matter-of-
course respect for the rights of everyone in America as a
human being and a citizen.

It is not easy to sum up the work of a philosopher with such a
broad intellectual range. It may be useful to introduce our discussion of Dewey's thought by emphasizing that he came to
pragmatism not, like James, through the British empiricist philosophers, but rather through Hegel, with his dialectical, holistic
idealism. Dewey's philosophy, despite his early abandonment of
Hegelianism, continues to exhibit certain fundamental Hegelian
emphases: on *continuity*, on *wholeness*, on *development*, and on the
power of ideas. However, Dewey transforms the Hegelian emphasis
on Reason or Spirit into an emphasis on *science* and its works.
Absolute Spirit is replaced, in Dewey's philosophy, by the operation of the scientific intelligence. It is science that develops from
problematic stage to problematic stage, unifying progressively the
tensions and difficulties that give birth to its motivating questions.
It is science, also, that transforms the world through its revision
of inherited concepts of nature and practice, setting the stage for
new conditions of social life. Science, moreover, has moral ramifications: by increasing man's capabilities, it increases his responsibility. For men are culpable in acquiescing to avoidable evils
whenever, evading the possibilities of intelligent reconstruction,
they swim along with the inertia of old ways or follow the momentary promptings of whim.

[1] Sidney Hook, *John Dewey: an Intellectual Portrait* (New York: John Day, 1939),
5–6.

Science, as Dewey conceives it, is not, however, to be identified with physics or with the special procedures of the laboratory. It is to be understood broadly, as the operation of intelligence in its ideal form. *Experiment*, for Dewey, is *experience rendered educative*,[1] and learning from experience is something that even a child can do. From the child's exploration of its environment to the scientist's theorizing about nature, the pattern of intelligent thought is the same: a problem provides the initial occasion of inquiry. Action is blocked, conflicts or difficulties create an unsettled situation. Deliberation is blocked action turned inward; the resultant elaboration and competition of hypothetical ideas sparks action once more. Such action tests the idea that initiated it, for if the action settles the initial difficulty, the idea has worked in reorganizing conduct in a more effective pattern. Otherwise, it has failed, and a new idea must be awaited.

In developing Dewey's ideas further, I shall here discuss the following four topics: (1) his notion of experience, particularly as he contrasts it with the ideas of older philosophies, (2) his psychological conceptions, (3) his concept of reflective experience, and critique of the distinction between means and ends, and (4) his social and educational theory.

---

[1] This formulation is suggested to me by John Dewey, *Experience and Education* (New York: Macmillan, 1938), 13; and *Democracy and Education*, 271–6.

II

DEWEY'S CONCEPT OF
EXPERIENCE

Three elements enter into Dewey's concept of experience: (a) the biological emphasis on experience as a product of the *interplay* between objective conditions and organic energies, (b) the scientific notion of *experiment*, as a deliberate alteration of the environment by inquirers, leading to new knowledge, and (c) the Peircean doctrine of *meaning*, according to which our conceptions are to be analysed in terms of the consequences of our actions, such conceptions serving therefore in the reflective regulation of our conduct.

Experience, as interpreted by Dewey, embodies all these elements. In his view, the essential ingredient in acquiring knowledge is the perception of relations, especially the relations between our actions and their empirical consequences. As we gain this type of perception, both our conduct and the environment grow in meaning. To achieve a grasp of relations, we require experience and the ability to store what is learned from experience. Experience is, however, more than a passive registering or beholding of phenomena; it involves deliberate interaction with environmental conditions, the consequences of which are critically noted and fed back into the control of future conduct. Such interaction is the mark of scientific thinking. It is characteristic of the most advanced forms of scientific experimentation but it may be generalized to embrace all varieties of intelligent thinking. Intelligent thinking is, moreover, not a thing apart from the moral life. For increased awareness of the empirical consequences of our choices expands our control of the future, and thus our responsibility for its character. Subjection to personal and social habits of the past, or haphazard action in accordance with caprice become immoral once we are able to affect the future significantly as a result of applied intelligence.

In *The Quest for Certainty*,[1] Dewey contrasts his conception of experience with older conceptions. We have inherited from the ancients a distinction between *mechanical* and *liberal* arts. The latter (inclusive of grammar and rhetoric) are concerned with *people* and with *ends*; the former are concerned with *things* as *means*. The mechanical arts are gained by apprenticeship, that is, by routine drill in imitation of the master. The liberal arts are for those who have leisure and are destined to rule; these arts are learned not by drill and imitation, but through the mind. Vestiges of this distinction remain evident in our contemporary separation of the learned professions from the work of shop and factory.

Beside the distinction between higher and lower arts, the ancients distinguished between all arts, as concerned with practice, and true science, which is a matter of the intellect. For Aristotle, the social arts were of a lower order of value than pure intellectual pursuits. With the expansion of the Church, this whole tradition, together with the fundamental split between body and mind, was transposed into a religious key: theology was seen as the supreme science of ultimate being.

The ancient conception of experience as merely 'empirical' and routine was an honest reflection of the general split between science and practice. This split was rationalized in ancient philosophy as due to a basic contrast between the body or the senses, and the spirit; between change and permanence; between the particular and the universal. The senses can perceive only the changing flux of particulars; only the intellect can grasp the permanent and the universal lying behind phenomenal change. Aristotle's concept of science was directed toward a knowledge of natural kinds or species as defined by their essences or ends. Change itself cannot yield knowledge but only opinion. Science needs to rise above the world of sense and change, in order to achieve a grasp of essences and universals.

In modern science, by contrast, knowledge is achieved in and

[1] John Dewey, *The Quest for Certainty: a Study of the Relation of Knowledge and Action* (New York: Minton, Balch, 1929) (*QC*), ch. IV.

through sensory observation. The limitations of sensory observation are not final and ultimate. They are only practical and relative, calling for supplementation and correction by further observation and by theory. Sensory observation, rather than setting a limit to the possibility of genuine knowledge, is indispensable to it. The older view, in sum, turned away from change. Modern science is, by contrast, precisely the search for correlations of changes in natural phenomena. 'Constants and relative invariants figure, but they are relations between changes, not the constituents of a higher realm of Being.'[1] The knowledge sought by science cannot be got by pure intellect. Rather, it involves practice essentially, either by direct experiment, or by control of the conditions of our observations as, for example, in astronomy.[2]

> . . . we cannot introduce variation into remote heavenly bodies. But we can deliberately alter the conditions under which we observe them, which is the same thing in principle of logical procedure. By special instruments, the use of lens and prism, by telescopes, spectroscopes, interferometers, etc., we modify observed data. Observations are taken from widely different points in space and at successive times. By such means interconnected variations are observed.

Action is essential to knowledge and not a contaminating factor. Rationality, in general, is not a quality of a separate organ of intellect, that is, a mind. Rather, it is a way of behaving in the light of perceived meanings, that is, under the guidance of anticipated consequences of action.

Doing is thus essential to knowing; experience, as educative, ought properly to be construed as experiment.[3]

> The rudimentary prototype of experimental doing for the sake of knowing is found in ordinary procedures. When we are trying to make out the nature of a confused and unfamiliar object, we perform various acts with a view to establishing a new relationship to it, such as will bring to light qualities which will aid in understanding it. We turn it over, bring it into a better light, rattle and shake it, thump,

[1] Ibid., 83.
[2] Ibid., 84.
[3] Ibid., 87.

push and press it, and so on. The object as it is experienced prior to the introduction of these changes baffles us; the intent of these acts is to make changes which will elicit some previously unperceived qualities, and by varying conditions of perception shake loose some property which as it stands blinds or misleads us.

Modern science enormously elaborates and refines the 'active doings'[1] available to us as resources of knowledge. By extending the use of instruments, by introducing systematic variation of conditions over a wider range than is characteristic of familiar situations, by devising reliable means of recording and measuring changes, science radically advances the capability of *doing* to disclose the relations among natural phenomena. The basic difference between modern science and ancient science is the dependence of the former upon[2] 'doing, doing of a physical and overt sort'.[3]

Ancient science, that is, what passed as science, would have thought it a kind of treason to reason as the organ of knowing to subordinate it to bodily activity on material things, helped out with tools which are also material. It would have seemed like admitting the superiority of matter to rational mind, an admission which from its standpoint was contradictory to the possibility of knowledge.

The fundamental contribution of modern scientific method is its *active* attitude toward the materials of sense. It is false to suppose that 'the difference between ancient and modern science is that the former had no respect for perception and relied exclusively upon speculation'. In fact, the Greeks did not disdain observation as such. They were 'keenly sensitive to natural objects and were keen observers'. However, they took sensed material 'as is', requiring only the provision of logical form, that is – processing by 'operations of logical definition, classification into species and syllogistic subsumption'.[4] They supposed that rational thought could[5]

[1] Ibid.
[2] Ibid., 88.
[3] Ibid.
[4] Ibid., 88–9.
[5] Ibid., 90.

take the material supplied by ordinary perception, eliminate varying and hence contingent qualities, and thus finally reach the fixed and immutable form which makes particulars have the character they have; define this form as the essence or true reality of the particular things in question, and then gather a group of perceived objects into a species which is as eternal as its particular exemplifications are perishable.

Hence, ancient science was familiar, aesthetic, non-technical, qualitative. Modern science, introducing extensive and systematic changes in the 'subject-matter of direct perception', thereby 'gets away not from observed material as such, but from the qualitative characteristics of things as they are originally and "naturally" observed'.[1]

Modern science strives for directed control of phenomenal changes to discover their conditions and consequences. Hence, it is not qualitative but rather abstract, mathematical, technical. Rightly conceived, however, it does not read qualities out of existence. It does not 'bifurcate nature' (in Whitehead's phrase),[2] but studies the *relation* of qualities to underlying conditions and further consequences. Although, unlike Greek science, it is not aesthetic or contemplative in character, neither is it opposed to appreciation of quality. In fact, it enables a more secure establishment of valued qualities, by a knowledge of their sustaining conditions.

Summing up the characteristic features of modern science, Dewey writes:[3]

The work of Galileo was not a development, but a revolution. It marked a change from the qualitative to the quantitative or metric; from the heterogeneous to the homogeneous; from intrinsic forms to relations; from esthetic harmonies to mathematical formulae; from contemplative enjoyment to active manipulation and control; from rest to change; from eternal objects to temporal sequence. . . .

The revolution opened the way to description and explanation of natural phenomena on the basis of homogeneous

---

[1] Ibid.
[2] Alfred North Whitehead, *The Concept of Nature* (Cambridge University Press, 1926), 26ff.
[3] *QC*, 94–7.

space, time, mass, and motion. . . . Heavenly bodies and movements were brought under the same laws as are found in terrestrial phenomena. The idea of the difference in kind between phenomena in different parts of space was abolished. All that counted for science became mechanical properties formulated in mathematical terms: the significance of mathematical formulation marking the possibility of complete equivalence or homogeneity of translation of different phenomena into one another's terms.

The philosophical empiricism of the seventeenth and eighteenth centuries revolted against the classical tradition, which emphasized the role of the intellect in knowledge. Empiricism produced an opposing emphasis, attributing all knowledge ultimately to sense experience. Although on its critical side a healthy development, such empiricism cannot, in Dewey's opinion, be considered a constructive theoretical alternative, particularly from the point of view of education. For it promoted an exaggerated conception of the role of sensation in knowledge, and tended to conceive learning as a passive reception of ideas. It underestimated thereby the active part of the learner in the acquisition of knowledge – his reconstruction of the environment in the very process of learning.[1]

Current science has, however, taught us that 'experimental knowledge is a mode of doing'.[2] Experimental ideas do not belong to a realm of intellect divorced from the senses, nor does sensation produce knowledge without the guidance of ideas. The empiricism of modern science is brought into connection with intellect through a recognition of the *activity* of ideas.[3]

> Ideas [says Dewey] are statements not of what is or has been but of acts to be performed . . . intellectually (that is, save for the esthetic enjoyment they afford, which is of course a true value), ideas are worthless except as they pass into actions which rearrange and reconstruct in some way, be it little or large, the world in which we live.

The active interpretation of ideas bridges the inherited division

[1] John Dewey, *Democracy and Education* (New York: Macmillan (original date 1916), 1961), 266–71.
[2] *QC*, 102.
[3] Ibid., 138.

between intellect and sensation. Scientific experimentalism gives us a new conception of experience, in which idea, sensation, and active purpose are brought into intimate connection.[1]

When we take the instance of scientific experience in its own field, we find that experience when it is experimental does not signify the absence of large and far-reaching ideas and purposes. It is dependent upon them at every point. But it generates them within its own procedures and tests them by its own operations. In so far, we have the earnest of a possibility of human experience, in all its phases, in which ideas and meanings will be prized and will be continuously generated and used. But they will be integral with the course of experience itself, not imported from the external source of a reality beyond.

[1] Ibid., 138–9.

III

DEWEY'S CONCEPT OF EXPERIENCE: CRITICAL COMMENTS

Dewey's use of experimental science as a basis for the reinterpretation of *experience* seems to me both persuasive and significant. Experimentation in modern science does bring theory and practice into close communication, showing thereby how ideas may be tested through activity and, at the same time, how activity may give rise to new knowledge when appropriately related to ideas. The sharp division of intellect from sensation indeed underplays the active character of inquiry; moreover, it reduces the power of ideas while unrealistically taking sense materials as fixed givens. Dewey's interpretation of experience as incorporating ideational, purposive, and active elements along with sense perception seems to me to project a more plausible conception of inquiry and, at the same time, to relate such inquiry to problems of conduct.

Nevertheless, in developing his interpretation, Dewey seems to me to overstate the case in certain respects. Theory and practice are indeed, as he argues, closely connected in science, but he seems to suggest, further, that the import of theory can be wholly encompassed within the sphere of action and observation. The latter suggestion cannot, I believe, be sustained. The points at issue are analogous to those raised earlier, in criticism of Peirce's attempt to construe the clarity (or content) of a statement in terms of its observable consequences.

Thus, Dewey's view that ideas in science are 'generated within' scientific procedures, as well as tested by scientific operations,[1] is too strong. *Testing* of ideas through scientific operations is certainly an important function of such operations. But there are no scientific procedures that capture the processes by which theoretical ideas are *generated*. These creative processes remain independent of routines and procedures; they can hardly be adduced as a reason for saying that 'ideas and meanings' are 'integral with the course of experience itself, not imported from the external source of a reality beyond'.[2]

Nor, indeed, is it plausible to hold that changes not only set the scientist's problems but that scientific 'problems are solved when changes are interconnected with one another. Constants and relative invariants figure, but they are relations between changes, not the constituents of a higher realm of Being.'[3] Science is concerned not only to determine the relations among observable changes, but also to explain these relations in a comprehensive and systematic manner. Relations do not, as Dewey puts it, 'constitute the proper objects of science as such',[4] if by this is meant that science restricts its explanatory efforts to observational concepts and hypotheses exclusively. Rather, to make sense of 'the happening of experienced things'[5] and their changes, at the level of observation or practice, science develops theoretical structures that go beyond this level, and are incapable of being reduced to it. Indeed, it is not inaccurate, I suggest, even to characterize science as postulating entities that belong to a 'higher realm of Being',[6] provided only that the connotation of moral or theological superiority is eliminated from this phrase. Theories with the same observational content are not, in general, identifiable with one another, for they may differ in a wide variety of other relevant features, among the most important of which are the postulations employed to systematize and explain observable processes.

It follows, I believe, that to conceive 'experimental knowledge' as 'a mode of doing'[7] is to overstate the case. Experimental knowledge is born both of doing and of theorizing, and theorizing is

---

[1] *QC*, 138.
[2] Ibid., 139.
[3] Ibid., 83.
[4] Ibid., 104.
[5] Ibid.
[6] Ibid., 83.
[7] Ibid., 102.

itself independent of the constraints of activity or observation at the level of practice.

It follows further that to say 'ideas are worthless' unless they 'reconstruct . . . the world in which we live'[1] is to say something either false or trivial. The statement is false if it means that ideas make no contribution in science unless they imply characteristic and distinctive predictions at the level of observation. For, as suggested, ideas that make no differential predictions may, in postulating new theoretical structures, profoundly affect the systematization and development of knowledge. The statement is, on the other hand, trivial if it means that ideas are worthless unless they effect any change whatever, *inclusive* of changes in our actions, attitudes, or verbal behaviour. For in that case, no idea fails the test, since any idea, once accepted, alters our attitudes, actions, or verbal behaviour in some way. Even the learning of a set of nonsense syllables has some effect on us.

Dewey's doctrine of experience is correct, I conclude, in *relating* theory to practice or observation through the mediating category of *activity*. It goes too far, however, in the direction of absorbing theory wholly into activity and construing science as concerned solely with observable change.

[1] Ibid., 138.

IV

DEWEY'S PSYCHOLOGICAL CONCEPTIONS

In dealing with Dewey's psychology I shall take his *Human Nature and Conduct*[1] as the basic text for consideration. This important and pioneering work is subtitled 'An Introduction to Social Psychology' and it exercised significant influence on the growth of the latter subject as well as on the social sciences generally in the United States.[2]

It is a systematic and balanced work, setting forth Dewey's views on mind and society, on deliberation and morality, on activity and freedom. Continuous with the thought of the other pragmatists we have discussed, it emphasizes the role of consequences in meaning, the stability and functional character of habit, and the individuation of minds formed in a particular social setting. But it also generalizes upon the notion of habit to yield the parallel social concept of custom, presents a new account of thinking and intelligence, and turns its descriptive analyses of conduct to use in developing an interpretation of goods, aims, and ends. Moreover, even where it is continuous with the discussions of other writers, it elaborates common themes in specific treatments of great subtlety and originality of statement.

The psychological conceptions developed in this book are social in emphasis, and they are based firmly in an evolutionary

[1] John Dewey, *Human Nature and Conduct: an Introduction to Social Psychology* (New York: Modern Library, 1922, 1930) (*HNC*).

[2] For an interesting recent study of the influence of pragmatism, see Charles Morris, *The Pragmatic Movement in American Philosophy* (New York: George Braziller, 1970), 168–73.

framework. The organism, that is to say, is considered always within its natural and social context. Habits, although they are acquired, are like physiological functions 'in requiring the cooperation of organism and environment'.[1]

> We may shift from the biological to the mathematical use of the word function, and say that natural operations like breathing and digesting, acquired ones like speech and honesty, are functions of the surroundings as truly as of a person. They are things done *by* the environment by means of organic structures or acquired dispositions. The same air that under certain conditions ruffles the pool or wrecks buildings, under other conditions purifies the blood and conveys thought. The outcome depends upon what air acts upon.

Moral activity is also to be viewed as involving the environment and not just the person.[2]

> Honesty, chastity, malice, peevishness, courage, triviality, industry, irresponsibility are not private possessions of a person. They are working adaptations of personal capacities with environing forces. All virtues and vices are habits which incorporate objective forces. They are interactions of elements contributed by the make-up of an individual with elements supplied by the out-door world. They can be studied as objectively as physiological functions, and they can be modified by change of either personal or social elements.

To effect change, we must take the facts of interaction into account. To suppose that we can achieve desirable ends simply by feeling strongly enough or wishing hard enough is a belief in magic.[3] It is often assumed, for example, that a man may correct his posture simply by wish and effort, but this assumption ignores the reality of habit, and the need to enlist independent factors to change this reality.[4]

> A man who does not stand properly forms a habit of standing improperly, a positive, forceful habit. The common implication that his mistake is merely negative, that he is simply

[1] *HNC*, 14–15.
[2] Ibid., 16.
[3] Ibid., 26–8.
[4] Ibid., 29.

failing to do the right thing, and that the failure can be made good by an order of will is absurd. One might as well suppose that the man who is a slave of whiskey-drinking is merely one who fails to drink water. Conditions have been formed for producing a bad result, and the bad result will occur as long as those conditions exist. They can no more be dismissed by a direct effort of will than the conditions which create drought can be dispelled by whistling for wind. It is as reasonable to expect a fire to go out when it is ordered to stop burning as to suppose that a man can stand straight in consequence of a direct action of thought and desire. The fire can be put out only by changing objective conditions; it is the same with rectification of bad posture.

Custom is a 'widespread [uniformity] of habit' and persists[1]

because individuals form their personal habits under conditions set by prior customs. . . . Each person is born an infant, and every infant is subject from the first breath he draws and the first cry he utters to the attentions and demands of others. These others are not just persons in general with minds in general. They are beings with habits, and beings who upon the whole esteem the habits they have, if for no other reason than that, having them, their imagination is thereby limited. The nature of habit is to be assertive, insistent, self-perpetuating.

To talk about 'society' or 'mind' in the abstract creates perplexities in conceiving the organization and development of individual habits. The mystery disappears if we replace such abstract notions with specific references to customs as ways of behaving that constitute the setting for individual growth.[2]

If we start with the traditional notion of mind as something complete in itself, then we may well be perplexed by the problem of how a common mind, common ways of feeling and believing and purposing, comes into existence and then forms these groups. The case is quite otherwise if we recognize that in any case we must start with grouped action, that is, with some fairly settled system of interaction among

[1] Ibid., 58.
[2] Ibid., 61-2.

individuals. The problem of origin and development of the various groupings, or definite customs, in existence at any particular time in any particular place is not solved by reference to psychic causes, elements, forces. It is to be solved by reference to facts of action, demand for food, for houses, for a mate, for some one to talk to and to listen to one talk, for control of others, demands which are all intensified by the fact already mentioned that each person begins a helpless, dependent creature.

Psychology needs to understand these special matters, rather than postulating abstract psychic forces.[1]

... we need to find out just how different customs shape the desires, beliefs, purposes of those who are affected by them. The problem of social psychology is not how either individual or collective mind forms social groups and customs, but how different customs, established interacting arrangements, form and nurture different minds.

In the organization of *Human Nature and Conduct*, part I is given over to *habit*, part II to *impulse*, part III to *intelligence*, and part IV to a conclusion concerned largely with moral questions. Having begun our exposition of Dewey's psychological notions with attention to habit and custom, as represented in his part I, we turn now to the question with which he begins part II: since habit is acquired, why does the book begin with habit rather than with the native and primitive capacities of human beings – with *impulse*, in other words?

The answer Dewey gives is that habit and custom are prior to the operation of impulse in the individual member of society and provide the very meaning of impulse as it becomes channelled through growth.[2]

In conduct the acquired is the primitive. Impulses although first in time are never primary in fact; they are secondary and dependent. The seeming paradox in statement covers a familiar fact. In the life of the individual, instinctive activity comes first. But an individual begins life as a baby, and babies are dependent beings. Their activities could continue at most

[1] Ibid., 63.
[2] Ibid., 89–90.

for only a few hours were it not for the presence and aid of adults with their formed habits. And babies owe to adults more than procreation, more than the continued food and protection which preserve life. They owe to adults the opportunity to express their native activities in ways which have meaning. . . .

In short, the *meaning* of native activities is not native; it is acquired. It depends upon interaction with a matured social medium. In the case of a tiger or eagle, anger may be identified with a serviceable life-activity, with attack and defense. With a human being it is as meaningless as a gust of wind on a mudpuddle apart from a direction given it by the presence of other persons, apart from the responses they make to it. It is a physical spasm, a blind dispersive burst of wasteful energy. It gets quality, significance, when it becomes a smouldering sullenness, an annoying interruption, a peevish irritation, a murderous revenge, a blazing indignation. And although these phenomena which have a meaning spring from original native reactions to stimuli, yet they depend also upon the responsive behavior of others. They and all similar human displays of anger are not pure impulses; they are habits formed under the influence of association with others who have habits already and who show their habits in the treatment which converts a blind physical discharge into a significant anger.

Although impulse depends for its *significance* upon the settled habits and customs of the environment, it is certainly required in order to explain the development of habit in the individual. Psychology, says Dewey, having for a long time ignored *impulse* in favour of *sensations*, tended later to postulate an initial inventory of *instinctive activities*. Such a postulation, says Dewey, may be considered an improvement over sensation-psychology, in that it recognizes an active factor in growth. But a direct appeal to instincts is still unsatisfactory: it is too general and abstract to explain the complexities of personal and social life.[1]

It is like saying the flea and the elephant, the lichen and the redwood, the timid hare and the ravening wolf, the plant with the most inconspicuous blossom and the plant with the

[1] Ibid., 91.

most glaring color are alike products of natural selection. There may be a sense in which the statement is true; but till we know the specific environing conditions under which selection took place we really know nothing. And so we need to know about the social conditions which have educated original activities into definite and significant dispositions before we can discuss the psychological element in society. This is the true meaning of social psychology.

Adult capacities need to be explained by specific *interactions* between impulse and environments. The diversity of adult practices is simply too great to be accounted for by any listing of instincts.[1]

Exaggerate as much as we like the native differences of Patagonians and Greeks, Sioux Indians and Hindoos, Bushmen and Chinese, their original differences will bear no comparison to the amount of difference found in custom and culture. Since such a diversity cannot be attributed to an original identity, the development of native impulse must be stated in terms of acquired habits, not the growth of customs in terms of instincts.

Dewey thus rejects the notion of an inventory of instincts. In place of such an inventory, he employs the term 'impulse', to refer to the unlearned active energy of the organism which is channelled through custom, but is also capable of reacting upon and altering particular customs. 'Impulses', says Dewey, 'are the pivots upon which the reorganization of activities turns, they are agencies of deviation, for giving new directions to old habits and changing their quality.'[2] He suggests that an interest in primitive human nature thus generally accompanies an interest in social change.[3]

It is fast becoming incredible that psychologists disputed as to whether they should choose between innate ideas and an empty, passive, wax-like mind. For it seems as if a glance at a child would have revealed that the truth lay in neither doctrine, so obvious is the surging of specific native activities.

[1] Ibid.
[2] Ibid., 93.
[3] Ibid.

But this obtuseness to facts was evidence of lack of interest in what could be done with impulses, due, in turn, to lack of interest in modifying existing institutions. It is no accident that men became interested in the psychology of savages and babies when they became interested in doing away with old institutions.

Impulse, then, is channelled through custom, but a *given set* of customs may fail satisfactorily to channel available impulse, whereupon such impulse becomes a 'pivot' for the alteration of customs, for the reorganization of habits. But how, in fact, can impulse reorganize established habits? The basic point is that habits are themselves fragile growths: they endure only through relearning, and this process produces change in any case.[1]

We speak of the peoples of southern Europe as Latin peoples. Their existing languages depart widely from one another and from the Latin mother tongue. Yet there never was a day when this alteration of speech was intentional or explicit. Persons always meant to reproduce the speech they heard from their elders and supposed they were succeeding. This fact may stand as a kind of symbol of the reconstruction wrought in habits because of the fact that they can be transmitted and be made to endure only through the medium of the crude activities of the young or through contact with persons having different habits.

Such continuous alteration of habit, largely unintended, illustrates the process of relearning, in which immature activity succeeds in changing adult organized activity. But the process need not always be accidental and unconscious. The idea arises of bringing about a new society through attention to the new uses of impulse – through 'deliberate humane treatment of the impulses of youth'. 'This is the meaning of education; for a truly humane education consists in an intelligent direction of native activities in the light of the possibilities and necessities of the social situation.'[2]

Adults have for the most part given training rather than educa-

[1] Ibid., 95–6.
[2] Ibid., 96.

tion, mechanizing impulse prematurely according to adult habits rather than permitting immature impulse[1]

> to exercise its reorganizing potentialities. The younger generation has hardly even knocked frankly at the door of adult customs, much less been invited in to rectify through better education the brutalities and inequities established in adult habits. Each new generation has crept blindly and furtively through such chance gaps as have happened to be left open.

Docility and plasticity of impulse have been identified with imitativeness rather than with the power to re-create. Critical and independent thought has been kept within bounds by sets of mind formed early and impressed deeply.

Childhood, however, continues to remind us that its immature and unformed activity allows the possibility of a better life. We continue to idealize childhood as[2]

> standing proof of a life wherein growth is normal not an anomaly, activity a delight not a task, and where habit-forming is an expansion of power not its shrinkage. . . . Our usual measure for the 'goodness' of children is the amount of trouble they make for grownups. . . . Yet by way of expiation we envy children their love of new experiences, their intentness in extracting the last drop of significance from each situation, their vital seriousness in things that to us are outworn.

Childhood affords outstanding proof of the possibility of renewing habit by impulse. Such renewal is not, however, limited to childhood. On the contrary, renewal must take place in adult life as well, or else 'life would petrify, society stagnate'.[3] Impulse is, in fact, often too intense to be smoothly channelled by adult custom. Such channelling, successful under ordinary conditions, may break down under extraordinary stresses. These stresses then release impulse in a rush of 'wild violent energy', showing 'how superficial is the modification which a rigid habit has been able to effect'.[4]

[1] Ibid., 96–7.
[2] Ibid., 99.
[3] Ibid., 100.
[4] Ibid., 101.

It is at this point that Dewey introduces his general theme of intelligent social reform. Is it not possible, he asks, to employ intelligence for deliberate and continuous reconstruction of institutions in advance of crises, so that change is not dependent upon accidental upheaval? In general, this has not been the case.[1]

> We have depended upon the clash of war, the stress of revolution, the emergence of heroic individuals, the impact of migrations generated by war and famine, the incoming of barbarians, to change established institutions. Instead of constantly utilizing unused impulse to effect continuous reconstruction, we have waited till an accumulation of stresses suddenly breaks through the dikes of custom.

Reconstruction can be continuous, for there is always unused impulse available for the task. Moreover, reconstruction is always in order, for existing habits have grown up under conditions that are subject to change. As a matter of fact, change is generally to be expected in the historical conditions under which prevailing habits first emerged as reasonably adjustive devices. The possibility of continuous reconstruction is typically overlooked because we are impressed with the manifest strength and stability of inherited customs. But the fixity of custom shows not that there are no unused impulses, but only that 'they are not organically taken advantage of'.

> As matter of fact, the stiffer and the more encrusted the customs, the larger is the number of instinctive activities that find no regular outlet and that accordingly merely await a chance to get an irregular, uncoordinated manifestation. Routine habits never take up all the slack. They apply only where conditions remain the same or recur in uniform ways. They do not fit the unusual and novel.[2]

To recognize the possibility of, and the need for, continuous reconstruction provides, of course, no assurance that the need will be met. We face the problem of developing a steady habit of reconstruction – a second-order habit of intelligent assessment and adjustment of custom to meet arising circumstances.[3]

[1] Ibid.
[2] Ibid., 102–3.
[3] Ibid., 104.

The moral problem in child and adult alike as regards impulse and instinct is to utilize them for formation of new habits, or what is the same thing, the modification of an old habit so that it may be adequately serviceable under novel conditions.

To speak of impulse as a *pivot* of reorganization of habit emphasizes that impulse is not self-sufficient in such reorganization, which may proceed intelligently or unintelligently. Intelligence is a mode of utilization of impulse. Interpreted as a higher level moral disposition, it is itself not opposed to habit. It is, rather, a superordinate habit of habit-improvement and reconstruction. Dewey defends neither a fixed scheme of customs, nor the idealization of raw impulse and spontaneity. 'Impulse', he insists, 'is a source, an indispensable source, of liberation; but only as it is employed in giving habits pertinence and freshness does it liberate power.'[1] Liberation is to be sought, not in a flight from habits, but in their improvement. Rigid habits petrify and constrict action, but raw impulse in itself yields no action, dissipating energy randomly and ineffectively. The course Dewey advocates is one of continual adjustment and renewal of available habits through intelligence. In sum, intelligence and habit can no more be opposed than can life and mechanism.[2]

All life operates through a mechanism, and the higher the form of life the more complex, sure, and flexible the mechanism. This fact alone should save us from opposing life and mechanism, thereby reducing the latter to unintelligent automatism and the former to an aimless splurge. How delicate, prompt, sure and varied are the movements of a violin player or an engraver! How unerringly they phrase every shade of emotion and every turn of idea! Mechanism is indispensable. If each act has to be consciously searched for at the moment and intentionally performed, execution is painful and the product is clumsy and halting. Nevertheless the difference between the artist and the mere technician is unmistakable. The artist is a masterful technician. The technique or mechanism is fused with thought and feeling. The 'mechanical' performer permits the mechanism to dictate the performance. It is absurd to say that the latter exhibits habit

[1] Ibid., 105.
[2] Ibid., 70–1.

and the former not. We are confronted with two kinds of habit, intelligent and routine. All life has its élan, but only the prevalence of dead habits deflects life into mere élan.

The renewal of habit, in one way or another, is inevitable, in Dewey's view. 'If conditions do not permit renewal to take place continuously it will take place explosively. The cost of revolutions must be charged up to those who have taken for their aim arrest of custom instead of its readjustment.'[1] Dewey insists, therefore, that 'The position of impulse in conduct is intermediary.'[2] It provides an *occasion* for intelligent reconstruction, which must be continuous if explosive renewal is to be replaced by steady, focused change. We must now ask, however, how intelligence proceeds in the work of reconstruction.

The operation of intelligence, as Dewey describes it, is reminiscent of the Peircean view of thought. A problem arises when a person's organized and confident activity is arrested. 'From the standpoint of an onlooker, [the person in question] has met an obstacle which must be overcome before his behavior can be unified into a successful ongoing. From his own standpoint, there is shock, confusion, perturbation, uncertainty.'[3]

The arrest of activity is an interference with habit, and frees impulse for recollection and exploration.[4]

The blocked habits . . . give him a sense of where he *was* going, of what he had set out to do, and of the ground already traversed. As he looks, he sees definite things which are not just things at large but which are related to his course of action. The momentum of the activity entered upon persists as a sense of direction, of aim; it is an anticipatory project. In short, he recollects, observes and plans.

The body of undisturbed habits meanwhile preserves a steady background of objects and meanings that qualify the setting of the problem. Sensations arise in consciousness as elements of the action that has been interrupted, but they occur always against a

---

[1] Ibid., 167.
[2] Ibid., 169.
[3] Ibid., 181.
[4] Ibid., 181–2.

background of undisturbed habits yielding perceived and remembered objects. These habits, along with those that have been impeded and define the locus of obstruction, gradually change mere shock into a 'figured framework of objects, past, present, future'.[1] Impulse moves forward, in the direction of overcoming the conflict constituting the obstruction of activity, and unifying conduct once more. In moving forward, it calls, however, upon definite objects and meanings as instruments of solution, and these 'are retrospective; they are the conditions which have been mastered, incorporated in the past',[2] embodied in the habits with which we know.

Impulse energizes deliberation, which is 'a dramatic rehearsal (in imagination) of various competing possible lines of action'. 'It starts from the blocking of efficient overt action. . . . Then each habit, each impulse, involved in the temporary suspense of overt action takes its turn in being tried out.'[3] Deliberation is an experiment in combining and recombining 'selected elements of habits and impulses' to see what lines of possible action are open and where each of them may be expected to lead. The experiment is, however, imaginative, not overt. 'Thought runs ahead and foresees outcomes, and thereby avoids having to await the instruction of actual failure and disaster. . . . An act tried out in imagination is not final or fatal. It is retrievable.'[4] That action is blocked means that the elements of action 'hold one another up'.[5] None succeeds in moving the organism but each prevents the rest from moving the organism as well. This paralysis of action transforms habit into thought. 'Activity does not cease in order to give way to reflection; activity is turned from execution into intra-organic channels, resulting in dramatic rehearsal.'[6]

The process of rehearsal proceeds by following out each suggested course of action in imagination. 'The objects experienced in following out a course of action attract, repel, satisfy, annoy, promote, and retard.'[7] These reactions of imagined objects give a concrete sense of the character of each projected course. They

---

[1] Ibid., 182.
[2] Ibid., 184.
[3] Ibid., 190.
[4] Ibid.
[5] Ibid., 191.
[6] Ibid.
[7] Ibid., 192.

also affect, in various ways, the diverse habits of the agent. The process of deliberation, in other words, has causal consequences. Deliberation is typically terminated when choice occurs, choice consisting in 'hitting in imagination upon an object which furnishes an adequate stimulus to the recovery of overt action'.[1]

Choice composes and harmonizes preferences into a coherent whole: some imagined combination of elements of habits is effective in unifying mental dispositions. It is wrong to suppose there are no preferences until choice occurs. Choice does not create preferences. Rather, it presupposes them. We are, from the outset, 'biased beings'. 'The occasion of deliberation is an *excess* of preferences, not natural apathy or an absence of likings.'[2] There is no problem of deriving values out of facts, as this problem is often conceived by philosophers. Rather, the problem in deliberation is to eliminate suspension among incompatible values or desires – to reorient competing preferences so that, instead of inhibiting one another, they may begin to move in the same direction, initiating action once more.

Emotion must therefore not be opposed to 'bloodless reason'.[3]

More 'passions', not fewer, is the answer. To check the influence of hate there must be sympathy, while to rationalize sympathy there are needed emotions of curiosity, caution, respect for the freedom of others – dispositions which evoke objects which balance those called up by sympathy, and prevent its degeneration into maudlin sentiment and meddling interference. Rationality, once more, is not a force to evoke against impulse and habit. It is the attainment of a working harmony among diverse desires. . . . The man who would intelligently cultivate intelligence will widen, not narrow, his life of strong impulses while aiming at their happy coincidence in operation.

Reflection, however, also has its vices.[4]

We may . . . become overinterested in the delights of reflection . . . afraid of assuming the responsibilities of decisive choice and action. . . . We may become so curious about

[1] Ibid.
[2] Ibid., 193.
[3] Ibid., 196.
[4] Ibid., 197-8.

remote and abstract matters that we give only a begrudged, impatient attention to the things right about us. . . . Humility and impartiality may be shown in a specialized field, and pettiness and arrogance in dealing with other persons. 'Reason' is not an antecedent force which serves as a panacea. It is a laborious achievement of habit needing to be continually worked over. . . . Deliberation is irrational in the degree in which an end is so fixed, a passion or interest so absorbing, that the foresight of consequences is warped to include only what furthers execution of its predetermined bias. Deliberation is rational in the degree in which forethought flexibly remakes old aims and habits, institutes perception and love of new ends and acts.

V

DEWEY'S PSYCHOLOGICAL CONCEPTIONS: CRITICAL COMMENTS

In succeeding sections, I shall treat further aspects of Dewey's psychology, relating, in particular, to his notion of reflective experience, his analysis of the means-ends distinction, and his interpretation of educational processes. But, having already outlined his major doctrines concerning habit, impulse, intelligence, and deliberation, I wish to devote the present section to critical remarks on these doctrines.

There is no denying the power and sensitivity of Dewey's discussions. The delicacy of his observations, the richness of his illustrations, the qualifications, contrasts, and nuances of his formulations, and the originality of his statements mark the work we have been considering as a genuine classic. Even where it is most reminiscent of Peirce, it goes far beyond Peirce's description of thought in its subtlety and comprehensiveness. As a psychological work, it is equalled only by James's *Principles*, and it goes much farther than James in fusing individual psychology with the social and moral dimensions of experience.

On its critical side, Dewey's work is impressive. The critiques he offers of sensationalistic psychology and instinct theory are important and, I believe, well taken. On the other hand, his positive views seem to me at times so vaguely expressed as to preclude determinate application. Thus, he describes deliberation as rational in the degree to which 'forethought flexibly remakes old aims and habits', characterizing the 'balanced arrangement of propulsive activities manifested in deliberation' as dependent upon a 'sensitive and proportionate emotional sensitiveness'; reason, he declares, implies a 'balanced distribution of thought and energy'.[1] How, one wants to know, is an instance of *flexible* remaking of habits to be recognized, in contrast with a *non-flexible* sort? How is one to establish a balance between thought and energy? How is one to determine when a piece of thinking embodies a 'balanced arrangement of propulsive activities', or reflects a 'proportionate emotional sensitiveness'?

Dewey tells us that reflection, as well as impulse, has its vices. We may be hurried into action by impulse and 'not look far enough ahead'; on the other hand, we may become 'overinterested in the delights of reflection' and 'become afraid of assuming the responsibilities of decisive choice and action'.[2] Presumably, one sort of balance to be attained in rational deliberation is a distribution of reflection and impulse that avoids vices of both kinds. Now it is trivial to say that *not looking far enough ahead* is a vice, for to say that someone has not looked far enough ahead is to imply he ought to have looked further. The counsel to avoid this vice amounts to the prescription that one should look as far ahead as one should. But how far is that?

Similarly, it is trivial to call *overinterest in reflection* a vice, since to say that someone is overinterested is to convey that he ought to be less interested. To counsel avoidance of this vice is to say that one ought not to be more interested than one ought to be. But when is someone more interested than he ought to be? Dewey remarks, indeed, that we may become afraid of decision, but how are we to mark the point at which desirable caution and prudence turn into undesirable fear? In sum, if the balance between reflection and impulse turns on the avoidance of their respective vices, the very notion of such balance turns out to be empty, or virtually empty, without additional specification. One can interpret the desired balance in various ways, depending upon how one independently reads the situation.

A more important, because more central, difficulty besets the notion of impulse as a pivot for the reorganization of habit. Dewey speaks of the need for constant utilization of 'unused

[1] *HNC*, 198.
[2] Ibid., 197.

impulse to effect continuous reconstruction'.[1] How are we to tell, however, when impulse is unused? Impulses, he says, are 'highly flexible starting points'[2] for diversified activities which employ impulses in various ways. Cultures channel impulses in fundamentally different directions. However, one cannot, presumably, infer merely from the selective canalization of impulses within a given society that it leaves some impulses unused. Dewey does not, certainly, intend to suggest that a society in which chess is unknown has, *ipso facto*, an unused chess-playing impulse to be put to use in reorganizing its customs. But neither does he offer any other way of judging whether impulse is fully utilized in a given society, or not.

It might be suggested that it is not 'unused impulse' but rather 'released impulse' that serves as Dewey's basic notion. Instinctive reactions may, he says, under ordinary conditions 'appear to be tamed to obey their master, custom. But extraordinary crises release them and they show by wild violent energy how superficial is the control of routine.'[3] Impulse, in normal circumstances bound by habits, is released when such habits break down under stress. Release of impulse, according to this conception, is a function of habit breakdown, and it is *released impulse* that, freed from its earlier channels, requires *new uses* and propels activity into the reorganization of habits. Such reorganization is, in other words, a response to difficulty, conflict, stress, or breakdown in prior habit, and it is energized by the impulse freed through the breakdown itself.

This is a discontinuous picture of habit reorganization and depends, as we have seen, on the release of impulse from prior habits. It is certainly true to much of Dewey's discussion. Yet Dewey also speaks of the 'unformed activities of childhood'[4] and sees in them a reminder of the possibilities of community reorganization and renewal. These unformed activities show the plasticity of the child's store of impulse – impulse that is *initially free* and unused at birth, not released by the breakdown of prior habit. To suggest that the child be taken as an inspiration for adult habit renewal is, however, to transfer to the adult situation the

[1] Ibid., 101.
[2] Ibid., 95.
[3] Ibid., 100–1.
[4] Ibid., 99.

notion of merely *unused* impulse, a notion that, as I have argued above, is very difficult to apply. Moreover, Dewey asks for the constant utilization of 'unused impulse to effect continuous reconstruction',[1] and the concept of *continuous* reconstruction seems at odds with the *discontinuous* picture earlier mentioned.

It may, in fact, be argued that there is a basic conflict between these two conceptions that runs through Dewey's treatment. It may, further, be suggested that this conflict reflects a parallel tension between Dewey's psychological and his moral views. For his psychological account is based predominantly on the discontinuous conception:[2]

> Escape from the clutch of custom gives an opportunity to do old things in new ways, and thus to construct new ends and means. Breach in the crust of the cake of custom releases impulses; but it is the work of intelligence to find the ways of using them.

On the other hand, Dewey's moral view stresses the imperative of continuous reconstruction, the need to anticipate and avert stresses and upheavals through intelligent foresight and revision of custom – *prior* to breakdowns. Yet how can such thoughtful anticipation be continuous if, by hypothesis, the difficulties releasing needed impulse have not yet arisen, but are only to be foreseen? What energizing impulses for reorganization are available prior to the release effected by breakdowns in habit? Deliberation, after all, 'starts', according to Dewey, 'from the blocking of efficient overt action';[3] how can thought continuously anticipate the difficulties occasioned by such blocking?

It is difficult to reconcile Dewey with himself on this point. He says, to be sure, 'There always exists a goodly store of non-functioning impulses which may be drawn upon . . . they may be drawn upon continuously and moderately.'[4] But how is this statement itself to be made consistent with the discontinuous account of habit reconstruction and with the notion that deliberation starts from a prior blocking of *overt* action?

One possible answer may be suggested by Dewey's comment

[1] Ibid., 101.
[2] Ibid., 170.
[3] Ibid., 190.
[4] Ibid., 102.

that the equilibrium between organism and environment is never perfect. There is a large-scale but imperfect balance which sustains the functioning of the organism but there is also, at all times, sufficient imbalance to produce a continuous release of impulse:[1]

> Normally, the environment remains sufficiently in harmony with the body of organized activities to sustain most of them in active function. But a novel factor in the surroundings releases some impulse which tends to initiate a different and incompatible activity, to bring about a redistribution of the elements of organized activity between those [that] have been respectively central and subsidiary.

May it not be, then, that a continuous flow of impulse, resulting from the always imperfect equilibrium of organism and environment, is available for the continuous reconstruction demanded by Dewey's moral theory?

The answer, I think, is no. For there is no provision in Dewey's account for putting impulse to use in revising habits that are currently functioning perfectly well and adequately. The impulse released is directed toward reconstruction of the *particular* habit whose breakdown has released it. It cannot be transferred to the prevision of difficulty and the advance reconstruction of habits whose functioning is presently unimpaired. In the sequel to the passage just cited, for example, Dewey illustrates his point as follows:[2]

> Thus the hand guided by the eye moves toward a surface. Visual quality is the dominant element. The hand comes in contact with an object. The eye does not cease to operate but some unexpected quality of touch, a voluptuous smoothness or annoying heat, compels a readjustment in which the touching, handling activity strives to dominate the action. . . . The disturbed adjustment of organism and environment is reflected in a temporary strife which concludes in a coming to terms of the old habit and the new impulse.

The unexpected quality of touch signifies some difficulty in the old habit or set. The released impulse is directed forward in a search beginning as 'vague presentiment of what we are going towards.

[1] Ibid., 179.
[2] Ibid.

As organized habits are definitely deployed and focused, the confused situation takes on form, it is "cleared up" – the essential function of intelligence.'[1]

In other words, although breakdowns occur continuously, each breakdown releases impulses directed toward *its* resolution, while the background habits functioning steadily carry the organism through the process. The continuous flow of impulse is not available for general use in advance reconstruction of potential breakdowns foreseeable only in imagination. It is difficult to avoid the conclusion that Dewey's psychological views are incapable of adequately supporting his moral advocacy of continuous reform based on a rational prevision of consequences. The difficulty here seems to parallel the difficulty noted above, with respect to Peirce's theory of inquiry, where the doctrine of real doubt as the starting point of inquiry seemed inadequate to support the descriptive analysis of scientific practice. In Dewey's case, the notion of thought originating from defects in overt habit-functioning seems incapable of supporting the doctrine of continuous habit-reform.

[1] Ibid., 180.

VI

REFLECTIVE EXPERIENCE AND THE MEANS-ENDS DISTINCTION

We have already seen the main outlines of Dewey's theory of thinking as originating in a problem. Action is arrested, transformed into thought. The resultant elaboration and competition of the ideas brought forth by thought sparks action once more. Such action tests the idea initiating it, for if the action settles the original difficulty, the idea has worked in reorganizing conduct in a more effective pattern. Otherwise, it has failed and a new idea must be awaited.

Action guided by thought is a special form of what is broadly referred to as 'experience'; it is experimental, that is to say, it is action capable of educating. In *Democracy and Education*, Dewey relates his view of experience to thinking. Experience has an active as well as a passive phase, he says:[1]

> On the active hand, experience is *trying* – a meaning which is made explicit in the connected term experiment. On the passive, it is *undergoing*. When we experience something we act upon it, we do something with it; then we suffer or undergo the consequences. We do something to the thing and then it does something to us in return: Such is the peculiar combination. . . . Experience as trying involves change, but change is meaningless transition unless it is consciously connected with the return wave of consequences which flow from it.

[1] John Dewey, *Democracy and Education* (New York: Macmillan (original date 1916), 1961), 139.

227

Experience in itself is not primarily cognitive. But 'the *measure of the value* of an experience lies in the perception of relationships or continuities to which it leads up'.[1]

All our experiences have an element of trial and error about them. Sometimes there is little else but a hit and miss quality in the experience, leading to a rule of thumb as a conclusion. Our perception of the detailed connections between action and consequence is 'very gross'.[2] In other cases, we develop our observations and analyses further, so that we begin to see how causes and effects are bound together, in detail. 'The deliberate cultivation of this phase of thought constitutes thinking as a distinctive experience. Thinking, in other words, is the intentional endeavour to discover specific connections between something which we do and the consequences which result, so that the two become continuous.'[3] In discovering such connections, thinking enables us to begin 'to act with an end in view'. That is, it enables us to take responsibility for bringing about some future as a consequence of present action. Thus, 'thoughtful action' is opposed to the attitude of routine which says, 'Let things continue just as I have found them in the past', and opposed also to the attitude represented by caprice, which says, 'Things are to be just as I happen to like them at this instant'. Both these attitudes 'refuse to acknowledge responsibility for the future consequences which flow from present action. Reflection is the acceptance of such responsibility.'[4]

The general features of a reflective experience are given by Dewey as follows:[5]

(i)   perplexity, confusion, doubt, due to the fact that one is implicated in an incomplete situation whose full character is not yet determined;

(ii)   a conjectural anticipation – a tentative interpretation of the given elements, attributing to them a tendency to effect certain consequences;

(iii)   a careful survey (examination, inspection, exploration, analysis) of all attainable consideration which will define and clarify the problem at hand;

[1] Ibid., 140.
[2] Ibid., 145.
[3] Ibid.
[4] Ibid., 146.
[5] Ibid., 150.

(iv)   a consequent elaboration of the tentative hypothesis to make it more precise and more consistent, because squaring with a wider range of facts;

(v)   taking one stand upon the projected hypothesis as a plan of action which is applied to the existing state of affairs: doing something overtly to bring about the anticipated result, and thereby testing the hypothesis.

Dewey calls attention to steps (iii) and (iv) in particular. For it is the extent and accuracy of these steps that distinguish a[1]

reflective experience from one on the trial and error plane. . . . Nevertheless, we never get wholly beyond the trial and error situation. Our most elaborate and rationally consistent thought has to be tried in the world and thereby tried out. And since it can never take into account all the connections, it can never cover with perfect accuracy all the consequences. Yet a thoughtful survey of conditions is so careful, and the guessing at results so controlled, that we have a right to mark off the reflective experience from the grosser trial and error forms of action.

The notion of ideas as plans of action is a key notion for Dewey, and he employs it to criticize the prevalent conception of means and ends. This conception holds ends to be fixed somehow, in advance, yielding normative criteria by which technical instrumentalities, i.e., means, are to be judged. The end, in short, justifies the means. Unless ends are decided upon in advance, no means can be justified, whereas if ends are chosen at the outset, the assessment of effective means to those ends can be rationally performed, thereby justifying certain means. The choice of ends, however, is an antecedent and mysterious affair, beyond the reach of rational considerations.

Criticizing this view, Dewey distinguishes between the *end* as actual outcome of a course of action, and the *end-in-view* as the envisaged end which currently serves to direct activity. The actual end may be 'fixed', but *it* is surely not available to us now, at the moment of deliberation. What *is* now available is the *idea* of a desired end or outcome, i.e., an end-in-view or plan, presently

[1] Ibid., 150-1.

estimated to lead to certain ends. Such an end-in-view is a hypothesis, a plan which guides *present* activity. It does not *close off*
further activity. Ends-in-view are, in effect, beginnings, to be
evaluated not by their origins but by their fruits. It is clear that,
in science, ideas are hypotheses, to be judged by their consequences. Dewey wants to extend this notion of hypothesis to all
ideas, in particular, to ideas in the domains of morality, education,
and social thought. He thus insists that ends-in-view are action-
guiding ideas, having the character of hypotheses.

Ends-in-view are prospective, and thus fallible. Having chosen
an end-in-view, we have thereby embarked on a course of action,
but we surely have not eliminated the possibility of subsequent
evaluation, and revision of our plan. Indeed, because the execution
of a plan typically brings errors and difficulties to light, it is important to be alert to possible alterations of an end-in-view
throughout the activity guided by it, rather than assuming such
activity to be a matter of mere technical implementation of an
antecedently fixed end. An end-in-view, in short, is itself a means
of organizing present activity; it is thus to be viewed as having the
character of a hypothesis, not a dogma. Its function is to guide us
into the future, and this very function subjects it, in principle, to
the test of future experience.

Having chosen a particular end-in-view, or plan, we do indeed
justify subsidiary ends-in-view, i.e., sub-plans, as means, *relative*
to the main end-in-view, when they are suitably connected with
the latter. But this does not imply that the main end-in-view is to
be held as a dogma, conferring justification but itself beyond the
reach of all rational criticism and review. For the contrasting process is also relevant; that is, we criticize the main end-in-view by
reference to the subsidiary ends-in-view that it seems to require.
The assessment of our chosen end, in other words, requires an
appraisal of related means: we need to reckon what it would *cost*
to put it into effect. Nor is the concept of *cost* to be taken in a
purely technical or material sense. For means are not merely
neutral ingredients of a plan; they have inherent values and disvalues. They have, in addition, causal consequences bearing not
only on the main goal sought, but also on independent outcomes
of various kinds, with their respective value characteristics. The
price of instituting any plan, in terms of the values and disvalues
associated with its subsidiary ends-in-view, is essential to estimate

in evaluating the end-in-view itself. The choice of means, in short, enters into and qualifies the nature of the end.

Moreover, the main end-in-view also has its side effects. To avoid wishful thinking, we must especially guard against looking at any given end-in-view, whether main or subsidiary, *solely* as means to a previously articulated desired end. For we then tend to give scant attention to unforeseen, and possibly undesirable, side effects. We must also avoid leaving *ourselves* out of the cost equation. Every social policy, in particular, has a reflexive effect on those who carry it forward. The idea of achieving a democratic utopia by authoritarian means typically leaves out of account the alteration in the persons themselves: a utopia thus achieved is one whose inhabitants have interiorized authoritarian methods and habits of mind – a critical cost that colours the nature of the actual end once achieved. 'If there is one conclusion to which human experience unmistakably points it is that democratic ends demand democratic methods for their realization.'[1] A final point Dewey makes is that *actual* ends are themselves not historical finalities; they continue to lead forward and must be viewed in the light of such leading.

All these various emphases are brought together in Dewey's phrase 'the continuum of ends-means'.[2] The notion of this continuum is, in effect, a denial of the popular fact-value division in the realm of action: ends are also instrumentalities, and means also have values and disvalues. Ends and means are, further, to be seen as connected if ends-in-view are to be effective guides to the alteration of present conditions rather than simply ways of rationalizing what exists. Critical thought in all realms involves critical thought regarding ends and means.

Dewey illustrates his analysis of means and ends in *Human Nature and Conduct* by considering the building of a house. Building a house is an intelligent activity directed by a plan, based upon foresight of future uses, assessment of present resources, and information retained from past experience. Nobody builds for the sheer fun of building; the activity is instrumental to the future comfort and security envisaged as provided by the house itself. 'Now if a legitimate case of subordination of present to regulation

---

[1] John Dewey, *Freedom and Culture* (New York: Putnam, 1939), 175.
[2] John Dewey, *Theory of Valuation* (University of Chicago Press, 1939), 40ff.

of the future may anywhere be found, it is in such a case as this.'[1]
Yet, even here, concern with the past and future is itself instrumental: it is 'for the sake of directing present activity and giving it meaning'.[2]

> Note that the present activity is the only one really under control. The man may die before the house is built, or his financial conditions may change, or he may need to remove to another place. If he attempts to provide for all contingencies, he will never do anything; if he allows his attention to be much distracted by them, he won't do well his present planning and execution. The more he considers the future uses to which the house will probably be put the better he will do his present job which is the activity of building. Control of future living, such as it may turn out to be, is wholly dependent upon taking his present activity, seriously and devotedly, as an end, not a means.

Education provides an important application, for Dewey. Its theme has traditionally been preparation; as a result, the present and its potentialities have been subordinated to a remote future, and have not been fully and properly utilized to attain the achievable. 'The professed exaltation of the future turns out in practice a blind following of tradition, a rule of thumb muddling along from day to day. . . .'[3] The future has not been seriously analysed and applied as a guide to present educational activity; the continuum of means and ends has been severed. 'If education were conducted as a process of fullest utilization of present resources, liberating and guiding capacities that are now urgent, it goes without saying that the lives of the young would be much richer in meaning than they are now.'[4]

Dewey applies his means-ends analysis also to economic life. Here he takes the major difficulty to be the divorce of production from consumption, a divorce of means and ends that empties work activity of meaning.[5]

---

[1] *HNC*, 268.
[2] Ibid., 268–9.
[3] Ibid., 270.
[4] Ibid.
[5] Ibid., 271.

Activity should be productive. This is to say it should have a bearing on the future, should effect control of it. But so far as a productive action is intrinsically creative, it has its own intrinsic value. Reference to future products and future enjoyments is but a way of enhancing perception of an immanent meaning. A skilled artisan who enjoys his work is aware that what he is making is made for future use. Externally his action is one technically labeled 'production.' It seems to illustrate the subjection of present activity to remote ends. But actually, morally, psychologically, the sense of the utility of the article produced is a factor in the present significance of action due to the present utilization of abilities, giving play to taste and skill, accomplishing something now. The moment production is severed from immediate satisfaction, it becomes 'labor,' drudgery, a task reluctantly performed.

Attending seriously to the present provides specific direction superior to that offered by vague ideal goals projected into the future.[1]

Men have constructed a strange dream-world when they have supposed that without a fixed ideal of a remote good to inspire them, they have no inducement to get relief from present troubles, no desires for liberation from what oppresses and for clearing-up what confuses present action. . . . Sufficient unto the day is the evil thereof. Sufficient it is to stimulate us to remedial action, to endeavor in order to convert strife into harmony, monotony into a variegated scene, and limitation into expansion. The converting is progress, the only progress conceivable or attainable by man. Hence every situation has its own measure and quality of progress, and the need for progress is recurrent, constant. . . . We find our clews to direction in the projected recollections of definite experienced goods not in vague anticipations, even when we label the vagueness perfection, the Ideal, and proceed to manipulate its definition with dry dialectic logic.

Here Dewey seems to be making a point that others have made in different terms, i.e., contrasting the vagueness of a 'positive' goal

[1] Ibid., 282.

such as happiness, with the specificity of a 'negative' goal such as the overcoming of pain. Indeed, the contrast to be made in this connection is independent of the difference between past and future. Yet Dewey connects these topics, suggesting that the emptiness of static positive ideals allows them to be used in such a way as to break the continuity of means and ends, present and future. Such ideals may fascinate the imagination but they are not focused enough to be used as instruments of reconstruction. Thus they drain away energy available for improving the present, thereby making action incapable of altering the future. He contrasts the appeal to static positive goals with the work of the physician, whose guiding ideals are specific in that he is concerned to help his patients overcome their particular difficulties, using their particular strengths and resources:[1]

> The physician is lost who would guide his activities of healing by building up a picture of perfect health, the same for all and in its nature complete and self-enclosed once for all. He employs what he has discovered about actual cases of good health and ill health and their causes to investigate the present ailing individual, so as to further his recovering; recovering, an intrinsic and living process rather than recovery, which is comparative and static. Moral theories . . . have reversed the situation and made the present subservient to a rigid yet abstract future.

Dewey here makes two general points at once: that the good of activity is to be sought in the present, and that it consists in an overcoming of specific problems and a liberating of particular powers. In so far as it functions in this way, activity expands in meaning.

Dewey relates these points to the general conception of happiness or welfare, since he holds that a person's happiness depends upon the degree to which his activity has meaning. And this, in turn, is a matter of the effectiveness of his choice or agency, his ability to meet the urgent difficulties of the present through actions that reconstruct the conditions of his future. Action is thus effective only if it is not isolated – only as it branches out in causal, emotional, and conceptual connections to other elements of life. From such a conception of happiness, Dewey concludes that it

[1] Ibid., 283–4.

cannot be *given* to others; welfare cannot 'consist in a soup-kitchen happiness'.[1] For happiness thrives upon enlargement of meaning, and such enlargement is, in turn, a matter of the expansion of perceived relations between one's activity and its consequences.[2]

> To 'make others happy' except through liberating their powers and engaging them in activities that enlarge the meaning of life is to harm them and to indulge ourselves under cover of exercising a special virtue. Our moral measure for estimating any existing arrangement or any proposed reform is its effect upon impulse and habits. Does it liberate or suppress, ossify or render flexible, divide or unify interest? Is perception quickened or dulled? Is memory made apt and extensive or narrow and diffusely irrelevant? Is imagination diverted to fantasy and compensatory dreams, or does it add fertility to life? Is thought creative or pushed to one side into pedantic specialisms? There is a sense in which to set up social welfare as an end of action only promotes an offensive condescension, a harsh interference, or an oleaginous display of complacent kindliness. It always tends in this direction when it is aimed at giving happiness to others directly, that is, as we can hand a physical thing to another. To foster conditions that widen the horizon of others and give them command of their own powers, so that they can find their own happiness in their own fashion, is the way of 'social' action. Otherwise the prayer of a freeman would be to be left alone, and to be delivered, above all, from 'reformers' and 'kind' people.

[1] Ibid., 293.
[2] Ibid., 293–4.

VII

DEWEY'S VIEW OF MEANS AND ENDS: CRITICAL REMARKS

Dewey's interpretation of thinking and his analysis of ends and means are important contributions to philosophical understanding. They are, moreover, fraught with significance for critical approaches to decision, planning, and policy-formation. The combination of shrewd description, brilliant criticism, plain common sense, and practical wisdom permeating his discussions of these topics is characteristic of Dewey's best writing and exemplifies his conception of the proper tasks and resources of philosophy. The lessons he teaches concerning the continuum of ends and means are particularly important, and have yet to be fully appreciated, in theory as well as in the public life.

It seems to me, nevertheless, that there is a fundamental difficulty in his views, arising from a tension between his account of reflective thought and his insistence on the continuum of ends-means. The difficulty is of a kind that has already been noted, in variant forms, in our discussion of Peirce, and in our earlier critique of Dewey's psychological conceptions. In the case of Peirce, we noted the conflict between his view that inquiry always originates in genuine doubt, and his recognition of the independent problem-seeking and autonomous theorizing characteristic of scientific practice. In our earlier criticism of Dewey's psychological conceptions, we suggested a conflict between the discontinuous conception of habit-reconstruction, dependent upon the release of impulse due to prior difficulty, and the practical advocacy of continuous reform, in advance of crises.

Dewey's View of Means and Ends: Critical Remarks

In the present case, there seems to me to be an analogous conflict between the discontinuity of the problem-theory of reflective thought, and the continuity of critical thinking that seems to be required by Dewey's interpretation of ends and means. Deliberation, says Dewey, 'starts from the blocking of efficient overt action'.[1] Reflective experience begins in perplexity and ends with adoption of a plan of action 'applied to the existing state of affairs'.[2] The reflectiveness of the experience depends especially upon the extent of the middle phases, in which the original problem is clarified and the tentative hypothesis elaborated. But the experience concludes with 'taking one stand upon the projected hypothesis . . . doing something overtly to bring about the anticipated result, and thereby testing the hypothesis'.[3]

With adoption of a plan or end-in-view, according to this analysis, thought should cease, since overt action has resumed; by hypothesis, the original block no longer exists. To be sure, the new plan may subsequently occasion new blocks, giving rise to new deliberations. But the moment action resumes under the new plan, reflection has resolved the initial perplexity, and must, according to this analysis, subside for it has lost its occasion.

On the other hand, the action guided by the new plan is continuous with the reflection that gave it birth; indeed, as Dewey insists, it tests the hypothesis under which it proceeds. The evaluation of the test provided by action requires an appreciation of its outcomes that relates its relevant features to the expectations of the guiding hypothesis. Such appreciation requires a continuous critical alertness precisely at the point of translation of idea into action. If action is to be critical, thought must not subside just when the test of its hypothesis begins. Having adopted a blueprint for the construction of a house, a man ought not thereupon to proceed unthinkingly with the work of construction. His end-in-view requires continual critical surveillance throughout the active process it initiates, for it may or may not work out as expected. Moreover, if he is to avoid wishful thinking, he needs to avoid fascination with isolated desired consequences and be

---

[1] *HNC*, 190.
[2] John Dewey, *Democracy and Education* (New York: Macmillan (original date 1916), 1961), 150.
[3] Ibid.

alive to unforeseen side effects, further consequences of the realization of his plan, and the unexpected as well as expected costs of subsidiary ends-in-view.

Nor is it adequate to say that, so long as his action proceeds effectively or satisfactorily, he has no need for thought, while as soon as a new overt difficulty is encountered, a new occasion for reflective thinking will prompt the needed deliberation. For if he is indeed a wishful thinker, he will act confidently, hypnotized by the envisaged consequences he desires, and oblivious to unforeseen side effects and hidden costs until it is too late to retrieve his errors. Whether he judges overt action as effective or satisfactory depends, in other words, upon the consequences he takes as criteria in appraising its course. If he is to act critically, Dewey suggests, the range of his preferred criteria ought to be broadened and it ought to be sufficiently open-ended to allow for the addition of relevant consequences in process. Moreover, he is, so far as possible, to anticipate and avert difficulties on the basis of past experience, rather than await 'the blocking of efficient overt action'.[1] If we stretch the notion of blocked overt action to include anticipated difficulties, we shall have weakened the problem-theory of thinking to the point of virtual emptiness. Even so, the intervals between difficulties are not to be free of thought, for a continuous alert monitoring of action for an indefinite range of consequences and costs is to be maintained.

It may perhaps be proposed that the conflict here outlined may be overcome if we distinguish Dewey's analysis of deliberation, proper, from his suggestion of the continuous surveillance of action in his discussion of means and ends. I do not think this proposal is satisfactory. For, in the first place, Dewey's analysis of deliberation itself acknowledges that the phase of action, which closes a cycle of reflective experience, tests the hypothesis in question, and it is such testing that requires the persistence of critical thought tying the action to the cycle preceding it. Thus the continuity of thought is suggested not only by Dewey's discussion of means and ends but also by his analysis of deliberation. In the second place, although deliberation proper, as Dewey describes it, may perhaps be analytically distinguished from the critical monitoring of action succeeding such deliberation, the

---

[1] *HNC,* 190.

question remains as to the scope of Dewey's theory of deliberation. Thus restricted, it can hardly be put forward as a general account of thinking or reflective experience. Moreover, it provides no psychological basis for the continuous critical surveillance of action which is so central to Dewey's general philosophy.

VIII

DEWEY'S SOCIAL AND EDUCATIONAL THEORY

The key to Dewey's social and educational theory is his emphasis on wholeness. He urges an increasing awareness of the infinite context of our action, a continual growth in meaning through an expansion of intelligent activity. Thus, he views education as continuous growth. Thus, he judges social and political institutions by their capacity to enable individual persons to develop in power and awareness. Thus, he demands of schools that they present the studies in relation to one another and link available knowledge with the live context beyond the classroom.

Dewey is not a religious thinker, but, in *Human Nature and Conduct*, he offers an interpretation of the theme of wholeness in religious terms:[1]

> Infinite relationships of man with his fellows and with nature already exist. The ideal means, as we have seen, a sense of these encompassing continuities with their infinite reach. This meaning even now attaches to present activities because they are set in a whole to which they belong and which belongs to them. Even in the midst of conflict, struggle and defeat a consciousness is possible of the enduring and comprehending whole.

> Such a consciousness requires symbols, but the symbols of the

[1] *HNC*, 330.

past no longer serve.[1] 'Religion has lost itself in cults, dogmas, and myths.'[2]

> Religion as a sense of the whole is the most individualized of all things, the most spontaneous, undefinable and varied. For individuality signifies unique connections in the whole. Yet it has been perverted into something uniform and immutable. . . . Instead of marking the freedom and peace of the individual as a member of an infinite whole, it has been petrified into a slavery of thought and sentiment, an intolerant superiority on the part of the few and an intolerable burden on the part of the many.

Although he is critical of actual religions, Dewey identifies the religious sense as a sense of the whole, and holds that 'every act may carry within itself a consoling and supporting consciousness of the whole to which it belongs and which in some sense belongs to it'.[3] In a vein reminiscent of James's discussion of the moral holidays afforded by belief in the Absolute, Dewey suggests that a consciousness of the whole allows an emancipation from its burdens, which is yet consistent with responsible action.[4]

> There is a conceit fostered by perversion of religion which assimilates the universe to our personal desires; but there is also a conceit of carrying the load of the universe from which religion liberates us. Within the flickering inconsequential acts of separate selves dwells a sense of the whole which claims and dignifies them. In its presence we put off mortality and live in the universal. The life of the community in which we live and have our being is the fit symbol of this relationship. The acts in which we express our perception of the ties which bind us to others are its only rites and ceremonies.

The community is, thus, a symbol of the whole, consciousness of which offers the only religious consolation Dewey acknowledges as significant. The whole is, however, infinite and so cannot be grasped as complete. We may approximate it in our experience

---

[1] Ibid.
[2] Ibid., 331.
[3] Ibid.
[4] Ibid., 331-2.

through the conception of growth, growth without end – in awareness, sensitivity, and meaning. The community ideally fit to symbolize the whole is one that frees itself and its members to grow.

An ideal society, for Dewey, is an association that allows for maximum growth of each person, through his own activity and self-development. Such an association aims to institutionalize intelligence in matters of conduct, as natural science institutionalizes intelligence in investigations of nature. It is free of artificial barriers dividing its members from one another, it fosters the free exchange of ideas, and it treats the ideas underlying its common activities as hypotheses – open to the test of experience, criticizable by all whom such activities affect, and revisable by procedures enlisting their common consent.

This is the ideal of democracy. The machinery of democracy is not an end in itself but a means directed toward such an ideal. The justification of democracy is not to be sought in some mythical infallibility of democratic procedures. Rather it is to be sought in the *quality* of human action promoted by institutions that acknowledge each person's dignity and judgment in forms of public exchange and participation in the public life.[1]

> The keynote of democracy as a way of life may be expressed, it seems to me, as the necessity for the participation of every mature human being in formation of the values that regulate the living of men together: which is necessary from the standpoint of both the general social welfare and the full development of human beings as individuals.

Democratic political forms are means to an end. They rest[2]

> upon the idea that no man or limited set of men is wise enough or good enough to rule others without their consent; the positive meaning of this statement is that all those who are affected by social institutions must have a share in producing and managing them. The two facts that each one is influenced in what he does and enjoys and in what he

---

[1] John Dewey, 'Democracy and Educational Administration' (an address to the National Education Association, 1937), *School and Society*, 45 (3 April 1937), 457–62. Cited passage reprinted in Joseph Ratner, ed., *Intelligence in the Modern World: John Dewey's Philosophy* (New York: Modern Library, 1939), 400.

[2] Ibid., 401.

becomes by the institutions under which he lives, and that therefore he shall have, in a democracy, a voice in shaping them, are the passive and active sides of the same fact.

When social institutions exclude certain persons from the development of their own powers, it is not only they as individuals who suffer, but 'the whole social body' that is deprived of their intelligence, judgment, and contribution. And there is one thing in particular that excluded persons are 'wiser about than anybody else can be, and that is where the shoe pinches, the troubles they suffer from'.[1] Authoritarian schemes assume that the value of a person's contribution may be judged[2]

by some *prior* principle, if not of family and birth or race and color or possession of material wealth, then by the position and rank a person occupies in the existing social scheme. The democratic faith in equality is the faith that each individual shall have the chance and opportunity to contribute whatever he is capable of contributing and that the value of his contribution be decided by its place and function in the organized total of similar contributions, not on the basis of prior status of any kind whatever.

Of all the freedoms required by the democratic outlook, freedom of *mind* is basic, for without it, individuals are not genuinely free to develop. 'Freed intelligence . . . is necessary to direct and to warrant freedom of action.'[3] Cultivation of intelligence under conditions of freedom is thus at once, for Dewey, the fundamental imperative of democracy and the main task of education.

Institutionally, education may, in fact, be viewed as the formal agency for fostering intelligence. Its primary aim is to develop the habits and mentality of critical thinking in application to all spheres of life. As an institution, it may itself be operated more or less intelligently. For it to be run intelligently, it should incorporate the general values of the democratic ideal, and its procedures should be developed and reviewed in a critical and scientific manner. This implies, fundamentally, that educational policy is to be stated and criticized in the public forum and that all concerned

[1] Ibid., 402.
[2] Ibid., 403–4.
[3] Ibid., 404.

in education ought to be heard. It implies also that educational procedures are to be judged by their fruits rather than their origins; curriculum and teaching methods, school organization and grouping, grading and testing – all are open to critical review in the light of empirical consequences scientifically assessed. It emphatically does not follow from Dewey's view that the educational past is to be rejected in a wholesale manner. On the contrary, the funded wisdom of the past provides a valuable guide to present activity. But guiding ideas are not dogmas; they are tested by the very activities they help to organize. They must continue to prove themselves by their consequences. If we are alert to this fact, we will profit from their guidance and we will also learn from critical experience how to improve upon them.

The aim of education, according to Dewey, is first and foremost to develop critical methods of thought. Its task is not to indoctrinate a particular point of view, but rather to help generate those powers of assessment and criticism by which diverse points of view may themselves be responsibly judged. In pursuit of this task, the school ought to *exemplify* the application of critical method to all the domains of human life. This implies the need to present these domains with an emphasis upon their *meaning*, that is, in their relatedness to one another but, most particularly, in their bearing upon the realm of purposive activity. For the more meaning we grasp, the greater the context we can take into account and the more we are able to evaluate critically. This is the central idea of Dewey's theory of education, which he develops into a notion of proper method and curriculum.[1]

> Study is effectual in the degree in which the pupil realizes the
> place of the . . . truth he is dealing with in carrying to
> fruition activities in which he is concerned. This connection
> of an object and a topic with the promotion of an activity
> having a purpose is the first and the last word of a genuine
> theory of interest in education.

Proper method requires that the subject be placed in a broad, and growing, context – a context that embraces the student's own purposes and potential activities as well as the urgent problems confronting the human community of which he is a part.

[1] John Dewey, *Democracy and Education* (New York: Macmillan (original date 1916), 1961), 135.

In the matter of curriculum, Dewey's emphasis is on continuity and meaning. Selection and specialization are, of course, necessary in modern schooling, but we must take care not to erect practical separations into hard and fast divisions among the studies. For every such division disrupts an array of real connections and so impoverishes the meaning of the subjects taught.[1]

The subject matter of education consists primarily of the meanings which supply content to existing social life. The continuity of social life means that many of these meanings are contributed to present activity by past collective experience. As social life grows more complex, these factors increase in number and import. There is need of special selection, formulation, and organization in order that they may be adequately transmitted to the new generation. But this very process tends to set up subject matter as something of value just by itself, apart from its function in promoting the realization of the meanings implied in the present experience of the immature.

Divisions between higher and lower studies, between theoretical and applied, between scientific and humanistic, between literary and technological studies – all are devices of convenience at best. Taken in any more serious fashion, they are all mischievous. We may need to use them, but we need also to help the student to see through them. For the full meaning of technology cannot be appreciated unless it is put into connection with its theoretical base and its human import; humanistic studies are, likewise, impoverished if they are isolated from contact with the social world and the science which is transforming it. A fundamental continuity of intimation, development, and human significance, moreover, unites studies that are elementary and advanced, basic and applied.

Integration of the curriculum is primarily a matter of recognizing that 'all studies grow out of relations in the one great common world'.[2] Studies are to be interrelated as varied avenues of access to this world and as valuable resources for the solution of common problems. In *Democracy and Education* Dewey argues that the school is not simply a mirror image of society; it represents a simplified,

---

[1] Ibid., 192.
[2] John Dewey, *The School and Society* (University of Chicago Press, 1899), 103.

idealized, and balanced environment with its own long-range goals of cultivating intelligent habits of mind.[1] Yet the impact of such cultivation is ultimately social, and the process of cultivation of such habits is one that requires genuine reference to environing social conditions within which the school has its being and role. It is this long-range social role that provides integration and coherence to the varied specialized activities of schooling.

[1] See Dewey, *Democracy and Education*, 20–2.

IX

DEWEY'S SOCIAL AND EDUCATIONAL THEORY: CRITICAL REMARKS

Dewey envisages a society that allows the maximum growth of each person through an expansion of his own capabilities for intelligent and effective action. Such a society, although it is based on the concept of indefinite and varied growth in its individual members, is far from indefinite and indeterminate itself. It requires institutions that foster free expression of ideas, toleration of diversity, and the participation of its members in 'formation of the values that regulate the living of men together'.[1] Moreover, such institutions themselves require supporting habits of mind, in particular, habits that are consonant with critical and scientific thought. Dewey has been criticized for taking growth as his basic value, without specifying the direction or ultimate goal of growth. But, as he might reply, the outcomes of growth cannot thus be restricted without substituting an uncritical constraint in advance for the operation of intelligence, thereby placing an unwarranted limitation upon the freedom of activity. Furthermore, as we have seen, the ideals of intelligence, growth, and freedom, open-ended as they are, are not amorphous or directionless; indeed, they make the most stringent of demands upon those who would embody them in human institutions and strive to rear their young by their light.

[1] Dewey, in Joseph Ratner, ed., *Intelligence in the Modern World: John Dewey's Philosophy* (New York: Modern Library, 1939), 400.

The schooling Dewey advocates is analogous in its rationale. It is designed to cultivate critical habits of mind. This aim, according to Dewey's general analysis of thought, requires the involvement of the pupil's own purposes in the learning process and the relating of the school's studies to problems of the environing society. But schooling, in Dewey's scheme, is not therefore amorphous or undemanding. It is organized around problems and it is directed toward internalizing in the pupil the discipline of critical and responsible thinking.

Dewey's educational views have been subjected to contrary criticisms. On the one hand, he has been charged with counselling extreme permissiveness – a kind of anarchy in the classroom. On the other hand, he has been accused of exalting the social role of the school to the detriment of individuality – urging a society of conformists. He has been held to be radically disruptive of the ordered ways and traditions of the past and also to be a conservative, stamping in an inflexible belief in the values of the surrounding society.

These opposed forms of criticism cannot be simultaneously held, for they cancel one another. Moreover, each overshoots the mark, exaggerating some element of Dewey's thought to the point of distortion and ignoring the fundamental allegiance to critical, experimental thought that lends balance to his educational doctrines.

Dewey wants to enlist the student's purposes in learning, so that the relation of the various studies to his own choices may become evident. Such a procedure requires a problem-organization of materials; it is calculated to enhance the meaning of the studies while increasing the student's sense of effectiveness as a purposive and intelligent agent. It is a crude mistake to take Dewey as advocating activity for its own sake. The whole point of activity in his scheme is that it should, in so far as possible, be made educative through the guiding power of ideas and the critical assessment of consequences. This undertaking may be very difficult to execute, or otherwise inadequate; it surely cannot be characterized as simply permissive. Not only does it retain the materials of adult studies under a new educational organization, but it imposes the structure inherent in definite purposes, requiring special instrumentalities for their realization. Dewey is not opposed to discipline; he wants the school, so far as possible, to strive for an internalization of intellectual discipline rather than construing discipline as primarily a matter of enforcement from without. As with scientific research or the practice of the arts, crafts and professions, discipline ought, he believes, to grow from the first-hand struggle to solve specific problems, encountering the resistance of available resources, experimenting with alternative ideas, putting them to the hard test of experience, evaluating them in the light of guiding purposes. To acquire the discipline born of struggle with problems is to incorporate habits of critical method; such incorporation is not a *laissez faire* or easy task – it both enlists and helps to foster dedicated effort, care, responsibility, and self-control. It is this conception of discipline as growing out of purposive problem-solving activity that ought, in Dewey's view, to predominate in education.

Nor is Dewey eager to foster a society of conformists, as should be evident from even a cursory reading of his work. Certainly, he wants the work of the school to be related to basic problems of the environing society. In this way, he believes, the meaning of school work may be enlarged and the effectiveness of knowledge made increasingly apparent; at the same time, the urgent difficulties of the common life may be illuminated and the moral habit of coping with them reliably may be encouraged in the young. To take social problems as a significant focus for schooling is, however, by no means to advocate inculcation of a social dogma. Dewey explicitly warns against social indoctrination; the fundamental allegiance of the school ought to be an allegiance to critical methods of analysis. Such methods are inimical to conformity: they demand responsible and independent judgment of social issues by canons of scientific reasoning and assessment of data.

Dewey emphasizes the social climate of the school, to be sure. His point, however, is not to foster conformity, but to alert teachers to the learning that goes on outside the formal lessons of the classroom. In so far as critical habits of mind and character are related to the human arrangements within which academic lessons are set, teachers need to be aware of the influence of such arrangements and to take responsibility for the moral and intellectual habits they foster. These habits ought, ideally, to be consonant with scientific and responsible thought, they ought to foster the independence of mind, the respect for others, and the capability of adjudicating differences by orderly methods that are characteristic both of democratic and of scientific attitudes. Allegiance to method rather than conformity to creed is the keynote.

Dewey's educational vision is designed neither to uphold the past, as such, nor to disrupt it, as such. Continuity with the past is, in any case, inevitable, as are departures from it, in one or another respect. The point is to strive to develop habits of intelligence that may be applied to life's problems. The deliverances of intelligent analysis may, in certain cases, counsel revision or rejection of inherited ways; in other cases, they may counsel retention. The widespread development of intelligent and responsible habits of mind would, however, in itself, constitute a large change in society, capable of bringing critical evaluation to bear on the problems and practices of our common life. It is this long-range development of intelligent habits of mind which is the school's role, in Dewey's view. To succeed in this development, the school must take society's problems seriously, but this by no means requires it to stamp prevalent social values into the minds of its children. The school must also strive to deepen reflection, strengthen independence, and develop critical skills in application to social issues, to a degree that has not yet been achieved. But this is by no means tantamount to counselling a wholesale disruption of the past. It is, rather, to conceive the school's task as enabling society to cope with its problems more intelligently, more effectively, more imaginatively, and more responsibly than it has so far done.

I should, myself, however, wish to offer certain criticisms of Dewey's views, despite my agreement with much of what he has to say on educational matters. Since I have elsewhere elaborated some of these criticisms,[1] I will here note them only briefly, and try to connect them with earlier critical points related to pragmatic themes.

First, I suggest that the notion of continuity is exaggerated in Dewey's treatment. Continuities are certainly important in education, and Dewey's emphasis on bringing together the humanistic

---

[1] I. Scheffler, 'Educational Liberalism and Dewey's Philosophy', *Harvard Educational Review*, 26 (1956), 190–8; and Scheffler, 'Reflections on Educational Relevance', *Journal of Philosophy*, LXVI (1969), 764–73. Both papers are reprinted in my *Reason and Teaching* (London: Routledge & Kegan Paul, 1973).

and the technical, the elementary and the advanced, the disciplinary and the problematic elements of the educational process is a salutary one. He is, I believe, certainly right in attacking the idea that the studies are independent and external entities, self-enclosed and somehow rooted in nature. He is right in advocating that technical matters be illuminated by theoretical knowledge and seen from the perspective of their human significance. He is right, too, in demanding that an appreciation of values be supplemented by a realistic understanding of their natural conditions and vicissitudes. Nevertheless, discontinuities and distinctions are as natural as continuities, and they need also to be acknowledged where they exist.

Theory is, for example, surely connected with observation and with practice, but it is also autonomous; it has its own career and life. The general tendency of pragmatism, as we have seen, is to interpret theory as intermediary between practical problem and practical resolution, and to construe its content wholly in terms of observable transformations of the world through practical effort. As indicated in earlier discussions of both Peirce and Dewey, this characterization of theory does not seem to me tenable. Neither the content nor the function of theory can be fully understood by reference to the resolution of practical problems through transformations of the world. One must, to appreciate the force of a theory, grasp more than just its practical ramifications; theories serve not simply to guide practice, but to afford us an intelligible and coherent representation of fundamental natural processes.

The process of theorizing is a creative process. It is not just a matter of cataloguing the functional relations among phenomenal changes, nor is it, in any plausible sense, generated out of experience. The theorist is free to invent, simplify, postulate, categorize, extrapolate, idealize – he may need to back away from the detail of phenomenal change and practical urgency in order to strive to 'see through' to underlying elements and patterns. Distance, in other words, is functional for the theorist, who strives for ever deeper insights and broader perspectives on nature. The value of theoretical distance must be acknowledged in education, and distinguished from mere remoteness and pedantry. In opposing the latter, we must avoid destruction of the former. Education ought, indeed, to encourage the theoretical motive, which, whether or not it promises to relate to practical solutions of social problems, aims to achieve a penetrating vision of natural structures.

Second, the problem-theory of thinking, as developed by Peirce and Dewey, seems to me inadequate. Problems cannot be identified with difficulties of practice; the problems that organize scientific research arise in a context of prior theory and experimentation. Moreover, the life of science is not exhausted in resolving problems that arise without effort; the scientist's thought does not subside when his questions have been answered. Problem-finding is as important as problem-solving, and scientific thought of the greatest significance is expended in seeking, formulating and elaborating questions that have not yet intruded on practice.

We have noted the difficulties in Peirce's conception of real doubt as the origin of inquiry, and his own recognition of the importance of feigned, hypothetical, and speculative questions. We have also seen the shortcomings of the problem-theory of reflection as support for Dewey's notion of continuous reconstruction and critical testing of ideas in action. If we reflect upon the import of these criticisms for education, we should need to acknowledge both the possibility and the importance of encouraging the pupil to seek problems, of helping him to a wider perception and a richer sensitivity, a more insistent curiosity and a more active imagination. We should continue to value problem-solving as a method of educational organization, but we should place it within the context of a growing awareness that reaches out steadily to problems unperceived before.

The problem-theory of thinking seems to me also difficult in attempting to give a uniform analysis of thought in all realms. I have argued that it does not even give an adequate picture of scientific thought, the preferred domain of pragmatic interpretations. Much less does it provide an analysis that can smoothly contain not only the scientific imagination, but the work of the artist, the historian, the poet, the translator, the inventor, the novelist, the mathematician. Much of our thinking is problem-oriented, but much is not, growing out of free speculation, playfulness, curiosity, or out of the need to express, describe, or create. One can attempt to force all these varieties into a common abstract framework, but the advantages of doing so would need to be so evident as to override the cost in artificiality and generality. I do not think the problem-theory is adequate in this respect; even if it were, we should need to provide, in education, a concrete and realistic awareness of the special features differentiating science from history, art from mathematics, poetry from legal reasoning, philology from philosophy. We should, in other words, need to transmit the several traditions of thought as we now possess them, rather than simply filtering them through an abstract philosophical schema of thinking as problem-solving.

Third, while I applaud Dewey's emphasis on meaning in his account of education, I suggest that it is of variable relevance in the educational process. That is to say, the meaning of subjects is indeed enhanced through their mutual connectedness as well as their incorporation into the student's context of purpose and potential action. Moreover, the teacher himself ought to have as clear a conception as possible of the aims, values, and criteria that animate his educational choices of curriculum as well as methods and organization. Nevertheless, learning does not need to proceed, at every point, through linkages to prior purpose; the pupil does not, I suggest, need to learn everything in the context of its meanings and uses. Children learn many things as they do language, or games – through participation, curiosity, or the sheer joy of the activity. The teacher ought to be clear as to the meaning and value of introducing a particular subject or educational activity and enlisting participation as if it were a game. But the child may well learn it, efficiently and joyfully, as a game. It is, in principle, an empirical question whether mathematics is better taught through elaborate reference to the meaning of fundamental concepts and operations than through intuitive and gamelike methods. This question ought, at any rate, not be begged by a philosophical predilection for meaning in education.

What is certainly of basic importance is that, no matter how a child has been introduced to a subject, his capacity for meaningful action, intelligent criticism, and growth in understanding should not be destroyed or stunted through his education. Whatever hospitals do, as Florence Nightingale is reputed to have said, they at least ought not to spread disease. No matter what schools do, they should not cripple educational growth. The child's questions, his attempts to understand, should always be respected and sincerely met. His efforts to criticize, to relate, to utilize, and to elaborate ought always to be strengthened and encouraged, so that he becomes ever more aware of his intellectual agency, its powers and responsibilities. This does not imply, however, that he needs to have all things explained to him before questions arise, that he is incapable of stepping out of the familiar circle of his projects and purposes to explore the world beyond without prior assurances of meaning.

Finally, I believe that Dewey's view of the school underestimates its autonomy, for it emphasizes as the primary role of the school its long-range transformation of society through its ultimate impact on problems of the larger culture. Dewey's view of the school is by no means a simple-minded one; he does not see the school as a mere reflection of society, nor does he suppose it to be an instrument for accomplishing social purposes set in advance. The social end that is served by the school is represented, for him, not by society as it happens to be but by a reformed society, illuminated by critical intelligence. Nevertheless, he emphasizes the intermediary role of the school, as an agency capable of transforming problematic conditions, through the cultivation of intelligence, into more harmonious and satisfactory arrangements. To this end, he stresses the continuity between school and society, placing social problems at the centre of the school's focus.

As is already apparent from my earlier remarks on the autonomy of theory, I believe the work of the school is not adequately represented by Dewey's account. In fostering theory, the school ought, in a basic sense, to stand apart from life, not by propagating pedantry and myth, but by encouraging the theoretical illumination of a world that is wider than the school and wider even than the society in which the school is placed. The school requires sufficient distance from society to enable it to develop intellectual concerns and cultural standards that have their own worth, quite apart from the resolution of social problems, and that may, moreover, place those very problems in a new perspective. The school may be viewed as an intermediary agency helping to improve society in the long run, but society may equally be viewed as an intermediary agency to be judged by its dedication to the autonomous values of intelligence, criticism, knowledge, and art, of which the school is the guardian. The school, in my view, ought to see itself *not simply* as instrumental to an improved society, although it ought to see itself in that way, surely. Its job is not only to serve but also to enlighten, create, understand, and illuminate, efforts which have intrinsic value and dignity, efforts which are themselves to be served by the society of men.

EPILOGUE

Every genuine accomplishment instead of
winding up an affair and enclosing it as a jewel
in a casket for future contemplation, complicates
the practical situation.

John Dewey[1]

It would be contrary to the spirit of pragmatism to attempt a
final summation, a delineation of the essential content of the
thinkers we have discussed, a reckoning of their merits and de-
merits. For pragmatism, there are no final summations, no essential meanings, no ultimate reckonings. A movement of thought is
not a jewel in a casket, enclosed for contemplation. It is part of a
continuous process. Where it is significant, it provokes new
problems, sets new paths.

There is no doubt of the significance of pragmatism as a movement of modern thought. It is indeed both a modern and a
comprehensive philosophy, modern in its dealing seriously with
science and its attempt to rethink basic philosophical issues in the
light of scientific logic and practice; comprehensive in taking all
of human experience as its province, not only the traditional questions of philosophers but the practical urgencies of contemporary
civilization. In both these respects, pragmatic thinkers pioneered
in coming to grips with issues that concern all reflective persons

[1] *HNC*, 285.

in the world of today. For surely, the logic and practice of science require interpretation to assess their import for inherited ways of thought. And surely, philosophy ought not to lose itself in the achievements of its own past, but should address itself to the novel predicaments of our current life in all their variety. The attempt to seal philosophy off from developments in science, mathematics, art, and society is an attempt to turn it into another technical speciality, curtailing its power to illuminate the present, and depriving other areas of its analytical force and its traditions of reflective discussion. Both the scientific interest and the human scope of pragmatism have become increasingly unpopular in the philosophical thought of recent decades. It is for this reason that the example of pragmatic thinkers has much to teach us.

Various of the doctrines put forward by the pragmatists cannot, in my opinion, be said to have succeeded in detail. As is evident from my critical remarks, I, at least, am not persuaded by the several analyses they offer of symbolism, of thought, and of inquiry. Yet their broad emphases seem to me both valuable and sound. Their relating of meaning to action and of cognition to emotion, their denial of intuitive self-evidence, their emphasis on purpose and language in knowledge, their connecting of knowledge and value – all seem to me fundamentally correct. If their detailed analyses of these themes cannot be sustained, they challenge us to do better, and they point us in the proper direction. The problems raised by the pragmatists cannot, in any case, be abandoned; they are problems that help to define the intellectual situation we face, and there is no alternative but to make further attempts to resolve them in a more satisfactory way.

The doctrines of the pragmatists are not dogmas. They invite criticism and evaluation in the light of further reflection, new knowledge, and new social circumstances. Though the problems the pragmatists dealt with are still pervasive and urgent, we must make use of the new knowledge and modes of analysis available to us in coping with them. Moreover, the social circumstances of the world in which we now live have undergone, and are undergoing, enormous transformations, bringing forth their own new predicaments and special perplexities. In coping with these new developments, we shall, I believe, find wisdom and intellectual guidance in the work of the pragmatic thinkers we have discussed.

If we follow their teachings, we will, however, avoid enclosing their doctrines in a casket. We will try, rather, to use the best resources of our intelligence and critical thought to make sense of our world, as they did of theirs.

INDEX

Index

International Library of Philosophy & Scientific Method

Editor: Ted Honderich

(Demy 8vo)

Allen
  PI
Allen, R. L. and Fancy,
  326 pp. 1970.
Armstrong, D.M., F
  A Materialis
Bambrough, R
  184 pp. 1
Barry, Brian,
Bird, Graham, Ku
Bogen, James, Wi
Broad, C. D., **Lectures**
  (2nd Impression 1966.)
Crombie, I. M., **An Examinat.**
  I. Plato on Man and Society 4o
  II. Plato on Knowledge and Reality
Day, John Patrick, **Inductive Probabi.**
Dennett, D. C., **Content and Consciousi.**
Dretske, Fred I., **Seeing and Knowing** *270 p,*
Ducasse, C. J., **Truth, Knowledge and Causat.**
Edel, Abraham, **Method in Ethical Theory** *379 pp.*
Farm, K. T. (Ed.), **Symposium on J. L. Austin** *512 pp.*
Flew, Anthony, **Hume's Philosophy of Belief** *296 pp. 1s*
Fogelin, Robert J., **Evidence and Meaning** *200 pp. 1967.*
Franklin, R., **Freewill and Determinism** *353 pp. 1968.*
Gale, Richard, **The Language of Time** *256 pp. 1967.*
Glover, Jonathan, **Responsibility** *212 pp. 1970.*
Goldman, Lucien, **The Hidden God** *424 pp. 1964.*
Hamlyn, D. W., **Sensation and Perception** *222 pp. 1961.*
  (3rd Impression 1967.)
Husserl, Edmund, **Logical Investigations** *Vol. I: 456 pp. Vol. II: 464 pp.*
Kemp, J., **Reason, Action and Morality** *216 pp. 1964.*
Körner, Stephan, **Experience and Theory** *272 pp. 1966.*
Lazerowitz, Morris, **Studies in Metaphilosophy** *276 pp. 1964.*
Linsky, Leonard, **Referring** *152 pp. 1967.*
MacIntosh, J. J. and Coval, S. C. (Eds.), **Business of Reason** *280 pp. 1969.*
Meiland, Jack W., **Talking About Particulars** *192 pp. 1970.*
Merleau-Ponty, M., **Phenomenology of Perception** *487 pp. 1962.*
Naess, Arne, **Scepticism** *176 pp. 1969.*
Perelman, Chaim, **The Idea of Justice and the Problem of Argument**
  224 pp. 1963.
Ross, Alf, **Directives, Norms and their Logic** *192 pp. 1967.*
Schlesinger, G., **Method in the Physical Sciences** *148 pp. 1963.*
Sellars, W. F., **Science and Metaphysics** *248 pp. 1968.*
  Science, Perception and Reality *374 pp. 1963.*
Shwayder, D. S., **The Stratification of Behaviour** *428 pp. 1965.*

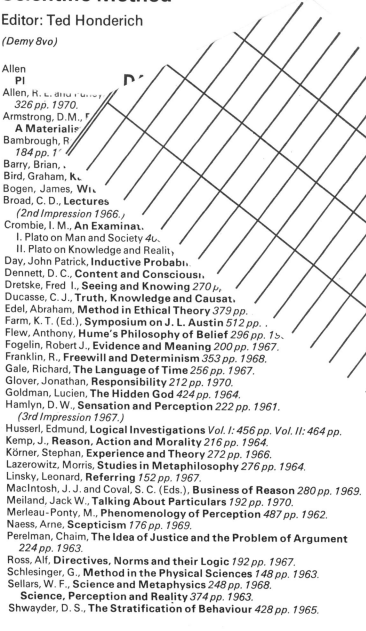